Coasting Schooner

The Four-Masted

Albert F. Paul

Albert F. Paul at sea, bound from Providence, Rhode Island, to Perth Amboy, New Jersey, June 6, 1939–taken from Merchants and Miners steamer *Kent*. (Photo by William B. Taylor, Courtesy The Mariners Museum)

Coasting Schooner

The Four-Masted

Albert F. Paul

Robert H. Burgess

Published for The Mariners Museum
Newport News, Virginia
by the University Press of Virginia
Charlottesville

The University Press of Virginia

Museum Publication No. 35

First Published 1978

Library of Congress Cataloging in Publication Data

Burgess, Robert H
Coasting schooner, the four-masted Albert F. Paul.

(Museum publication ; no. 35)
Includes index.
1. Albert F. Paul (Schooner) 2. Coastwise shipping–North America–History. I. Title.
II. Series: The Mariners Museum, Newport News, Va.
Museum Publication ; no. 35.
VM395.A38B87 387.2′2 77–10554
ISBN 0–917376–31–5

Printed in the United States of America

Contents

Acknowledgments

This volume is the result of assistance from many individuals. Samuel Johnson once wrote, "Knowledge is of two kinds; we know a subject ourselves or we know where we can find information upon it." I knew the *Albert F. Paul* well, having seen her and boarded her in Baltimore over a decade. During the past thirty-five years since she was lost, I gathered material about that schooner and learned of others who had followed her career in one way or another. The trip book from the Paul office and the historically valuable items from the late James S. McCullough and his wife were the beginning.

When I was working on my *Purnell T. White* book *Sea, Sails and Shipwreck*, in 1969, I was in touch with Charles C. Paul, grandson of the founder of the Paul fleet. He loaned me the record of the *Albert F. Paul*'s voyages during her twenty-four-year ownership by his family, clippings, photos, and other data about the schooner.

Mrs. Herbert H. Bryant, Sr., Captain Jones's daughter who sailed on the *Paul* as a child from 1925 to 1941, shared her recollections, photos, and clippings, as did her mother and her brother, Col. Albert F. Paul Jones, USA. They should be able to write a book just about their experiences on the schooner.

Schooner enthusiasts and historians Robert H. I. Goddard and Capt. W. J. L. Parker, USCG (Ret.) and marine artist John A. Noble were willing to assist when I called upon them. Mrs. Agnita B. Phillips was helpful in lending a photo of one of her relatives, Capt. William M. Martino, who was lost with the *Paul*.

The late Lloyd H. Lewis I mention later, but I must acknowledge him here for allowing me to copy the trip book. The late Mrs. James E. Bailey, sister of Charles C. Paul, made a trip in the *Paul* in 1935 and kept a journal. She allowed The Mariners Museum to copy this for its library, and I referred to it to learn something about the daily activities of the Jones children at sea. The sister of Albert F. Paul, Bessie Paul Bacon—who christened the schooner—loaned me the photos of the launching.

Bill Swan, of the Norfolk office of Wm. H. Swan & Sons, ship chandlers, which serviced the schooner at times, found the letter, addressed to Captain Martino from his sister, which had remained in his files unopened for three decades. Al Humes of Milford, Delaware, kindly researched the *Milford Chronicle* to shed some light on the *Paul*'s launching.

Thanks are due also to William T. Radcliffe, photographer of The Mariners Museum, for his skillful work in copying and printing many of the photos in this book. And to that museum, for recognizing the historical worth in this material, my gratitude for publishing it.

Foreword

"Arrived: Schr. A. F. PAUL, Georgetown." Back in the 1930s, any such shipping page note would send a sea-struck boy (me) biking to the distant Brooklyn waterfront. To observe and photograph schooners showing up in the New York area was, to me, an overriding interest.

I feel fortunate in having been able to witness these wooden ships from Maine, Nova Scotia, Delaware, Maryland, and Florida shipyards. Seen at the tag end, they were gone in another decade, and two hundred years of American wood shipbuilding ended with them.

Perseverance in tracking down the vessels and hanging around paid off. In time, I was riding out to the anchorage and returning with the tug, and I finally made several coastwise trips in the *Annie C. Ross*, a four-master similar in size, type, and trade to the *Albert F. Paul*. As a result, reviewing the material in this book has been a fascinating experience that certainly broadened my understanding and appreciation of that class of ship in areas I never saw, but wanted to know about.

B. B. Crowninshield, designer of big schooners in the zenith of the sailing coal trade, wrote in 1907 in the *Transactions of the Society of Naval Architects and Marine Engineers* this testimonial to the era represented by vessels such as the *Paul*:

> The men who turned out the wooden tonnage usually constructed the entire hull, frame, plank, ceiling, decks, and joiner work. They were frequently caulkers, painters, spar-makers, and riggers as well as carpenters—men of wonderful recourse, self reliant and skillful. They had been trained by long experience and by traditions of their forefathers, and had learned from many failures and disasters what to avoid. Progress had been attained almost wholly by development. The model of each vessel was derived from, and was in fact, the natural growth of those immediately preceding it. Anything radically different was properly discouraged, there being no thoroughly workable knowledge of the

natural laws of stability, flotation, or application of the law of composition and resolution of forces as applied to the problem of propulsion by sails.

The *Albert F. Paul* was one of the last representatives of that rich heritage of wooden ships, and though she shared the common characteristics of the final form of the American schooner, she also had a distinct personality. I had no greater thrill, when I was a boy seeking a vantage point, than when I could identify the hidden hull of some schooner whose masts towered above the high lumber piles. No knight of old ever sought the Holy Grail more enthusiastically than I sought to get a good look at some vessel I had not yet seen, for they all had individual personalities.

Fortunately, others more qualified than I were recording the sailing coaster. John Noble, also in the environs of New York harbor, captured completely their aura in his sketchbooks that covered not only the decline of the wooden walls but also the worn Scandinavians and others in the fo'c'sles—true schoonermen—needed to keep them going.

Additional adherents of the schooners, still around in those days before World War II, collected material which has been published over the years and in so doing performed an overdue and timely service to American sailing history. On the east coast, W. J. L. Parker, Giles M. S. Tod, Robert H. Burgess, Robert H. I. Goddard, Francis E. Bowker, Charles S. Morgan, John P. Parker, and John F. Leavitt are to be thanked by anyone who has an inkling of what those final schooners stood for, and what disappeared when they went.

This book is another significant work by Bob Burgess, adding to the other marine historical publications (two on the Atlantic coasters) he has so carefully researched and assembled. He was already well underway in his monumental documentations of Chesapeake sailing craft when I was just starting out with my Brownie and bike expeditions. The larger four- and five-masted schooners were included in his sharp lens and systematic documentations, and he knew the *Paul* well for the last decade of her life.

What greatly enhances this book is a virtue in all of Burgess' works: his recognition of the people behind the ships—builders, captains, owners, shipyard operators—vital to the overall picture.

We are indeed fortunate that Bob Burgess never faltered in collecting or photographing what others thought commonplace. His accomplishments can never be duplicated; the time has passed, and the records are scattered.

I believe an appreciation of the place of the American coastwise trade in marine history is necessary to put the *Albert F. Paul* memorabilia into perspective. The usual concept of the "old American Merchant Marine" has usually been expressed in terms of clipper ships and distant ports, or whaling barks and tropic isles. However, the American longshore fleet, for years larger and more important than our deepwater sailing commerce, tends to be overlooked. It resisted economic decay and misfortune long after the Yankee deep-sea square-rigger went hull down as a commercial reality. Coal for Bermuda or salt from Turks Island are not necessarily unromantic or uninteresting; such voyages were real and attainable to sea dreamers in the last half of the 1930s. I am sure that the hope of sailing in a schooner bound "offshore" must have thrilled Bob Burgess as it did me.

The longevity of the coastwise trade in schooners may call for explanation. Since the earliest days of this Republic, commerce between American ports has been "protected," that is, restricted by law to United States flag vessels. It was a situation which a century later contributed to the development of that unique vessel, the large American schooner, long after European iron and steel drove the wooden offshore square-riggers from the seas.

At the turn of this century, the Atlantic coasters constituted a vast armada. Built mostly in New England, the wooden bottoms carried every conceivable commodity of their times: coal, ice, lumber, bricks, logwood, phosphate rock, lime, salt, naval stores, locomotives, pins, sewing machines, notions—the list is endless. The ubiquitous schooner was in truth the national rig that thrived for many decades when powered vessels or more complicated rigs could not begin to pay their way.

The availability of the small steam deck engine made it possible to increase the size of the schooners without greatly adding to the number of sailors to set and handle the tremendous gaffsails or to heave in the massive ground tackle. Later vessels, when their size was not too great, could simplify crew manning even more by using a gasoline-driven donkey engine that did not require a licensed steam engineer. The *Paul* was one of those handy four-masters small enough to effect that very significant economy when crews were scarce and freights low.

By the time of World War I, the large coastwise schooner was highly developed by the process that Crowninshield described above. The rigging, hull form, and general layout varied only to a relatively minor degree, as ship classes went. Their economy of construction, basic simplicity, and low operating costs made them practical during the shipping emergency from 1916 through 1921. The resurgence of the type saw the reactivation of long-dormant wooden shipbuilding yards and the construction of new facilities to build literally hundreds of wooden schooners on all coasts of North America, including the Maritime Provinces of Canada.

Not all the vessels were by any means as well constructed as the *Albert F. Paul*; few withstood the economic shoals of the depression, and most were laid up permanently as the boom faded. In the last decade, then, of the *Paul*'s long service, only a few dozen American and Canadian representatives of the once vast coastwise fleet remained. If the ability of a wooden vessel to hold her sheer line after over two decades of hard service indicates a well-built vessel, then the product of Abbott's yard on the Mispillion River of Delaware, the *Albert F. Paul*, certainly compared with the best of them.

Not only were the large schooners unique in the world of ships but in them was bred an unusual body of men who were able to navigate and handle with comparatively few sailors the big fore-and-afters on both American coasts. On the Atlantic side they experienced intense cold, heavy gales, and the ever-present risk of stranding or being driven ashore. On top of these factors, the expectation of big dividends stimulated in the "great schooner" coal trade the maximizing of the "trips" per year (never "voyages" if coastwise). If the captain couldn't or wouldn't drive her, there would soon be a new one on the poop deck of the five- or six-master.

The *Paul* was of a later generation, the lean twenties and thirties, which hardly encouraged undue wear and tear on vessels or gear. While old schoonermen remembered the halcyon days of the coal trade, prudence and freedom from trouble (repairs and replacements) were vital for survival. A "quick trip," however, still gave reason for pride among the shrunken sailing fraternity of the latter days.

The special seamen commanding the schooners were, in large measure, of Yankee or Nova Scotian origin. Many, however, were from other parts of the seaboard: New Jersey, Maryland, etc. Ambitious foreign-born seamen—Scandinavians, Germans, Latvians, Yugoslavians, and other nationalities—rose to command vessels and did well. It was not unusual, on some trips, for an American schooner to have no native-born Americans aboard.

Regardless of national origin, before the mast or after, captain, mate, bosun, steward, engineer, or sailor—all were alike in courage, hardihood, and mastery of a hard trade. Capt. Robert O. Jones of the *Paul*, a Welshman by birth, was certainly a long-standing and respected member of the schoonermen on the Atlantic coast.

Mr. Burgess gives in this book a significant and first-source collection that provides an insight not presented elsewhere to this date. It encompasses the financial, technical, economic, pictorial, and navigational aspects—the total record of a single, large American coaster—in one package. It was, in my case, particularly fascinating as the windows of memory opened on occasions between 1935 and 1941 (Trip #71 at Cross, Austin, Ireland Yard in Brooklyn; Trip #73 at Rankin and Tyson's, Georgetown; Trip #76 in Brooklyn; Trip #97 at Redman and Vane's, Baltimore) when I boarded the vessel and engaged Captain Jones, or the mate, or the steward in conversation in my on-going thirst for schooner lore.

The overall historical summary of the *Paul*'s life nicely frames the material that follows. Particularly appropriate, in my opinion, is the poignant, undelivered letter from Captain Martino's anxious sister Dora Bell, for it deals with a *fact*, one that the present gush of belated enthusiasm (Operation Sail, etc.) for past sailing glories does not appreciate. Sailing ships were often but precarious refuges from the hazards of storms, economics—and war. While a hardy breed of men were developed on these vessels, no small fraction of them were hurt or killed in the process.

The Bicentennial public has been presented a "picture of sail" in the Tall Ships parade, which was indeed thrilling, spectacular, emotion-provoking, and a timely tonic. But those scrubbed decks of teak, shining dacron sails, and crowds of uniformed cadets should not be construed as representative of commercial sail in America (or anywhere, really). The correlation, I would say, is about zero. However, the *Albert F. Paul,* the *Doris Hamlin,* the *Annie C. Ross,* or the *Edward R. Smith* and the *Lucy Evelyn,* or any of a score of others of that class in the late thirties *were* representative, significant, and very real links with our seafaring heritage under sail. When they were gone, that chain was broken, but Mr. Burgess's book does much to anchor fast the memory.

The "Trip Book," or financial record, of the *Paul* indicates what was taken physically from a sailor in those tired, old vessels by noting expenditures such as "Doctor for sailor—$3.00," or "Taxi to take sailor to hospital—$2.80." You see in the book how the husky Norwegian-American mate set two topsails by himself because the two men in his watch on that four-masted schooner were unable to haul on a rope (sprained ankle, bad hand).

That these ships were lovely to look at is a fact; however, they were also workhouses that exacted a toll of the men who had to sail them—old sailing-ship seamen or the young Georgetown greenhorns who signed on the *Paul* out of curiosity or to fulfill a dream of adventure on the high seas, which they received in full measure if they tried to stow a flapping topsail aloft, and alone, in a breeze at night.

The journal of James S. McCullough (most assuredly an unusual resident of a schooner's fo'c'sle house) is a unique record from a latter-day coaster. Similar accounts of day-by-day vessel activities from the sailors' viewpoints have been published (*The* Sea Serpent *Journal,* The Mariners Museum, 1975) dealing with California clippers, or Down Easters. Usually, these were written by very literate youths from Harvard or other schools, young gentlemen seeking their fortunes in the gold fields or striving to become officers in the glamorous sailing paragons of the clipper days. But few men before the mast in schooners appear to have been so interested in the vessels that they dutifully recorded the activities of a vessel or what it was like physically, as McCullough has done.

It is regrettable that McCullough did not describe in his *Paul* journal his shipmates and other personal aspects, as he did in his *Purnell T. White* record (*Sea, Sails and Shipwreck,* by Robert H.

Burgess). He stresses well in his loglike chronology the working of the vessel as she and the crew struggle to make the next port despite the vagaries of wind and current. We learn much of the working of a large fore-and-after, but not much of the men aboard her.

McCullough's technical descriptions clearly and truly describe what such a ship required of the sailormen in her, for thirty dollars a month. Small wonder that the gear on the *Paul* was tired and worn with something carrying away every watch. It was *working*—pulling, straining, and wearing every minute that the schooner was at sea. Even at anchor (or especially so, when the hook was down in a seaway), the ceaseless cycle of give and take continued. The seamed old sailormen—the Sore-Eyed Martins, Russian Ottos, and Mad Mike Jensens that McCullough sailed with—were in harmony with the groaning schooner as they all shared their last ailing days together.

Possibly all readers will not appreciate the listing provided by McCullough of the nicknames of the men sailing in the schooners in the 1930s. But it is from life. I only wonder why he did not include Old Charley (or Manville Charley, or Big Charley), who sailed in 150 schooners and could, in his sixties, still do the work of any two men; he did as much (between periods in Bowery hotels) to keep the last schooners going as anyone in the world.

Among the men listed, I certainly remember Russian Otto, but McCullough fails to mention Finn Arthur, Flagpole Barney, or Liniment Larsen whom I knew in the *Annie C. Ross*. Happily, shipping master Black Charley (Charles Hoyt—$5.00 for half shipping fee for sailor, Trip #89 in 1939 in the *Paul*'s Trip Book) is included. From his shipping "office" in the back of his tailor shop near South Street, he located and handled sailing-ship men on the beach when captains of schooners and barges needed them.

The stores list (Trip #92) put aboard the *Paul* brings back recollections of similar piles of all manner of items which I helped carry aboard the *Annie C. Ross* at the same Newtown Creek pier where the *Paul* discharged many cargoes. We were also sailing to Georgetown, South Carolina, and aboard we carried or rolled the "family beef" (salt pork) in barrels, the cabin jam and the crew jam, the cabin coffee and the crew coffee—all reminders of days when the gap between poop deck and the fo'c'sle was much greater than today. I can't help but recall what the *Ross*'s steward called "Merchants and Miners strawberries," in fifteen-pound packages; never since have I heard prunes so designated or thought of the term until reading the *Paul*'s stores list in this book.

The chandlery list also links even the 1940 schooner with a bygone technology so different from today. Mast grease, 30-inch mast hoops, barrels for drinking water—all are items that were put aboard American schooners from earliest Colonial days. I can still smell the pine tar for oiling decks, the kerosene in tins for sidelights and lamps, and the fragrance of the wood-burning galley stove after I helped saw up an old gaff while the mate and a sailor completed a new one. It was a routine repeated an infinity of times after the first schooner was born until the last survivors such as the *Albert F. Paul* disappeared.

The financial records in the trip book, documenting ninety-nine trips under the C. C. Paul house flag from 1917 through 1941, are illuminating in depicting the "Golden Days" (as Captain R. B. White of C. C. Paul & Company described them to me, when, in 1947, I was endeavoring to purchase his two-masted schooner *Ida B. Conway*) wherein the *Paul* was launched. One readily traces the decay of the shipping boom and the hardening of times in the depression years, concurrent with the tiring of the ships and the disappearance of schoonermen to man them. Then freights picked up as the war in Europe started and sizable dividends became possible again. It was World War I that made the *Paul* economically feasible when she was built, and World War II that finished her off.

In perusing the expenditures, most are as to be expected—routine operational costs. Even though they are hardly representative of ship economics today, they are of historic interest. However, here and there intriguing items appear; not explained, they certainly lead one to wonder about the probably interesting or curious stories behind them, for they certainly would further illuminate the character of the vessel and the people in her.

For example, consider the $78.00 for photographs of the ship in 1919 (for whom?) or the 30 meals for stowaway ($9.00) on a voyage to Rio Grande do Sul, Brazil, in the early days. The 108 bushels of salt for preserving the vessel in 1923 are understandable, but the $38.50 for detention of deserters in Halifax is something else.

The numerous, but small, medical expenses for mate, sailors, captain, etc. indicate how healthy life in a schooner with a high deck load in winter off the North Atlantic coast might be. The sulphur candles I do understand, having been driven from my berth by bedbugs in the *Ross* on my first night aboard her (raw gasoline and salt on the bunk boards and springs did a much better job, though).

As we read on, inspectors and Naval Control Commanders are "entertained," and stevedores receive cigars as the "good will" of the vessel is maintained in foreign ports. However, in 1926 while at Portland, due to "informer's retainer" ($125.00), an unopposed $745.00 settlement with the United States Government, $100.00 in fines to mate and skipper, plus a whopping $2,177.44 paid out in lawyer's fees were certainly extraordinary. The outlay far transcended the usual gratuities required of the vessel in out-of-the-way places and shows how, in the prohibition era, the promise of easy money led some unidentified parties aboard to place the vessel in a bad position with the law.

The years go on and the expenses to keep the *Paul*, now well on in years, sailing continue—timber for booms, gaffs, jibboom (64-foot stick), oak for bitts, and knees. It is necessary to put in foremast pieces (dutchmen) at $28.00; also to buy sheet copper, oak frames, cypress planks, and rudder gudgeons for the motor yawlboat, damaged no doubt by some big following sea.

By 1940, the end was approaching. The repair requirements continue, and Captain Jones travels by road from Portland to Boothbay Harbor to select gear from the Crowell and Thurlow schooners junked there. A wildcat, water tank, Russell pump, topmast, gaff, rope, and mast hoops were brought from those long-laid-up vessels and went to sea again in that stout Milford-built hull that was to outlast so many New Englanders as characterized by the Boothbay fleet.

The *Albert F. Paul* is soon thereafter sold to new owners. Various repairs are entailed and other expenses show up before she changes hands and makes her last departure through the Virginia Capes.

There is "1 box candy—$2.00." For whom, after the vicissitudes of twenty-four years hard sailing, is that item intended?

However, the wooden schooners on the coast were always capable of producing surprises, and besides being picturesque and historically significant, they were downright fascinating. The world changed, as I suppose it must, but without the wooden schooners it did not become more interesting.

We thank Bob Burgess and The Mariners Museum for this book, which nails down so big a chunk of those days.

Fred F. Kaiser

Introduction

I took my first photo of the *Albert F. Paul* on May 10, 1931, as she lay at Pier 5, Pratt Street, Baltimore. That summer she was idle due to lack of cargoes, a brief respite for a busy schooner. I had occasion to visit her many times during that period, but come September 1 she was off to Georgetown, South Carolina, again for more lumber. During the next decade I went to see her whenever she put into Baltimore, taking my last photo of her in 1941 just before C. C. Paul and Company sold her and she left the Chesapeake on her last voyage.

The *Albert F. Paul* was one of a fleet of four-masted schooners owned in and operating out of Baltimore in the 1930s. The others were the *Sally Wren*, the *Purnell T. White*, the *G. A. Kohler*, and the *Doris Hamlin*. I boarded them all during that period, either to photograph them or to talk to their crews. One might say I was obsessed with sailing craft. The smaller Bay schooners and rams and the other Chesapeake sailing types were still plentiful then and could be seen around Baltimore harbor. But when one of the four-masters came in, I was soon down at the dock. Their size and longer voyages at sea surrounded them with a more romantic and adventurous aura than the Bay's "small fry." Eventually, only a trip on one of those schooners could satisfy me.

But those big sailing craft were passing quickly. In the summer of 1930 the *Sally Wren* grounded off Bermuda and was towed into port there and abandoned. In August 1933 the *G. A. Kohler* was driven onto the Outer Banks of North Carolina by a hurricane and was lost. The next year the *Purnell T. White* was abandoned at sea, with the loss of four of her crew, but was later towed to Baltimore and abandoned. I had to act fast. Only the *Hamlin* and the *Paul* were left registered out of Baltimore. The latter's calls at Baltimore were infrequent, so I concentrated on the *Doris Hamlin*, became acquainted with her skipper, Capt. George H. Hopkins, and did make my voyage in her in 1936 to Bermuda and Haiti. My association with the big coasters paralleled that of Fred Kaiser and my experiences were similar to his around New York harbor.

The office of C. C. Paul and Company, in the Stewart Building at Gay and Lombard Streets in Baltimore, was my goal on many occasions. I wanted to talk ships with some of the men there, but they rarely had time for a youngster interested in maritime history. Making money through moving cargoes in their ships was uppermost in their minds. The visits did afford me an opportunity, however, to view the many photos and paintings, and the half model of the *Albert F. Paul,* hanging in the office. That half model is now owned by Capt. W. J. L. Parker, USCG (Ret.), of Camden, Maine.

In the late 1940s the Paul firm was sold to Lloyd H. Lewis, who had worked in the office and who continued the business under the Paul name. He was more talkative and outgoing, and I had some interesting visits with him. While I was making a call on him in 1953, he went to the huge office safe and brought out a ledger identified as the "Trip Book" of the *Albert F. Paul.* I started to glance through its pages, and there in handwriting appeared the entire economic history of that schooner from 1917 to 1941: just about every penny she ever earned and spent.

The book was then placed at the rear of the safe and was left there. Fortunately, it was never cast out during an office cleanup, as were, apparently, all of the *Paul*'s logbooks. I asked Lewis if I could borrow it so that I might copy it, a chore my wife and I carried out over a period of months. In the meantime, Lewis died before I could return the ledger to him. But he had advised C. Howard Paul, one of the owners of the *Albert F. Paul,* that I had the book. Mr. Paul requested its return, and it is now in the hands of his son Charles C. Paul. When I thought of doing this book on the *Paul,* I knew the revealing contents of the trip book would play a big part.

About 1953 I wrote an article on the schooner *Purnell T. White* for the nautical magazine *Ships and the Sea.* After it had appeared, I received a letter from James S. McCullough, advising of his service in that vessel in 1933. Thus started a correspondence that lasted until his death in 1965. His wife passed along to me some of his material related to vessels on which he had sailed. Some of that concerned the *Purnell T. White* and was extremely valuable to me for my book on that schooner. Then after that book was published in 1970, Mrs. McCullough sent me additional information about the *White*. Now, realizing that data would be of interest to schooner fans, I include it as Appendix D in this volume. Other McCullough material included a journal he had kept during two trips on the *Albert F. Paul*; photos, sketches, detailed measurements of fittings, and the color scheme of that schooner—all his work—are also incorporated within this book.

The McCullough journal is a day-by-day record of shipboard and port happenings, all routine events in the operation of a large schooner. There is none of the yo-heave-ho, shoreside skylarking one might encounter in some modern schooner tales. Just plain, hard work with little pay and not the best of food; a true, revealing account of a way of life that some seamen returned to time after time.

The *Albert F. Paul* was unusual not only in her constant activity and longevity but also in that she was a family ship. Not long after Capt. Robert O. Jones took over command in 1924, he brought on board his wife and six-month-old baby girl. From then on, the after cabin was to resound with the voices and laughter of children—three of them eventually—particularly in the summer-vacation months. They sailed along the east coast, to Bermuda, and to Haiti right up to 1941, when Captain Jones left the vessel.

Even though Baltimore was the home port of the *Paul*, her visits there were few in the 1930s. After a six-month lay-up there in 1932, she departed for Wilmington, North Carolina, and did not return to Baltimore again until January 1938. Then, after sailing from the Chesapeake later that month, it was March 1940 before she came back to her home port again.

In 1940 the *Paul* made frequent voyages to Bermuda with coal from Newport News, Virginia, then sailed light down to Cap Haitien, Haiti, to load logwood for the return trip to Baltimore. That was a popular triangular trade out of Baltimore in the 1930s. I had made the same voyage in the *Doris Hamlin*. In fact, the *Paul* picked up that trade after the *Hamlin* was tied up in Baltimore in need of repairs. As Fred Kaiser has pointed out, there is romance in coal and salt cargoes. I might add logwood to that list—a hard, dark, heavy, gnarled wood valuable in the extraction of a purple dye.

This was cut in the mountains of Haiti and was brought to the island's seaports for export. There it was weighed on primitive scales, loaded aboard barges in Cap Haitien, and towed to the anchored schooner. Stages were build up the schooner's side so that the logwood could be passed by hand, stick by stick, up to the deck and then down into the hold to be stacked. When that was filled, the wood was piled on deck to complete the cargo. It required two to three weeks to load a schooner.

I recognize the names of individuals in the *Paul's* trip book, in Bermuda and Haiti, whom I met when I was in the *Hamlin.* Through the book's entries I could visualize what had taken place in the discharging of the coal at St. George, the trade-wind sail down to Haiti once through the calms of the horse latitudes, the anchorage in Cap Haitien, warm nights with fragrant aromas and the sounds of tom-toms off the land. So much is written between the lines of each entry in the trip book for those who knew the coasting schooners and their trades. And it can be enlightening for those who missed that period.

Robert H. Burgess

Coasting Schooner

The Four-Masted

Albert F. Paul

Chapter I

The *Albert F. Paul* is Launched

1829 N. Calvert Street
Baltimore, Maryland
March 23, 1942

Dear Brother–

I had a letter from Grace* this morning. She was all worried over you so I called up Mr. Paul and he told me the *Herbert Rawding* had arrived off North Point† this morning and he was sure you would be getting in today or tomorrow in Norfolk. We have all been worried for there are so many things out in the water today. Lou‡ came down from Boston to see us before sailing for the Far East. His boy sailed a week before. He said he enjoyed his meeting with you in Bermuda. Said he had not seen you looking so well or in such good spirits as you were for years. . . . Are you coming up to Baltimore when you get in Norfolk? We would love to see you. . . . Grace says she wishes you would stop going on those trips. You have worked long enough. I am glad you left the *Heidritter*§ when you did as she was lost off Hatteras. Do try to come up to see us when you get in Norfolk.

Lovingly,
Sister Dora

For thirty years that letter remained sealed in the files of the ship chandlery office of William H. Swan and Sons, Norfolk, Virginia. It had been addressed to Captain William M. Martino, master of the four-masted schooner *Albert F. Paul,* which was due in Norfolk from Turks Island, Bahamas, with a cargo of salt. But the *Paul* never reached port. In fact, that schooner had been torpedoed a week before the letter was written, on March 15, 1942, by the German submarine U-322, in the northwest Atlantic, at 26 north lati-

*Capt. William Martino's daughter.

†On the north side of the Patapsco River, at the entrance, on the approach to Baltimore.

‡Probably Captain Martino's brother Luther.

§Four-masted schooner *Anna R. Heidritter* stranded off Ocracoke, North Carolina, on March 2, 1942, and became a total loss. Her crew was rescued.

tude, 72 west longitude, with the loss of all hands. In April, Captain Martino's family received word from the United States government that he was missing while in the service of his country. Later, the United States Navy publicly announced the vessel as missing.

The *Paul* had left Turks Island on her last passage about February 21. The four-masted schooner *Herbert L. Rawding* referred to in the letter had left Cap Haitien, Haiti, for Baltimore in February and had encountered heavy weather. It was felt that the *Paul* had met the same storm and was delayed. And the hopeful clung to this belief as long as possible, expecting the schooner's late arrival in the Chesapeake. When the vessel's loss was finally announced, all hope was given up for finding any survivors.

It seems ironic that Captain Martino should have been lost with the *Albert F. Paul.* He first captained that schooner as temporary master in August 1920 on voyages #10 and #11 from Hampton Roads to Guadeloupe with coal and return from Miragoane, Haiti, to Camden, New Jersey, with a cargo of logwood. Then after the *Paul* had had a long and successful career and was sold by her original owners just before the United States became involved in World War II, Captain Martino took over command again and was lost on the schooner's first voyage for her new owners.

Just twenty-five years before, in 1917, work on the *Albert F. Paul* was being rushed at the shipyard of William G. Abbott, Milford, Delaware, to have the schooner overboard by the last of June. That date was missed, but the July 27, 1917, issue of the *Milford Chronicle* carried the following notice:

> On Wednesday next, August 1, 1917, there will be launched from the shipyards of William G. Abbott in South Milford, a large four-masted schooner which has been rushed to completion by the builder, without regard to the cost. For several months admission to the yard had to be by permit, but on Wednesday, Mr. Abbott has announced, those desiring to look through the yard will be welcomed and shown through by calling at the office where guides will conduct visitors over the plant and the new schooner.
>
> The dimensions of the vessel are as follows, 160 foot keel, 37 foot beam, and 14 foot depth of hold. She is built of white oak and heart

Half model of the *Albert F. Paul,* scale 3/8″ to 1′, owned by Capt. W. J. L. Parker, USCG (Ret.), Camden, Maine. (Photo by William Bunting, Courtesy Capt. W. J. L. Parker)

pine, and the joinery work which is especially fine is the work of the Downing Planing Company of Milford.

If the men employed in the yard take a holiday on Soldiers Day, Tuesday July 31, Mr. Abbott stated that it will be necessary to postpone the launching for one day, or until Thursday, August 2nd.

Apparently the men took their holiday, for the *Milford Chronicle* of August 3 reported:

The most beautiful vessel launching seen in Milford in years occurred at the Abbott shipyard in South Milford yesterday morning when the schooner *Albert F. Paul* was put in the water. The vessel started down the ways immediately after she was sawed loose and glided beautifully into the water.

She was built for New York parties and notwithstanding her exceptionally large size, was completed in less than a year. Every man who has been on the job since she was started was presented with a check for $100 soon after she was launched. Mr. Abbott will immediately lay a keel for another large boat.

Although the news item stated that the *Albert F. Paul* had been built for New York parties, she was actually constructed for the Baltimore ship brokerage firm of C. C. Paul and Company, her managing owners. They already owned the three-masted schooners *Bayard Hopkins, R. B. White,* and *William Linthicum,* and the two-masted schooners *Charles G. Joyce, Ada J. Campbell,* and *F. P. Murphy.*

The Paul firm was one of the more successful sailing-vessel operators of that period on Chesapeake Bay. The firm was established in 1894 by Charles Cornelius Paul as Paul and Wathen, at Pratt and Gay streets—known as Gaff-Topsail Corner—in Baltimore. The founder was born in St. Marys County, Maryland, in 1845, on a tobacco plantation. But his calling was toward the Chesapeake, and at age fifteen he joined a schooner commanded by his father, Capt. Charles Jackson Paul. The younger Paul worked up through the ranks and eventually went to sea in sail and became a master. He was associated with the construction of the two-masted schooner *Emily E. Johnson,* built in 1883 in Mathews County, Virginia, and was her master for a period. It is reported that his last command was the three-masted schooner *Venus,* built in Cambridge, Maryland, in 1883. Capt. Charles Cornelius Paul is said to have stated that when he reached the age of fifty he would stop sailing, because a man lost his nerve after that. He actually came ashore in 1894, not to get away from ships, but to become more involved with them as owner and manager. The captain made his home at 47 South Exeter Street in Baltimore, and there, in 1878, his first son, Albert F. Paul, was born. In 1900 the elder Paul moved to a home on Chase Street, later moving to 1708 North Broadway, Baltimore.

Albert, who had been attending business college, joined his father's firm in the mid 1890s. Soon after he became associated with the Paul Company, the business moved from Gaff-Topsail Corner to a building on the southwest corner of Gay and Lombard streets. The great Baltimore fire of 1904 ravaged that structure, but it was rebuilt, known as the Stewart Building, and C. C. Paul and Company continued their operations from its second floor.

The *Milford Chronicle* announcements conveyed a feeling of a festive atmosphere at the time of the launching of the *Albert F. Paul.* And it was. The launching party had assembled in Baltimore and consisted of Mr. and Mrs. Albert F. Paul; Mr. and Mrs. Charles M. Struven and their son; Mr. and Mrs. R. B. White and their son Russell (the senior men were also shareholders in the schooner); Miss Meta L. Koop; Captain Charles F. Southard, a shareholder and the *Paul*'s future commander; and Miss Bessie Paul, who was to christen the schooner.

After driving by motorcar to Seaford, Delaware, to stay for the night, the party continued next morning to Milford for the ceremonies. August 2 was bright and clear, and the town folk had turned out to witness the launching of the largest sailing vessel built in Milford up to that time. The launching time was set for 10:00 A.M., when the tide would be at its highest in the Mispillion River to accommodate the depth of the large hull. The river at Milford was less than two ship lengths in width, and to restrain the momentum of the schooner as she glided to the other side after sliding down the ways, stout lines from the ship to the yard kept her under control.

Miss Paul, sister of the ship's namesake, took a position at the forefoot of the schooner, and upon a signal she smashed a bottle of champagne—draped with red, white, and blue ribbons—against the blunt wooden stempiece and said, "I christen thee *Albert F. Paul.*" Shipyard workers then released the hull, and it slid down the ways, pushing a crest of water astern. Flags streamed from a line running the length of the ship, adding a holiday air to the event as steam whistles at the shipyard and nearby plants sounded off. Following the launching, guests were entertained at a luncheon provided by shipbuilder William G. Abbott.

The *Paul* was launched without masts and was towed to Baltimore to be rigged at the shipyard of J. S. Beacham and Brother. Through the late summer and early fall, the schooner was made

Hull of the four-masted schooner *Albert F. Paul* poised on the ways at the William G. Abbott Shipyard, Milford, Delaware, August 2, 1917. (Courtesy Mrs. Bessie Paul Bacon)

Albert F. Paul (left) and shipbuilder William G. Abbott. (Courtesy Mrs. Bessie Paul Bacon)

Launching party of the *Albert F. Paul* at Milford. Left to right—unknown, Mrs. Albert F. Paul, unknown, Mr. and Mrs. Charles M. Struven, Miss Bessie Paul, Mrs. and Mr. R. B. White, Russell White. (Courtesy Mrs. Bessie Paul Bacon)

Looking aft on the *Albert F. Paul,* prior to launching. (Courtesy Mrs. Bessie Paul Bacon)

Workmen prepare for the launching of the schooner. (Courtesy Mrs. Bessie Paul Bacon)

Miss Bessie Paul poses with the bottle of champagne at the forefoot of the schooner, just before the launching. (Courtesy Mrs. Bessie Paul Bacon)

The *Albert F. Paul* is restrained after sliding down the ways into the Mispillion River. (Courtesy Mrs. Bessie Paul Bacon)

ready for sea. She was then towed to Norfolk, Virginia, where she took on a cargo of 1,129 tons of coal for Pernambuco, Brazil, departing on October 28, 1917. Then began a succession of voyages that took her to several South American ports, Bermuda, the West Indies, Nova Scotia, and Gulf and east coast ports.

At the outset she was to profit from the freights resulting from World War I, $26.50 per ton of coal on that first passage. Seventeen years later that rate had tumbled to $1.10 per ton for coastwise delivery of the same commodity. But the *Albert F. Paul* has been described as one of the most successful and active of the World War I–built, east-coast four-masted schooners, never having experienced any lengthy periods of lay-up and in many instances with charters lined up for her two or three voyages ahead. She was also relatively free from any destructive mishap until her final loss as a result of war action. This was a result of excellent management, which found paying cargoes, and of capable shipmasters, who maintained her in good condition and navigated cautiously.

In Appendix A appears a listing of all her voyages, totaling ninety-nine under the C. C. Paul flag. This represents an extremely busy schooner, carrying a variety of cargoes to many ports. This running list was kept in the Paul office. It does not, however, reveal the personality of the ship. This is better discerned through the "Trip Book" maintained in the C. C. Paul office during the entire career of the schooner, detailing just about every penny expended or earned by the *Albert F. Paul*. The trip book appears as the lengthy but informative Appendix B.

Chapter II

A Schooner's Career Begins

Albert F. Paul was built of oak, yellow pine, and hackmatack, salted, and secured with iron and copper fastenings. She was classed A1 for fifteen years in the Record of American and Foreign Shipping, the highest rating given to a new ship. To achieve this distinction she had to be built under the supervision of the American Bureau of Shipping. She retained this rating through the time of her last survey in April 1941, at which time she was dry-docked and caulked. A survey made in 1939 showed that she had hogged only 6½ inches since her launch in 1917. The schooner measured 174 feet in length, 37 feet in beam, and 14.3 feet in depth, with a gross tonnage of 735 and a net tonnage of 661. Her stockless anchors each weighed 3500 pounds, and her anchor chain measured 1¾ inches in diameter. These were handled by a 16 horsepower Mianus engine mounted in her forward house. Her foremast was 26 inches in diameter, mainmast 25 inches, mizzenmast 24 inches, and spankermast 24 inches; each was 90 feet in length. The *Paul* lacked the finer lines of some of the other four-masted schooners built during her period. Her sheer was not too pronounced, and she had a "stubby" appearance about the bow. But apparently she was strongly built, which made up for her looks.

The original owners of the *Albert F. Paul*, their share of ownership, and costs of shares are as follows:

42/180	Charles M. Struven, Baltimore, Md.	$17,755.50
42/180	George N. Reed, Reedville, Va.	17,755.50
37/180	C. C. Paul and Co., Baltimore, Md.	15,641.75
28/180	R. W. Tunnell, Philadelphia, Pa.	11,837.00
12/180	Charles F. Southard, Baltimore, Md.	5,073.00
6/180	A. W. McNeal, Reedville, Va.	2,536.50
4/180	W. H. Edwards, Baltimore, Md.	1,691.00
3/180	G. H. McNeal, Reedville, Va.	1,268.25
3/180	J. W. McNeal, Fairport, Va.	1,268.25

3/180	H. W. Randolph, Richmond, Va.	1,268.25
	Entire cost	$76,095.00
	$422.75 for 1/180th Share	

It is interesting to note that virtually all of these names were associated with ships in one way or another—ship broker, chandler, shipmaster—and half of them were involved in the Reedville menhaden fishery.

The shipmaster was Capt. Charles F. Southard, who was to be in command of the *Paul* on her first nine voyages, until mid-1920. This was a fortunate situation, since a captain who held shares in a vessel would be apt to be more exacting in all phases of his charge, freights, expenses, and navigation.

In August 1920 Capt. William M. Martino became master of the schooner, taking her from Norfolk to Guadeloupe with coal. A return cargo from the Caribbean to the States made this a profitable voyage—logwood from Haiti to Camden, New Jersey. Capt. G. U. Fletcher was in command of the *Paul* when she sailed from Mobile in January 1921 with lumber for San Juan. Within the next several years the schooner was to have as masters, Capt. Richard Copsey, Capt. B. A. Warren, Capt. G. G. Carkow, Capt. George C. Carlson, and Capt. Alonzo S. Wallace.

On August 26, 1924, Capt. Robert Owen Jones took over command on a passage from Fall River, Massachusetts, to Baltimore. He was to remain in her, except for brief periods when he was hospitalized, for the balance of her career under the C. C. Paul flag, through 1941, a long time for a man to be in one ship. Captain Jones was born in Muria Llangdwll, Pwelheli Carnarvonshire, North Wales, on October 8, 1896. A newspaper account in 1936 reported that he ran away to sea on a square-rigger in 1914 and that he was a member of the crew of the British four-masted bark *Grenada,* sunk by a German submarine off the English coast on November 22, 1916. He went into steam after World War I for a period. In March 1924 he was mate on the four-masted schooner *Dorothea L. Brinkmann,* bound from Boston to Darien, Georgia. On the twenty-second of that month the schooner ran ashore near Oregon Inlet, North Carolina, and became a total loss.

Five months later, almost to the day, Captain Jones was in com-

Left to right, C. Howard Paul, Captain Webster Foxwell of the four-masted schooner *Salisbury*, and Albert F. Paul, c. 1915. (Courtesy Charles C. Paul)

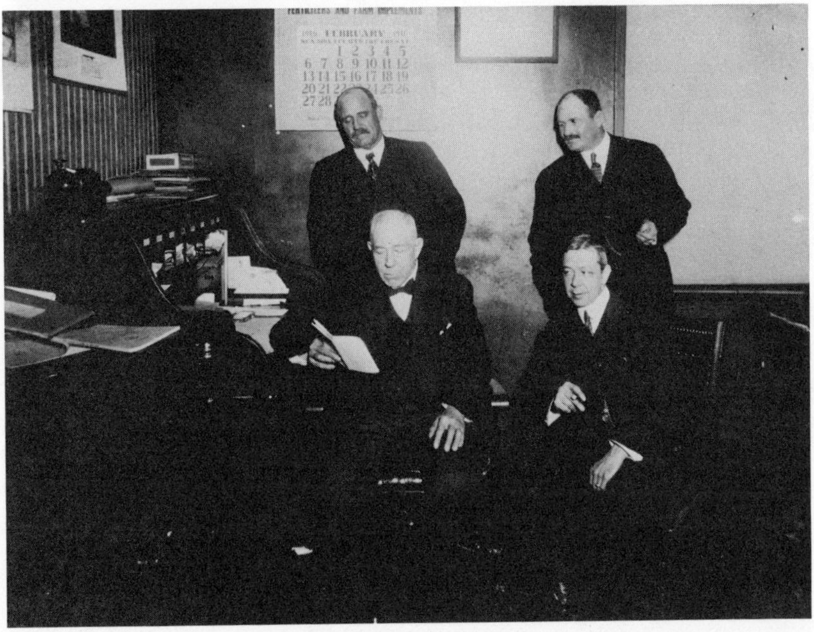

Seated at left is Charles Cornelius Paul, founder of the C. C. Paul firm; at right, Albert F. Paul. Standing at left is Captain Charles F. Southard, first master of the *Albert F. Paul*; at right, Captain J. Warren Simmons, in 1916. (Courtesy Charles C. Paul)

mand of the *Albert F. Paul,* and thus started a long and interesting association between a ship and a man. No doubt Captain Jones had put into Georgetown, South Carolina, for lumber while in schooners on the Atlantic coast. That port was one of the chief lumber-loading towns for coasting schooners. And it was there that he met his future wife. On December 21, 1924, the couple was married. The *Paul* was the scene of their honeymoon as the schooner departed from Georgetown on December 25 with a cargo of lumber for New York. Mrs. Jones, a native of Wilmington, Delaware, whose family had moved to Georgetown in 1913, had never sailed before. However, she was destined to sail on the *Paul* on most of her voyages until their children reached school age, and she admits to having been seasick every trip for about four days and in rough weather.

At the time of a visit of the *Paul* to Portland, Maine, in May 1926, there appeared in a local newspaper an article headlined "Personnel Of The *Paul* Has Increased Since Last Visit" and its first paragraph read:

> When the four-masted American schooner *Albert F. Paul* arrived here from Turks Island in July 1925, Captain Robert Jones brought with him a bride of but a few months. When the same vessel arrived here yesterday afternoon from the [same] port in the British West Indies, Captain Jones brought not only his wife but a wee baby girl as well. The infant [Maude Luella Jones] was born on land but now travels wherever Captain and Mrs. Jones are sent with the big schooner.

From January through November 1927, the *Paul* had been sailing regularly between New York, Baltimore, and Georgetown. The latter port was where Captain and Mrs. Jones maintained a home, and he always welcomed a brief spell away from the schooner to carry on activities enjoyed by his land-bound brethren. While the *Paul* was loading lumber for New York and Stamford, Connecticut, in early November, Captain Jones took a day off to go hunting with some friends. On November 8, while trudging through a swamp, his gun discharged prematurely, and he was hit in the left leg, above the knee. He was sent to the Florence (S.C.) Hospital, where it was found necessary to amputate the leg near the thigh. At first, Captain Jones's condition was critical, but a blood transfusion from a friend assisted in his recovery.

Capt. Charles Nicklas replaced Captain Jones in command of the *Paul* on November 16. Captain Nicklas was born Karl Nickel in Dortmund, Westphalia, Germany, on August 1, 1864, and came to the United States when he was nineteen years of age to search for gold. That treasure eluded him, so he turned to the sea, with which he had some experience. He sailed on vessels of the coffee fleet trading between Baltimore and Rio de Janeiro. He eventually gained command of coasting schooners and had been master of the Baltimore-owned four-masted schooner *Purnell T. White,* which also flew the C. C. Paul house flag, in the mid-1920s. In the summer of 1927 he had resigned from command of the *White* to retire to a farm he had purchased near Westminster, Maryland, to raise chickens. Three months later he was back at sea, if only temporarily, in charge of the *Albert F. Paul.*

Captain Nicklas sailed the *Paul* to New York and Stamford, leaving the schooner in the latter port on December 17 to return to Baltimore. Mate John Snelgrove took over the *Paul,* but by December 30 Captain Jones was again in command of the schooner, rejoining her in Stamford. The loss of a leg was not to impede him in navigating his vessel. A wooden leg enabled him to get about the decks as well as he had in the past.

Captain Nicklas did return to the sea again, resuming command of the *Purnell T. White.* He was lost off that schooner with three other members of the crew on February 9, 1934, when it capsized off the North Carolina coast while in tow of the Coast Guard cutter *Mendota.* The *White* had become waterlogged during heavy weather while bound from Georgetown to New York with a cargo of lumber.

The *Paul*'s name was rarely associated with mishaps of any kind, and the schooner seems to have been devoid of trouble in the 1920s —at least as far as getting her name in the papers. But in early March 1925 the *Paul* arrived in Baltimore from Georgetown with a story unique in her career. Captain Jones reported that, after the schooner had passed in the Virginia capes, a submarine chaser manned by members of the Coast Guard approached his ship and placed a searching party on board. The quest was for contraband liquor, but none was found. As the *Paul* proceeded up the Chesapeake, a second submarine chaser was sighted off York Spit. The craft headed

Albert F. Paul, as a new vessel and possibly just prior to her first voyage, anchored off the Norfolk and Western coal piers, Norfolk, Virginia. (Courtesy The Mariners Museum)

for the schooner and struck her mizzen chains, starting several of them and damaging the monkey rail. Again the *Paul* was boarded, but the search for liquor was fruitless. This was the bootleg and rum-running era, and the schooner is recorded as being the first sailing vessel to reach Baltimore after being subjected to such search.

The next year, however, the *Paul* was not to be as fortunate. The *Portland* (Me.) *Press Herald* reported on May 22, 1926: "The *Paul,* which dropped anchor in the lower harbor Thursday evening [May

20], was delayed a week by fierce winds and fogs which she encountered during her trip up the coast. The vessel is here with 30,000 bushels of Turks Island salt and will discharge at the W. H. Shurtleff plant."

May 27: ". . . completed discharging yesterday afternoon. All of the crew with the exception of the captain and mate have been paid off. There are several charters in view and probably she will sail for Halifax, N.S., to load for New York in the near future."

May 28: ". . . She is libeled for $10,000 on account of contraband cargo which was found in her hold."

June 3: ". . . The agents are here from Baltimore and it is thought the case will be cleared up in a few days."

June 5: ". . . is still under bonds, and activity aboard the boat has ceased. The owner, C. C. Paul, of Baltimore, was in Portland recently, and it is thought the case will soon be settled."

June 10: ". . . still remains idle at the end of Union Wharf. The case has not been settled as yet, and the skeleton crew is made up of the captain, his wife, a six-month old baby, and the mate."

June 12: "The schooner *Albert F. Paul* which has been tied up at the end of Union Wharf for the last three weeks will sail today for Halifax for a load of lumber for Philadelphia.

"The schooner which arrived here from Turks Island with a full cargo of salt for the W. H. Shurtleff Company, was discharging at the pier when seven cases of liquor were found in the hold wrapped in burlap bags. The captain and the mate were taken into custody and held on the charge of unlawful possession and the schooner was libeled for $10,000 and taken into the custody of the United States marshal.

"Yesterday the captain and the mate appeared before Judge Clarence Hale and were fined $50 each and a fine of $745 and costs were placed on the boat. A new crew was shipped aboard yesterday and today she will sail on her new charter."

In mid-August 1926 Captain Jones wrote to C. C. Paul and Company from New York:

> At 7 PM, while the schooner was lying at the foot of Tiffany Street, Brooklyn, we were struck by a whirlwind. Instantly, the vessel and vicinity were in the center of a "blue flame" which began destruction and within five minutes had disappeared. All mooring lines, including

Captain William M. Martino as a young man; he was master of the *Paul* on trips 10 and 11 in 1920 and was later lost with the schooner in 1942. (Courtesy Mrs. Agnita B. Phillips)

Captain Robert O. Jones as the young master of the schooner *Albert F. Paul,* c. 1924. (Courtesy Mrs. Robert O. Jones)

Captain and Mrs. Robert O. Jones on board the *Albert F. Paul,* c. 1932. (Courtesy Mrs. Robert O. Jones)

"Black Charlie." The last shipping master for sail in New York, who at times supplied crew members for the *Albert F. Paul.* "Black Charlie" was really Charles Hoyt. He is shown here seated on the waterways of the four-masted schooner *Annie C. Ross,* c. 1933. Standing is Edward Jordan, a distant relative and a steward on the *Ross.* (Photo courtesy of John A. Noble)

a new hawser, were snapped like twine. Two sail covers and the awning tied to the spanker boom were torn into shreds. The hatches and ship's hatches were picked up as if paper and hurled through the air. They were later recovered 700 feet from the ship. But for the quick service of the two men I had on board, the *Paul* would have brought up on a rocky beach. Timber and trees, carried away by the violence of the wind, were carried over the lofty masts of the schooner.

On November 22, 1932, after a summer's lay-up in Baltimore, the *Paul* departed from that port for Wilmington, North Carolina. As the schooner sailed down the coast, she was beset by heavy weather about 175 miles east of Wilmington. A sea boarded her and struck Captain Jones, hurling him against a deck house and mast. The *Paul* was driven far off her course, to the parallel of Jacksonville. For nine days Captain Jones suffered from a slight concussion of the brain and a four-inch gash in his forehead and was blinded for thirty-four hours. The schooner was finally brought to an anchorage off the Charleston lightship, where Captain Jones signaled the fishing smack *Maud* to take him ashore to a doctor. The smaller craft replied that it couldn't go in yet "as seven men were on board and they'd caught but one bluefish." Finally, the schooner's master was taken ashore by the boat. After the delay, the *Paul* arrived at Wilmington on December 12.

In early July 1933, a Bridgeport, Connecticut, newspaper devoted some space to the schooner. The *Paul* had arrived in that port in tow of the tug *Ferret*, of the Bridgeport Towing Company, from Stamford. It was reported that at the latter city she had been aground for several days before being able to continue her passage to Bridgeport.

In the summer of 1933, the *Albert F. Paul* successfully rode out two hurricanes in sheltered waters. These accounts appear in the section of the journal kept on board the schooner by seaman James S. McCullough making up chapter IV.

On April 6, 1935, the *Paul* was anchored off Beach Haven, New Jersey to await a favorable wind on a passage from New York to Georgetown. When her crew attempted to weigh anchor the next day, they found the windlass inoperative. Unable to make the necessary repairs on board ship, Captain Jones flew a signal of distress. A surfboat from the Squan Lifesaving Station went to her aid but found the vessel in no danger. In the meantime, the British steamer *Australind* had observed the schooner's plight and radioed for aid. The Coast Guard cutter *Comanche* was dispatched from New York to assist the schooner in making repairs. At 3:30 P.M. on the seventh, repairs had been completed, and the *Paul* weighed anchor and proceeded on her passage south.

October 1937 found the *Paul* in Jacksonville, loading lumber for Providence, Rhode Island. On the twenty-third she departed for her northern destination and made good time, for five days later she was off the mouth of Chesapeake Bay. Captain Jones had been stricken with pleurisy and required hospitalization, so the Coast Guard was contacted and a cutter was sent out to tow the schooner into Lynnhaven Bay, near Cape Henry, Virginia. On November 2 the *Paul* continued on her passage to Providence, momentarily in charge of a new master, Capt. George Jones.

Even though Baltimore was the schooner's home port, years would pass before she had occasion to call there to deliver a cargo. Her busy schedule kept her ranging the east coast from Florida to Maine, but on January 8, 1938, she departed from Jacksonville for Baltimore, her first visit there since the summer of 1932, when she had been laid up there for several months. On January 16, leaking and disabled, the schooner was found and taken in tow by the Coast Guard cutter *George M. Bibb* 390 miles southeast of Cape Hatteras. The Coast Guard cutter *Sebago* was dispatched to the scene to relieve the *Bibb*, which had been ordered to return to Norfolk. Heavy weather and rough seas delayed the tow, but on the twentieth the safety of Hampton Roads was reached. There the schooner was turned over to a commercial tug for the final leg up Chesapeake Bay to Baltimore.

Albert F. Paul was fortunate in being able to avoid actual confrontation with hurricanes, except for the incidents in the summer of 1933—when she was able to find anchorages in nearby sheltered waters or was in port when these storms passed over. In November 1939, however, she ran into a hurricane shortly after she left St. George, Bermuda, for Jacksonville. Captain Jones heard on his radio that a hurricane was moving northward out of the Caribbean area. Realizing the storm would cross the path of the schooner, he altered his course to place the ship into the northwest, or less severe,

Tug *Relief* and *Albert F. Paul* at New York, July 20, 1933. (Photo by P. L. Sperr, courtesy The Mariners Museum)

quadrant. But the hurricane changed its direction, and the *Paul* was steering directly into the center of the storm. The schooner was caught with too much sail on and was pressed over on her beam's end. She lost two jibs, and before the rest of her sails could be secured, she lost her spanker. She arrived safely in Jacksonville on November 11.

On November 29, 1939, the *Paul* left Jacksonville for Providence, but anchored off Jacksonville Lightship until December 1, when she set sail. On her way north the schooner held to the west until off Barnegat, New Jersey, to take advantage of the northwest wind and arrived in Narragansett Bay on December 8 and in Providence the next day. While anchored in that bay, the *Paul* was cast aground about a mile north of Poppasquash Point by northwest winds reaching sixty miles an hour. The Coast Guard patrol boat AB-59 went to her aid from Newport but was unable to assist her. The lighthouse tender *Shrub* later went to the scene and stood by her through the night. She was easily pulled clear on the ninth.

Chapter III

The *Paul* and Her People

In the days when commercial sailing craft were prominent at sea, it was fairly common for the captain to have his wife and often his children accompany him on voyages. The *Albert F. Paul* was a link with that period in that she was a family ship—Captain Jones taking his wife with him, and his three children during school vacations in the summer.

As mentioned earlier, the first of the Jones's children was Maude Luella, born on November 27, 1925. When she was two months old, her mother brought her on board the *Paul,* and they sailed with the schooner until the youngster was of school age. On April 27, 1929, a son was born, and he was named after the schooner, Albert Foxwell Paul Jones. That is living proof of the fondness Captain Jones had for his ship. On January 8, 1933, Jane Catherine was born. Another daughter, Laura Elizabeth, was born on January 4, 1945, after the schooner had been lost.

With the closing of school, the Jones family would join the *Paul.* Their quarters on the ship were ample, with two cabins off the main saloon—which served as a family room—and a bath. The ship's cook prepared all the meals which the family ate in the dining room off the saloon. The cook and mate also had cabins in the after quarters; the mate had his meals with the family. Mrs. Jones sent her laundry ashore when the ship reached port.

The Joneses claimed that none of the children except Albert suffered from seasickness, and they had full run of all the ship but forward where the crew was housed. At sea the youngsters played games on deck in fine weather, played with the dogs and cats that were always part of the schooner's complement, or fished. At times a swing was rigged under the mizzen boom. In rough or stormy weather the children were confined to the cabin, where more games would be played or they would listen to the radio or to stories read by their mother.

Up to the latter part of 1936, the *Paul* invariably called at Georgetown for lumber cargoes. There the Jones family would reside in their home while the schooner took two to three weeks to load, and their lives were as normal as any other citizen of that town. But in ports away from home, the family went sight-seeing, attended movies, or entertained on board the ship. Quite often they were guests of port officials at functions ashore. On one occasion, in Haiti, a government official staged a concert and dance in honor of Captain and Mrs. Jones and daughter Maude Luella.

In June 1935 Miss Mary E. Paul, daughter of C. Howard Paul, one of the schooner's owners, made a voyage in the vessel as passenger, signing on as stewardess, from New York to Charleston, Georgetown, and return to New York. She kept a daily journal which sheds some light on the shipboard and in-port activities of the Jones family. Miss Paul noted that she and the children played tag on deck and games in the cabin. At one period, as the schooner heeled while sailing, water rushed through the scuppers and formed puddles deep enough to permit the children to wade and to sail small boats. While the seamen were mending the spanker one day, the children made a tent out of a portion of it to shade them from the hot sun.

With so many children on board ship and with the variety of ways for them to get into mischief—climbing in the rigging and over deckhouses and cargo, and the possibility of falling down open hatches or overboard—the Joneses were fortunate that no injuries occurred. One incident, however, is still recalled: about 1929, when the *Paul* was entering St. George harbor, Bermuda, four-year-old Maude Luella—who had been holding onto a line attached to one of the schooner's booms—found herself suspended over the sea as the boom swung outboard. She was hauled back onto the ship quickly and was banned from the deck for a period.

Up through 1927 the *Albert F. Paul* had operated at a profit. In the late twenties the freights had been less and the expenses greater compared to her earlier career. But there were always dividend checks for her owners. In September 1928 there were eighteen shareholders in the schooner, most of whom were among her original owners or were members of their families.

In 1928 and continuing the next year, the schooner began to incur debts. On March 4, 1930, the *Paul* was libeled and sold at a

U.S. Marshal's sale, being taken in by C. C. Paul and Company and Charles Howard Paul, the latter a brother of Albert F. Paul, and associated with the Paul firm. From that time until the schooner's final sale away from the Paul house flag, C. C. Paul and Company was to hold 89/90 of the vessel and Charles Howard Paul 1/90.

Capt. Charles Cornelius Paul, founder of the company, died in the spring of 1927 and was buried in Loudon Park Cemetery, Baltimore. His son Albert F. Paul took over the business. Another son, Charles Howard Paul, had been associated with his father but had withdrawn from the firm in 1926 to join the Southern Transportation Company in Philadelphia. Neither son ever had an inclination to go to sea as a career.

Later, Albert F. Paul was to have R. B. White with him in the C. C. Paul firm. Between the two of them, they owned and operated quite a sizable fleet of pure sailing vessels out of Baltimore. The roster changed occasionally as new vessels were added and others were sold, lost, or abandoned. In the 1925 issue of the *Record of American and Foreign Shipping,* C. C. Paul and Company appear as owners of the two-masted schooners *Ada J. Campbell, Charles G. Joyce, F. P. Murphy, L. E. Williams, Ruth Decker,* and *Walter;* the three-masted schooners *John L. Martino, Lucie Wheatley, Lydia Middleton, William Linthicum,* and *William T. Parker;* the rams *B. P. Gravenor, Edward R. Baird, Jr., Edwin and Maud, Jennie D. Bell,* and *Levin J. Marvel;* and the four-masted schooner *Albert F. Paul.* In the same volume R. B. White is listed as owner of the three-masted schooner *Ida O. Robinson,* the ram *Clarence A. Holland,* and the four-masted schooners *Charles D. Stanford* and *Purnell T. White.* That is a goodly number of vessels to keep busy, and C. C. Paul and Company was able to do that, finding cargoes all round the Chesapeake area, coastwise, and down to the West Indies—principally lumber, coal, fertilizer, and logwood for the larger vessels.

The 1930s took a heavy toll of the fleet through losses, sales, and abandonments. Several voyages of the *Albert F. Paul* in 1937, 1938, and 1939 incurred small debts, but the schooner had sufficient funds from previous trips to carry her over. The latter year the Pauls almost sold the schooner. In August of 1939 the well-known Nova Scotian schooner operator Capt. James L. Publicover, of Dublin

Shores, began negotiations for the purchase of the *Albert F. Paul.* His four-masted schooner *Laura Annie Barnes* had been wrecked on Tuckernuck Shoal, Nantucket Sound, on January 17, 1939, while loaded with a cargo of wood pulp destined for New Haven, Connecticut, and he sought the *Paul* as a replacement. He still operated the four-masted schooner *Lillian E. Kerr* but found her too small for the wood-pulp trade. The acquisition of the *Paul* had just about been completed when the United States Maritime Commission halted the transfer of the schooner to British registry. Perhaps it was fortunate for C. C. Paul & Company that the sale was not approved.

The years 1940 and 1941 were good to the vessel, as she was voyaging offshore more often with payloads on a complete voyage, such as coal to Bermuda and logwood back from Haiti, in addition to coastwise trips. War clouds were gathering, and for the second time in her career, the *Albert F. Paul* would be sailing under wartime conditions. The United States had not yet become involved in World War II, but the Paul firm took out war risk insurance on the schooner and her cargoes. Maintenance was running high as the ship approached her first quarter century. On her last voyage under the Paul flag, to Haiti for logwood in 1941, the schooner got ashore at Cap Haitien. She was refloated and sailed back to Baltimore with her cargo intact. Upon her arrival in her home port, a diver was employed to inspect her bottom.

After discharging, the *Paul* was towed to Norfolk on October 28, 1941, where she was hauled out and repaired at the Norfolk Shipbuilding and Dry Dock Company. Then she was towed back to Baltimore again. Further repairs were made to the schooner in December at the Redman and Vane Shipyard. The latter part of November 1941, the schooner was sold to the Albert Shipping Company, Inc., of New York. The schooner was sold for $40,000, less $2,000 commission, leaving $38,000 for her owners. C. C. Paul and Company received $37,577.78 as its share. Charles Howard Paul was given $422.22 as his 1/90 part.

The sale of the *Albert F. Paul* marked the end of the operation of deep-sea sailing ships by C. C. Paul and Company. But that firm still had the rams *B. P. Gravenor, Edward R. Baird, Jr., Edwin and*

Maud, Grace G. Bennett, Jennie D. Bell, Levin J. Marvel, and *Mabel and Ruth,* and the two-masted schooners *Ida B. Conway* and *Ruth Decker.* Also on their roster were the power boats *Emily Margarette* and *E. Madison Hall,* the latter the former steam side-wheeler of that name which formerly operated out of Washington, D.C. The rams traded primarily on Chesapeake Bay, freighting lumber from the Carolina Sounds area to Baltimore and Philadelphia by way of the Albemarle and Chesapeake Canal and the Chesapeake and Delaware Canal. In addition, the company continued to secure charters for powerboats, tugs, and barges.

Albert F. Paul died in 1946. The fleet was sold, four of the rams, the *Edwin and Maud, Grace G. Bennett, Levin J. Marvel,* and *Mabel and Ruth,* being converted into "dude cruisers" taking out sailing parties. *B. P. Gravenor* had been sold earlier, was renamed *Mayfair,* and was lost on the North Carolina coast in 1942. R. B. White appears as owner of the *Baird* and the *Bell* in 1948, but they, too, changed hands and freighted on the Bay into the 1950s. The *Conway* was eventually converted into a powerboat and the *Decker* was abandoned. Arrangements had been made for Lloyd H. Lewis, an employee of the Paul firm, to take over the brokerage end of the business. This he pursued until his death in 1953, and then the Paul name faded from active participation in Chesapeake Bay shipping. Charles Howard Paul died in 1968.

As recorded here earlier, the *Paul* was lost on her first voyage under new ownership. Capt. Robert O. Jones had left the schooner when the Pauls sold her and had returned to his Georgetown home. It had been many years since Captain Jones had served in steamers. At the end of World War I he had worked on troopships bringing American soldiers home and subsequently stayed in the United States and became a citizen. Then he drifted into coasting schooners, where he remained until the *Paul* was sold. But after he gave up command in sail, he went back into steam again as first or second mate. His family has vague recollections of his being torpedoed off the Florida coast early in 1942. He is also said to have been torpedoed off Nova Scotia but was again rescued. In 1947–48 he sailed as second mate on the Liberty ship *Samuel Nelson.* His son was an able-bodied seaman on the ship at the same time.

Captain Jones later came ashore and began to work as night mate in Charleston, South Carolina, and as agent in Wilmington, North Carolina, for the Masters, Mates, and Pilots of America. He retired from that organization in January 1962 and died at Georgetown on May 24, 1963.

Chapter IV

Two Trips in the Schooner

James Smith McCullough, seaman, made two trips in the *Albert F. Paul* in 1933, from May to the latter part of September. He maintained a journal on board the schooner which is interesting from the seaman's viewpoint. This follows in its entirety. McCullough was not one merely trying to get experience on sailing ships for adventure's sake. He was a merchant seaman going to sea for a living. He had started in coasting schooners in 1923, in the three-masted schooner *Annie M. Murphy,* followed by service in other schooners and barkentines along the east coast.

McCullough was born at Brockway, Pennsylvania, on November 5, 1900. At the age of sixteen he ran away from home and joined a ship at Erie to inaugurate his seagoing career, which was to last almost half a century. Following World War I he made two trips to Europe from the States in the wooden steamer *Agria.* Then followed service in steamers to the Far East and the South Pacific. He kept diaries, and therein he mentioned seeing sailing ships at sea and in port, an indication of his fondness for sail. Through the 1920s he divided his service between sail and steam. Following his voyages in the *Paul* in 1933, he sailed on the four-masted schooner *Purnell T. White.* His account of his trip in the *White* appears in my book *Sea, Sails and Shipwreck* (Cambridge, Md.: Cornell Maritime Press, 1970).

Observant of his surroundings, McCullough was most unusual for a seaman of his day: he had a sense of history. Not only did he keep journals of his maritime activities but he also photographed his ships. The illustrations in this volume of the shipboard scenes of the *Paul* at sea are the results of his photographic efforts. In addition, he was a skillful artist and sketched the schooner, interior and exterior, to supplement his photos. Examples of his art are also included here.

In 1941–42 McCullough was a member of the crew of the two-masted schooner *Amendra,* formerly *Anna Sophia,* on a voyage from

James S. McCullough on the *Albert F. Paul* as able-bodied seaman, 1933. (Photo by James S. McCullough)

James S. McCullough at the wheel of the *Albert F. Paul,* 1933. (Photo by James S. McCullough)

Delaware River to Ciudad Bolivar, Venezuela, with explosives, and return to Norfolk. That was his last experience in sail. He then resumed his seagoing career in steamers, freighters, and tankers. On June 28, 1942, he was an A.B. on the tanker *William Rockefeller* when that ship was sunk by a U-boat sixteen miles east-northeast of Diamond Shoals, North Carolina. Following his rescue, he attended officer training schools and acquired his master's license and the rating of lieutenant commander in the U.S. Naval Reserve. During the war and until his death in New York on May 6, 1965, McCullough served as mate and master in tankers. His account of two voyages in the *Albert F. Paul* follows.

Detailed view of the mizzen crosstrees and topsail on *Albert F. Paul*, 1933. (Photo by James S. McCullough)

Looking aft on deck of the *Albert F. Paul*, 1933. Vessel is light, bound south to load lumber. Hatches are open for airing. (Photo by James S. McCullough)

Looking aft from the back ropes on the *Albert F. Paul* in 1933. Vessel under all lower sail, with sheets slacked well off in a fresh breeze. (Photo by James S. McCullough)

Albert F. Paul closest to the dock at Georgetown, South Carolina, almost loaded and ready to sail. *Purnell T. White* to her starboard, ready to take on a cargo of lumber when the *Paul* departs, November 1933. (Photo by James S. McCullough)

The Jones children on the *Albert F. Paul*; the eldest, Maude Luella, Albert Foxwell Paul, and Jane Catherine, c. 1935. (Courtesy Mrs. James E. Bailey)

The cook, Fred, with pie and food basket, 1935. (Courtesy Mrs. Robert O. Jones)

Mrs. Robert O. Jones with her children, Maude Luella, Albert, and Jane Catherine standing on the quarterdeck of the *Paul*, 1938. (Courtesy Col. Albert F. Paul Jones, USA)

Leaking and disabled, the *Albert F. Paul* is found on January 16, 1938, by the Coast Guard cutter *George M. Bibb*, 390 miles southeast of Cape Hatteras. (Photo by U. S. Coast Guard, courtesy The Mariners Museum)

The *Albert F. Paul* in tow of the cutter *George M. Bibb*, as the Coast Guard cutter *Sebago* approaches at left to take over the tow to Hampton Roads, Virginia, January 16, 1938. (Photo by U. S. Coast Guard, courtesy The Mariners Museum)

Albert F. Paul at Providence, Rhode Island, May 8, 1939. (Photo by Robert H. I. Goddard)

Looking aft from the forward house of the *Paul,* at Providence, May 8, 1939. (Photo by Robert H. I. Goddard)

The *Paul* sails light, bound from Providence to Perth Amboy, New Jersey, June 6, 1939. (Photo by William B. Taylor, courtesy The Mariners Museum)

Port-quarter view of the *Albert F. Paul,* showing the arrangement of the cabin trunk, at Providence, 1939. (Photo by Robert H. I. Goddard)

Albert F. Paul at Providence, August 14, 1939. (Photo by Robert H. I. Goddard)

Poop deck and motor yawl boat of schooner *Albert F. Paul* at Providence, 1939. (Photo by Robert H. I. Goddard)

Port bow of the *Albert F. Paul*, at Providence, 1939. (Photo by Robert H. I. Goddard)

Looking forward on *Albert F. Paul* at Providence, October 7, 1939. (Photo by Robert H. I. Goddard)

The *Paul* at anchor in Providence, December 9, 1939, after being aground off Poppasquash Point, Bristol, Rhode Island. (Photo by Robert H. I. Goddard)

Tug *Maurania* alongside the *Albert F. Paul* at pier of Wallace and Tucker Lumber Company, Providence, October 7, 1939, preparing to leave port. (Photo by Robert H. I. Goddard)

At the pier of the Redman and Vane Shipyard, Baltimore, Maryland, the *Paul* receives attention before departing for Jacksonville, Florida, for a lumber cargo, September 28, 1940. (Photo by Robert H. Burgess)

Albert F. Paul, after whom one of the more successful American coasting schooners was named, c. 1943. (Courtesy Charles C. Paul)

Albert F. Paul on the marine railway at Booz Shipyard, Baltimore, April 22, 1941. (Photo by A. Aubrey Bodine, courtesy The Mariners Museum)

Open seam in the rugged forefoot of the *Paul* is filled with compound at the Booz Shipyard, Baltimore, April 22, 1941. (Photo by A. Aubrey Bodine, courtesy The Mariners Museum)

After almost a quarter century of trading along the Atlantic coast, the bows of the *Paul* reveal signs of age. Her nicely carved trail boards and billethead remained in position to the end. Shown at Redman and Vane Shipyard, Baltimore, 1940. (Photo by Robert H. Burgess)

Captain and Mrs. Robert O. Jones, November 1953. (Courtesy Mrs. Robert O. Jones)

May 1, 1933

Vessel discharging at Church E. Gates Lumber Company, 152 Street and East River, New York. Robert O. Jones, Master. Turned to at 8 A.M. Took off sail covers, rove off the sheets. Patched main topsail, sent it aloft, and bent it. Set up the starboard mizzen rigging. Covered the hatches, swept down the deck, and knocked off at 5 P.M. Signed on after supper. Wages $30 per month. The ship is ready for sea and the tugboat will be alongside in the morning.

May 2, 1933

Due to a heavy fog the tug could not take us out with the morning tide. Spent the afternoon cleaning up the hold and piling the dunnage up alongside the keelson. Served and covered the mizzen turnbuckle threads in the afternoon. The tug *Relief* came alongside at 3 P.M. Filled up our fresh water tanks from the tug's supply. After our tanks were filled, gave the tug our hawser, cast off the mooring lines, and the towboat started down the East River with the vessel in tow. Anchored off Red Hook at 6 P.M. Wind is still south and it is foggy. Set anchor watch at 8 P.M. Clear and calm at midnight.

May 3, 1933

Rain squalls and fog; vessel anchored off Red Hook, New York. Turned to at 8 A.M. Washed the white paint work; started aft and worked forward to the break of the poop, then worked from the fo'c'stlehead aft to the poop. Finished and knocked off at 3 P.M. Clear at 3 P.M., rain squall at 6 P.M. Set anchor watch at 8 P.M.

May 4, 1933

Clear at 3 A.M. northwest wind. Called all hands at 6 A.M. Signalled for the tow boat (ensign bent half way up in the spanker rigging). Hove the anchor up short and loosed the head sails. Breakfast at 7:30 A.M. Tug *Relief* came alongside at 7:45 A.M. Passed the hawser to the towboat and hove up the anchor and got under weigh. Set the mainsail, forestaysail, jib, foresail, and mizzensail. On the port tack. Set the spanker, flying jib, and outer jib. Ship going wing and wing. In the lower bay the tug let go the hawser and gave us a parting salute (three blasts of her whistle) and we were on our way to Georgetown, South Carolina. Scotland Lightship abeam about 9:30 A.M. Streamed the log. Ship on the starboard tack and making about 6 knots. Set the fore, main, and mizzen topsails. Cleared up the deck and picked the watches. Port watch below 11 A.M. Spliced eyes in two old hawsers. Light north wind at 2 P.M., course south by west. Clewed up the topsails and wore ship at 4 P.M., port tack, shifted and set the topsails, wind southeast, course by the wind. Clewed up the topsails and wore ship again at 5 P.M., starboard tack. Barnegat Lightship abeam at 6 P.M. Shifted and set the main and mizzen topsails at 6 P.M., also loosed and set the spanker topsail and tied up the fore-topsail. Vessel going by the wind, moderate breeze.

May 5, 1933

At midnight, clear, light west wind, course SSW. Flat calm at 1 A.M. Clewed up the topsails, over the stays, and let them hang. Light breeze from the east at 1:30 A.M. Wore ship, shifted and set the topsails. Calm again at 2 A.M. Clewed the topsails up over the stays. Moderate breeze from the southeast at 3 A.M. Set the topsails, also loosened, shifted, and set the fore-topsail at 8 bells. 8 A.M. trimmed the sheets and stretched the throat and peak halliards. The four-mast schooner *Alvena* off to leeward, bound north. A Coast Guard cutter overhauled and spoke us about 10 A.M. "Where are you from?" asked the cutter. "New York," said the captain. "Where are you bound?" "Georgetown." "All well aboard?" "All is well." With that the cutter headed inshore.

Kept all hands on deck after dinner to send the mooring lines down in the hold, coil them, and lash them. At 3:30 P.M. it was blowing fresh from the southwest with passing rain squalls. Vessel going by the wind heading about W by N. Called all hands to clew up the topsails and tie them up. Hauled down the outer jib and tied it up. Hove the lead—17 fathoms of water. The skipper came on deck with his oil skins on, a boot on his right foot and a shoe on the left (he had a wooden leg). Fenwick Shoals Lightship abeam at 6 P.M., wind from the south and sailing by the wind. The sky is completely overcast with passing rain squalls. Winter Quarter Lightship abeam at midnight.

Lieutenant Commander James S. McCullough, USNR, 1900–65 (Courtesy Mrs. James S. McCullough)

At some time James S. McCullough had hoped to publish a volume on schooners. He made a series of pen and ink drawings and prepared a foreword and a lengthy caption for each drawing. The book's title was to be "Schooners of the Past in Picture and Story," and it was dedicated to his late wife Elinor, who resided in Tallahassee, Florida, until her death in September 1976. The drawings included portraits of the better known schooners along the east coast during the early part of this century. Other scenes were sketches of shipboard activities, particularly of the schooners *Albert F. Paul, Purnell T. White,* and *Emerett,* vessels in which he sailed. A selection of these is reproduced here. McCullough put much effort into his drawings to ensure accuracy of detail. His human figures are somewhat primitive, but his perspective is good. Most of these show men at work. He was unable to photograph some of these activities, since he was part of the crew involved in the labor. But he later sketched the scenes, in 1935, 1947, and 1949.

The *Albert F. Paul* (Drawn by James S. McCullough)

May 6, 1933

Moderate gale from the southeast, heavy rain squalls at 1:30 A.M., sailing by the wind. Called all hands at 2 A.M. to take in sail. Lowered the spanker, hauled down the flying jib, lowered the foresail, hauled down the jib, lowered the mainsail. Moderate breeze from the southwest, course SW by S. Heavy swell running. Heading for the beach under forestaysail and mizzen, taking soundings every few minutes. Got the anchors ready to let go. Last sounding 15 fathoms. Hauled the forestaysail down, brought the vessel up into the wind under the mizzen, let go the starboard anchor and lowered the mizzen. Ninety fathoms of chain out, all we have. It is quite cold and the rain came down in torrents. All hands worked until 6:30 A.M. tieing up the wet sails, then went below for coffee. Cleared up the deck. Heavy swell running and the vessel is rolling heavily. Two cloths in the head of the foresail split when taking it in. Stopped raining and the wind moderating. Patched the foresail. Breakfast. Wind went around to the southwest, light breeze. Clothes, bunks, and everything soaking wet. All hands turned in to get some sleep.

Called all hands at 2:30 P.M. to set sail. Wind from the west, moderate breeze, heavy swell, sea choppy. Hove in the anchor, set the forestaysail, mainsail, jib, flying jib, foresail, mizzen, and spanker. Cleared up the deck. Supper. Shifted and set the mizzen topsail.

May 7, 1933

Shifted and set the fore and main topsails about 2:30 A.M. Eight bells on the morning watch set the outer jib and swayed up the jib and topsail halliards, Ship just making steerageway. Heavy swell running with light breeze from the north-northwest, course SSW.

Stretched the spanker peak halliards at one bell. Light air, ship rolling heavily, clewed up the topsails, fore, main, and mizzen. Shifted and set the main and mizzen topsails about 5:30 P.M.

Clewed the main and mizzen topsails up over the stays at 8 P.M., hauled down the outer jib and wore ship, starboard tack. Calm or light air from the eastward, vessel rolling heavily. Flashing light off to the southwest.

May 8, 1933

Moderate breeze at 4 A.M., sailing by the wind on starboard tack, wind southeast by south. At 8 A.M. hauled down the outer jib, clewed down the topsails, and wore ship. Called out the watch below at 8:30 A.M. to haul down the outer jib as the seams along the head started to go. The watch on deck were aloft tieing up the topsails. Patched the outer jib and tied it up. Vessel going full and by heading about S × W½W.

Fresh breeze from the southwest at noon. Vessel heading W on the port tack under flying jib, jib, forestaysail, foresail, mainsail, mizzen, and spanker. The ship is laying over and the water is boiling up through the scuppers. Making about 10 knots. Crew painting the inside of the bulwarks.

Land in sight at 3:30 P.M. Wore ship. Vessel now close hauled heading about S. Swayed up the mizzen peak and forestaysail halliards at 6 P.M. Wind went around to the northwest and the vessel is again on her course, SW. Bodie Island Light ahead, about five miles off at 8 bells. Clewed up the topsails, main, mizzen, and spanker. Tied up the spanker topsail. Some of the seams in the spanker started to go. Lowered it and tied it up. Wore ship (port tack). Shifted and set the main and mizzen topsails. Loosened and set the fore-topsail. Vessel rolling along right before the wind.

May 9, 1933

At midnight moderate breeze from northeast, sea smooth, clear, cold, steering ESE. Bodie Island Lighthouse abeam at 2:45 A.M. Wind from the east at 10 A.M., course S × W½W. Diamond Shoals (Relief) Lightship abeam half mile off at 10:30 A.M. Changed the course to SW × W, light breeze.

Patched the spanker in the forenoon watch and set it. Painted the bulwarks inside. Went around the lightship. Very warm. The vessel is in the Gulf Stream. Edge of the Stream visible off to leeward. Plenty of seaweed and schools of flying fish. The sand flies came aboard off Cape Hatteras in great swarms. Ship going along about 2 knots.

Set the spanker topsail at 4 P.M., wind northeast, course S × W½W. Trimmed the sheets at 5 P.M., sailing by the wind as

THE FORECASTLE. The forward deckhouse in schooners was usually divided into three compartments: galley, donkey-engine room, and fo'c'sle or crew's quarters. The space allocated for seamen's accommodation, as required by law, was 120 cubic feet per man, with not less than 16 square feet of deck space. This necessitated careful planning in order to use the space to best advantage.

In well-designed vessels the customary double-decked bunks were placed fore and aft, decidedly a comfort to the sailor who was in his bunk when the vessel was listed over on the other tack. In a thwartship bunk he would find his feet higher than his head.

A hinged table, which could be folded up against the after bulkhead when not in use, and benches built along the lower bunks, with drawers beneath them, made up the furniture.

A small sliding door in the bulkhead at table height, called the pie-hole, opened up into the galley. At mealtime the cook rapped on the little door, signifying that he was ready to pass in the grub.

[Schooner depicted is unidentified.] (Drawn by James S. McCullough)

the moderate breeze from the south comes in. Sea choppy, clear. Vessel making about 8 knots.

Weather fore lift carried away, put a long splice in it and rove it off again. Clewed up the fore-topsail and tied it up. Cape Lookout Lighthouse about 2 points on the lee bow at 10 P.M. Clewed up the main, mizzen, and spanker topsails. Wore ship. Ship going by the wind, heading about SE. Shifted and set the main, mizzen, and spanker topsails at eight bells.

The captain is apparently a superstitious man. When we have a head wind he draws a pin or two out of the taff rail and lays them down on deck pointed in the direction he wants the wind to blow. This is an old sea superstition and he must believe in it.

May 10, 1933

Full and by at 4 A.M., wind from the southwest. Called all hands at 7:30 A.M. to shorten sail. Clewed up the topsails and hauled down the outer jib. Squalls all around the ship. Tied up the jib and topsails. Vessel going full and by on the port tack heading about W. Land in sight. Wore ship at eight bells.

Called all hands at 9:30 A.M. Lowered the spanker, foresail, hauled down the jibs and forestaysail. Let go the starboard anchor. Fifty fathoms of chain out. Let the main and mizzen sails set. Port spanker lift and forestaysail lifts carried away. Rove off a new spanker lift and spliced the staysail lift. Kept all hands on deck patching the spanker. At 10:30 A.M. heavy squall off to windward. Lowered the main and mizzen sails. Started to tie up the sails which had been left hanging in the lifts. A violent squall hit us, rain and wind, water smoking, impossible to do anymore at tieing up the sails in the driving, blinding rain and strong wind. Payed out more chain. Good thing the sails were down when the squall struck or we undoubtedly would have lost some sail. After the squall passed we finished tieing up the sails—a tough job. Knocked off all hands after dinner. Set anchor watch at 8 P.M.

May 11, 1933

Light breeze from the west, clear, at midnight. At 8 A.M., calm, turned the crowd to. Sent them down in the hold to caulk the seams in the ceiling along the bilges and bottom. All hands on deck at 11:30 A.M. to get under weigh. Light air from the northwest. Hove the anchor short, set the mizzen and mainsail. Flat calm again. Turned to after dinner and painted inside the bulwarks. Knocked off at 3 P.M.

At 6:30 P.M. lowered the main and mizzen sails and covered the hatches. A cover is taken off the fore and mizzen hatches every day that the weather is nice, to help dry out the inside of the vessel. Set anchor watch at 8 P.M.

May 12, 1933

8 A.M., hove short, set mizzen, main, and foresail. Anchor clear and hove up, set the forestaysail, jib, spanker, flying jib, outer jib, main, mizzen, and spanker topsails. Vessel on the starboard tack going by the wind, heading about E × S. It took just two hours to heave up and set sail. All sail set but the fore-topsail.

All hands set to work scraping and painting the inside of the bulwarks. The wheel was put in the beckets and the vessel steered herself. Clewed up the topsails and wore ship at 11:30 A.M. Shifted and set the main and mizzen topsails. Vessel going by the wind, heading about W × N. Clewed up the topsails and wore ship again at 2:30 P.M. Shifted and set the main, mizzen, and spanker topsails.

The captain takes the wheel when we wear ship. Otherwise the ship has been steering herself all day while all hands including the mate have been scraping and painting around the bulwarks. Clewed up the topsails and wore ship at 3:30 P.M. Shifted and set the main and mizzen topsails. Clewed up the topsails and wore ship again at 5 P.M. Shifted and set the main and mizzen topsails. Clewed up the topsails and wore ship at 6:30 P.M. At 8:30 P.M tied up the topsails, hauled down the outer jib and tied it up.

Hauled down all the head sails, lowered the foresail, and when the ship came up into the wind let go the starboard anchor. Lowered the main, mizzen, and spanker. Put peak stops on the sails and a turn around the jibs. No anchor watch set and all hands turned in at 9 P.M. Cape Lookout Lightship bearing SW × W and Cape Lookout Lighthouse bearing about NW × W.

THE CABIN. The afterhouse, or cabin—a spacious and elaborate place compared with the forecastle, and looked upon by sailors as a kind of holy of holies—quartered the Master and the ship's officers.

The typical cabin was divided into several parts. The forward cabin was used as a dining room for the after guard. The mate's room opened off it on the port side, followed by the steward's room, followed by the pantry. These were small and simply furnished rooms.

The after, or main, cabin, usually slightly larger than the forward cabin, was used by the Master as a sitting room or parlor. Guest rooms, one on each side, opened off this sitting room.

Abaft the main cabin on the starboard side was the Master's bedroom. It was quite spacious and was furnished with a large four-poster bed screened by curtains, a chest of drawers, and ample locker space. A small chart room was located at the foot of the after companion ladder, and across from it, on the port side, was the Master's bathroom with the customary fixtures including a small bathtub.

The cabin interior was usually paneled, and the wood was either finished in natural color or painted white. The decks in the main cabin and Master's bedroom were fitted out with rugs, and the forward cabin was covered with linoleum.

[Schooner depicted is unidentified.] (Drawn by James S. McCullough)

May 13, 1933

Wind southwest, ahead, but the weather is fine. All hands turned to at 8 A.M. painting bulwarks, masts from deck to saddles, sheet blocks, and blocks on the gaffs. Oiled the gaffs. Finished painting at 2:30 P.M., swept down the deck, and knocked off.

Set anchor watch at 8 P.M. Anchor watch is stood between 8 P.M. and 4 A.M. One man on the deck at a time to watch that the anchor does not drag, or to report the wind in case the vessel is anchored waiting for a fair wind, watch that the anchor lights do not go out, and keep a lookout for heavy squalls. With four men in the fo'c'sle, each man has two hours anchor watch to stand between 8 P.M. and 4 A.M. At 4 A.M. the mate, or bos'n if the ship carries one, is called. The cook is also called at 4 A.M.

About 10:30 P.M. the ship took some chain. Before the man on watch got back to call the mate, the captain came forward in a rage, called all hands and proceeded to bawl them out, using much profanity. He issued new orders—Two men on deck at a time and strike the bell aft every half hour.

May 14, 1933

Took the covers off the hatches at 8 A.M. Crew spent the day, this being Sunday, washing clothes, mending, airing bedding, and cleaning out the fo'c'sle. Wind southwest. Set anchor watch at 8 P.M. One man on watch at a time. Strike the bells aft every half hour.

May 15, 1933

Moderate northwest breeze, clear, at 3 A.M. Called all hands at 4:30 A.M. to set sail. Hove up the anchor and set the forestaysail, jib and flying jib. The wind shifted around to light northeast. Set the mainsail, foresail, and mizzen. Vessel going SW × S on the port tack. Set the fore and main topsails and outer jib. Cleared up the deck and went to breakfast. Set the spanker and mizzen topsail at 8 A.M. Scraping and sandpapering the blistered paint on the cabin trunk, getting it ready for a coat of paint. Lookout Lightship abeam about 9:30 A.M., a mile or so off.

Clewed up the topsails and gybed over on the starboard tack at 12:30 P.M. Shifted and set the topsails. At 4 P.M. clewed up the topsails and gybed over on the port tack. Shifted and set topsails. Ship making about 4 knots. Loosened and set the spanker topsail at 6 P.M. The wind hauled around to the south'ard about 6:30 P.M. All hands trim the sheets by the wind. Clewed up the fore-topsail and tied it up so that the vessel would head closer up into the wind. Cape Fear Lighthouse on the lee bow at 10:30 P.M.

May 16, 1933

At 4 A.M. cloudy, moderate breeze SW × W, sailing by the wind. Clewed up topsails and wore ship at 6 A.M. The wind is about southwest, head wind. Shifted and set the topsails, the ship heading about W × N (port tack). Frying Pan Shoals Lightship dead to windward at 8 A.M. Swayed up the jib and topsail halliards at 8 bells. Called out the watch below at 10:30 A.M. to clew up topsails and wear ship. Shifted and set the main and spanker topsails. Vessel on the starboard tack. Called out the watch again at 11:30 A.M. to haul down and tie up the outer jib. The jib was hauled down so that the vessel would point up closer to the wind. The vessel is heading about S½W and making about 1½ points leeway. Frying Pan Shoals Lightship broad on the starboard bow at 2 P.M.

Clewed up the topsails and wore ship at 2 P.M. Port tack. Shifted and set main and spanker topsails. Painted on the cabin trunk. Clewed up the topsails and wore ship again at 8 bells. Shifted and set the topsails. Starboard tack.

At 6 P.M. clewed up the topsails and wore ship. Shifted and set the topsails. The main topsail was torn in setting. Clewed it up and sent a man up to patch it. When the sail was fixed, tied it up. Clewed up and tied up the other topsails. Hauled down the jibs and staysail. Lowered the foresail, mainsail, and spanker. Brought the vessel up into the wind under the mizzen and let go the starboard anchor. Seventy-five fathoms of chain out. Lowered the mizzen. Tied up the jibs, put peak stops on the lower sails, secured everything for the night and went below at 10 P.M. Set anchor watch, one man on watch at a time.

May 17, 1933

Moderate breeze from N × E at 4:30 A.M. Called all hands at 5 A.M. to get under weigh. Fair wind. Hove short the anchor, set the

THE HELMSMAN. Steering was one of the most important jobs a sailor had to do. In a light breeze and smooth sea it was usually quite easy, but when the wind was strong and the sea rough, the task required the skill of an experienced seaman. If the wind was fair, the helmsman steered a compass course, but when the wind was ahead and the vessel could not make her course, the steering order was "by the wind."

Many vessels would hold their course with very little assistance from the helmsman when the wind was abeam or forward of the beam, if the sails were properly set and trimmed. A dangerous point of sailing, in a schooner, was directly before the wind with the sails trimmed, "wing and wing." In heavy weather two men were often needed to keep the vessel on her course. Under extreme conditions, when the vessel was hove to, the wheel was sometimes put in beckets and required no attendance from the helmsman.

At night the compass was illuminated by a small, brass binnacle lantern, which was not very efficient. On clear nights the helmsman often picked out a bright star ahead, which was in line with the masts when the vessel was on her course, and steered by it. This was an old seafaring practice.

[Schooner depicted is unidentified.] (Drawn by James S. McCullough)

fore, main, and mizzen. Hove the anchor in and set the forestaysail, jib, and flying jib. The outer jib needed some repairs so did not set it. Set the fore, main, and mizzen topsails. Put a patch on the outer jib and set it. Set the spanker. Breakfast. Put a patch on the spanker topsail and set it but clewed it up again. The vessel would not carry it without running up into the wind.

Called out the watch below at 3 P.M. Clewed up the topsails and wore ship. Shifted and set the topsails. Sent up the towing hawser and mooring lines from the hold. Georgetown sea buoy in sight off the lee bow. Clewed up the topsails. Rounded the buoy about 5:15 P.M. Wore ship. Hauled down the jibs and forestaysail. Lowered the spanker and foresail. When the ship came into the wind, let go the starboard anchor. Forty-five fathoms of chain out. Lowered the main and mizzen. Supper. Tied up the jibs, topsails, and put peak stops on the lower sails. Cleared up the deck. Set anchor watch.

Wind freshened into moderate gale from the northeast. Paid out more chain—80 fathoms out.

May 18, 1933

Fresh breeze but moderating, called all hands at 5 A.M. Coffee. Hove in some chain. Put a harbor furl on the jibs. Sea going down. The tugboat *W. H. Andrews* came out about 10 A.M. The pilot, Captain Porter, came aboard. Passed the hawser to the tugboat, hove in the anchor, and got under weigh. Set the main, mizzen, and forestaysail. The tug could not keep ahead of the vessel. Hauled down the forestaysail and dropped the peak of the mizzen. Fifteen miles up Winyah Bay to Georgetown. About two miles below the town lowered the main and mizzen sails and tied them up. Unhooked the jib sheets and coiled then down close up in the bow to be out of the way. Unshackled the lower fore, main, and mizzen sheet blocks, pulled them up two blocks, and coiled the sheets over the ends of the booms. Hove the main and mizzen booms up well clear of the deck to be out of the way when loading. Put shores under the boom jaws and unhooked the throat halliards which will be used in loading. When the vessel was abreast the town the tug blew three long blasts of the whistle to let the townspeople know a vessel had arrived in town.

Tied up to the Atlantic Coast Lumber Company dock about 3 P.M. Cleared up the deck, swept down, and knocked off. The captain's family, friends, and relatives of the crew were down on the dock to meet the ship. The arrival of the *Albert F. Paul* seems to be an important event.

Georgetown May 19, 1933

Turned to at 8 A.M. Only the mate and two men aboard the vessel. Two of the Georgetown members of the crew did not come aboard last night. Lowered the yawl boat. Took a spare foresail out on the dock to repair it. Put rope-yarn stops on the topsails and hoisted them up to have the crosstrees and mast doublings clear for painting. Swept down the decks and knocked off at 4 P.M. Started to load the vessel today. The longshoremen (colored) work ten hours a day. The wages range from 70 to 90 cents a day.

May 20, 1933

Turned to, one seaman and the mate, at 8 A.M. Started to paint the forecrosstrees. The mate worked on the foresail. Knocked off at noon. The longshoremen worked all day. The lumber comes aboard on a loader which is an endless chain conveyor and works very successfully. The tide has a range of about 4 feet.

Sunday May 21, 1933

Did no work except pump the ship. The pump is operated by a little gasoline engine.

May 22, 1933

Turned to at 8 A.M. Painting in the crosstrees and mast doublings. All hands back to work. Mate sewing on the foresail when he has time.

May 23, 1933

Turned to at 8 A.M. Two of the crew did not show up this morning. The painting in the crosstrees is not finished yet although it is only a short day's work for a man to paint one mast head. Painting on the poop deck.

TRIMMING THE SPANKER SHEET. The spanker was the largest sail in a schooner and the hardest one to handle. It often had an area of 4,500 square feet or more in the bigger vessels. It required plenty of "Norwegian steam" or a handy-billy to take in the spanker sheet if there was much wind. Using the handy-billy was a slow process, and when time did not permit its use, the watch below was called out to give assistance. A good helmsman could ease the vessel close to the wind, relieving the pressure on the sail and lightening the strain on the sheet. When the sea was rough, careful steering was necessary to keep from getting the sails aback or jibing over, which might result in damage to the sails or rigging.

[Schooner depicted is unidentified.] (Drawn by James S. McCullough)

May 24, 1933

Turned to at 8 A.M. Got up the chain deck lashings from the forward lazarette and shackled them in the bails in the waterways. Set up the stanchions along the bulwarks. Painted the waterways. Painting on the poop.

May 25, 1933

Mate and one man turned to. Mate sewing on the sail, the AB painting on the poop deck. Hauled the vessel up the dock to make room for a steamer that is coming alongside the dock in the morning. Longshoremen assisted in moving the vessel.

May 26, 1933

One man besides the mate turned to this morning. Longshoremen did not work the vessel today.

May 27, 1933

Turned to 8 A.M. Painting on the poop. Only one man in the crew working. The mate working on the foresail. Swept down and knocked off at noon. Longshoremen did not work today.

Sunday May 28, 1933

No work today.

May 29, 1933

Turned to at 6 A.M. and hauled the vessel down the dock to the loader. Longshoremen worked today.

May 30, 1933

Turned to at 8 A.M. Three men and the mate aboard. One man, W. Moore, quit at noon.

May 31, 1933

Turned to at 8 A.M. Shipped a new seaman, Henry Leonard. This is his first ship. Made up the foresail, brought it aboard, and stowed it in the after lazarette. The longshoremen finished loading at noon, 793,000 feet of pine and cypress lumber (kiln dried) aboard. The pilot Captain Porter came aboard and the towboat *W. H. An-*

drews came alongside at 2 P.M. Towed down to an anchorage off Frasiers Point, Winyah Bay, to await for fair wind. Captain went back ashore with the tug.

June 1, 1933

Moderate breeze from the north, cloudy. Turned to at 8 A.M. Secured the deck load with chains, wire, and turnbuckles. Used every bit of spare chain and wire aboard to secure the load which is piled about 8 or 9 feet above the deck and completely covers the cabin trunk extending aft to the after end of the cabin trunk. Only by the grace of God will we get this cargo to New York intact. Just before the vessel left the dock yesterday another boy, Jenkins Cooper, joined the crew. He is also a greenhorn. No wonder they call this the Georgetown training ship.

June 2, 1933

Turned to 8 A.M. Loosened the main and mizzen sails and took a reef in them. The sails had to be reefed before they could be set on account of the high deck load. Sails on lumber schooners usually have what is called lumber reefs in the main and mizzen. Built a temporary rail along each side of the deck load. Shackled in the sheet blocks, pennants for the boom tackles, put strops in the rigging for snatch blocks to be used for fair leads in setting sail, and in general got the ship ready for sea.

June 3, 1933

Light breeze from the north, clear. Turned to 8 A.M. Greased down the masts. Stowed away the gear, swept down, and knocked off at 2 P.M. The captain came aboard about 4:30 P.M. but went back ashore again. Wind shifted around to the southwest, light breeze, fair wind. Expect the captain aboard and the tug to be down at high water.

June 4, 1933

The captain came aboard at 2:30 A.M., clear, full moon, high water, and fair wind from the southwest. Called all hands to get under weigh. Hoisted the yawl boat up in the stern davits and secured it. The tugboat *W. H. Andrews* came alongside with the pilot

Captain Porter. Hove short the anchor and passed the hawser to the towboat. Hove in the anchor and got under weigh. Set the mainsail, forestaysail, foresail, mizzen, jib, and flying jib.

Off the sea buoy 7:30 A.M., the tug whistled to shorten the tow. Put the wheel down and hove the vessel to. Hauled in the hawser and the pilot bid "fair wind and a fast passage" and boarded his small boat to pull over to the *Andrews*. The tug, standing by on the starboard quarter waiting for the pilot, gave us a parting salute, three long blasts on her whistle, and we filled away on the port tack heading for Frying Pan Lightship, 81 miles E × N. Set the spanker and the fore and main topsails. Made 6½ miles on the forenoon watch by log.

The wind veered around to the south'ard about noon, gybed over on the starboard tack at one bell. Calm and light airs all afternoon. Shifted and set the fore and main topsails on the dogwatch. Got a gentle breeze from the SSW on the first watch. Made 14 miles by log on the watch. 8 P.M. wind from the south southwest, course E × N½N.

June 5, 1933

Frying Pan Lightship abeam about 2 miles off at 4 A.M. Changed the course to E so as to get out in the Gulf Stream and have the advantage of a favorable current. Painted the jaws of the booms and oiled the booms with raw oil. Clewed up the topsails at noon and gybed over on the port tack at one bell. Shifted and set topsails. We are well out in the Gulf Stream now with the seaweed and flying fish. We are about 35 to 40 miles offshore heading on a course, NE × E, parallel with the shore line. Calm at the end of the afternoon watch. Clewed up the topsails and let them hang. Light air from the eastward. Gybed over on the starboard tack. The wind veered around to S × W on the dog watch. Set the fore, main, and mizzen topsails.

June 6, 1933

At 4 A.M., light breeze from southwest by west, course ENE, clear, sea smooth. We are well offshore and in the Gulf Stream. Sighted a steamer this morning which is unusual as we are well away from the steamer lane. The wind veered around to the west about 8 A.M.,

LOOKING AFT. A sailing vessel under way makes a fascinating picture to a sailor perched on the end of the jibboom looking aft. The four-masted schooner *Albert F. Paul* presented this view as she moved through the water on the starboard tack, with all plain sail set and drawing well in a fresh quartering breeze.

Porpoises or dolphins racing, jumping, and diving in front of the bow might further distract the sailor's attention from his immediate job. Undoubtedly he was sent out on the boom for a purpose and would be rudely reminded by the mate to finish his task, as there were still other things to be done. (Drawn by James S. McCullough)

course NE½E. Clewed up the topsails and gybed over on the port tack. Painted on the forward deckhouse.

Wind went around to the southwest about 4 P.M. Clewed up the topsails and gybed over on the starboard tack at 8 bells. Shifted and set the topsails. The vessel is going almost dead before the wind. The helmsman must mind the wheel closely to keep from gybing over. There isn't much wind but the old topsails must be handled carefully. The wind went around to the west about 8 P.M., course NE. Light variable wind all day but a favorable current carries us along about 2 knots per hour.

Clewed up the topsails and gybed over on the port tack at 8 bells. Shifted and set the topsails. Diamond Shoals Lightship flashing off on the weather beam about 10 P.M. After a half hour or so of calm a light breeze came from the north-northeast about 11:30 P.M. Course by the wind on the port tack.

June 7, 1933

Sailing by the wind, moderate breeze from east-northeast at 4 A.M. Making 1½ points leeway, moderate sea, clear, vessel on the port tack. Clewed up the topsails at 4 A.M. Heading about east-southeast and directly offshore. The vessel is jammed up into the wind as close as she will go, making very little headway but the current is still favorable. Hauled down the outer jib at 6 bells and tied it up in an effort to bring the vessel closer into the wind.

Tarred down the standing rigging on the foremast. Tarred only the serving and seizing and oiled the wire. Tacked ship at eight bells (noon) and set the mizzen topsail. Vessel going by the wind on the starboard tack heading about north-northeast. This is the first time we have tacked ship since I joined the vessel on May 1st.

The Panama Line's *Ancon* passed us close aboard, bound south, about 4 P.M., as we were sailing closehauled heading NNE. Many passengers lined the rail to have a look at an old windjammer under sail. No doubt it is the first and perhaps the last and only sailing vessel under sail that many of them will see.

The wind shifted around to the east on the dogwatch (6 P.M.) Vessel heading on a course NE½N. Gentle breeze, sea smooth with a moderate swell. Shifted and set the main topsail and tied up the fore topsail.

June 8, 1933

At midnight there was a moderate breeze from southeast by south, sea choppy, sky clear, course NE × E½E. The wind shifted around to southwest about 4 A.M. Clewed up the topsails and wore ship at 8 bells. Shifted and set the main and mizzen topsails. Light and baffling airs on the forenoon watch. Vessel will not stay on the course.

Clewed up the topsails and wore ship, starboard tack, at 4 bells. Shifted and set the main and mizzen topsails and the outer jib. Tarred down the main rigging. The captain took a sight for latitude at noon at which time the ship was on a N × W course, wind west by south.

Clewed up the topsails at one bell and wore ship. Shifted and set the topsails. Vessel on the port tack. The captain caught two dolphins weighing about 15 pounds each this afternoon. Set the foretopsail at 4 bells on the dog watch. At 8 P.M. wind from west by south, gentle, clear and cool, smooth sea. Course N × W ½ W. We are well north of Hatteras now and the nights are quite chilly. Took a sounding at midnight but got no bottom at thirty-five fathoms.

June 9, 1933

Made 12 miles by log on the first watch. Day breaks clear, cool, and grey foretelling fine weather. Light westerly wind and the sea very smooth with a long even swell running. Washed the white paint around the poop deck and wet down the cabin top and poop deck. Great schools of porpoises (puffing pigs some fishermen call them) all around the vessel.

Flat calm at 7 bells (7:30 A.M.). Clewed the topsails up over the stays and let them hang. The skipper took a sight for longitude about 8 A.M. Tarred down the spanker rigging.

Light breeze from the southwest about 2 P.M. Set the topsails. Course NW. Made 5 miles by log on the afternoon watch. Plenty of porpoises still playing around the ship. The ship's dog, Gypsy, a big police dog, gets very excited when the porpoises come near the vessel and races along the rail barking at them.

Sighted a steamer to windward, hull down, on the dogwatch. Steamers are scarce out here. Most of them keep closer inshore. Very little wind all day but the current is favorable.

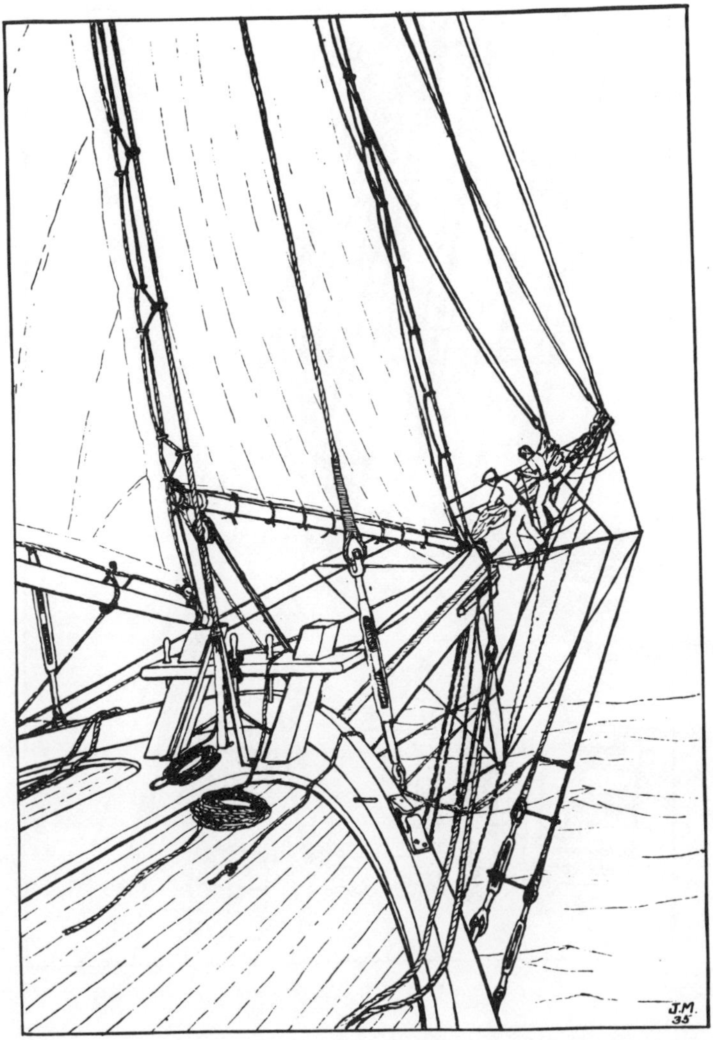

Furling the Flying Jib. More men have been lost attempting to secure the jibs than any of the other sails on a vessel. Furling a jib was not a difficult job if the weather was fine and the sail dry, but when a vessel was deep-laden and pitching in a rough sea, duckings were common, and sometimes all the men on the jibboom were washed overboard by one heavy sea.

Headsails on schooners are named differently from head sails on square-rigged vessels. Beginning with the forestaysail, on the schooner, they are named in the following order: standing jib, flying jib, outer jib, and often a fifth sail called the jib topsail.

[This scene probably depicts the schooner *Purnell T. White.*] (Drawn by James S. McCullough)

The Mate on Watch. It is the second dogwatch, 6 to 8 P.M.; the wind is fair and the weather fine. The sidelights have been trimmed, lighted, and set out. The watch on deck is coiling down the topsail gear clear for running in case of a sudden squall during the night.

The mate may look alert with his eyes on the sails and distant horizon, but his mind is far ahead of the vessel; it's already in the next port, anticipating the age-old pastime of sailors—wine, women, and song. Unfortunately for the poor sailor, his dreams seldom come true, and he finds himself back at sea, after a spell on shore, with little more than a big head and a flat pocket—but he never seems to give up hope.

[This scene probably depicts the schooner *Purnell T. White*.] (Drawn by James S. McCullough)

June 10, 1933

At midnight light breeze from the west, cool and hazy, steering a NW course. Fog set in about 2 bells in the middle watch. Got the fog horn up on the fo'c'sle head and started it going—two blasts for the port tack. Trimmed the sheets in flat, by the wind, at 7 bells. Sails setting flat and drawing well due to the dampness.

The wind shifted around to the southeast about 6 A.M. Clewed up the topsails and wore ship. Vessel heading on a course north, starboard tack. The moderate southeast wind cleared the fog away. Shifted and set the topsails at 8 bells. Painting on the fo'c'sle head.

About 10 A.M. a heavy squall hit us on the lee bow, taking all sail aback. Put the wheel hard down and let the topsail halliards go by the run. The squall was almost upon us before the man at the wheel saw it. The mate, whose watch it happened to be, was busy painting. There was very little rain and no unusually dark cloud to foretell the approach of the squall, except the white caps and driving spray that followed in the wake of the first blast of wind. The squall was past in a couple of minutes but the wind went around the compass and caught us aback before the vessel would answer the helm. Hauled down the outer jib and trimmed the sheets in flat. If we had been square-rigged instead of schooner-rigged we would be in a hell of a mess now. After the squall the wind came from north-northwest, a moderate breeze, and the course, full and by, the vessel heading W × N½N. During the squall H. Leonard tripped on a deck load lashing and sprained his ankle.

It was clear enough at noon for the old man to get a sight for latitude. Set the outer jib, main and mizzen topsails, at 1 bell (12:30 P.M.). Light breeze.

The first part of the dogwatch the vessel had steerageway, by the wind on the starboard tack, but at 4 bells it was a flat calm and the sky looked very threatening, squalls all around us. Clewed up the topsails and hauled down the outer jib. Tied up the jib and topsails at 8 bells. Calm. Hauled in the log line.

June 11, 1933

Calm and clear with a few high cumulus clouds. Horizon very hazy. Sea smooth. The vessel rolling easily in the long moderate swell and drifting off to the northeast, being still somewhat under the influence of the Gulf Stream. This being Sunday, and a fine day, the crew is busy cleaning out the fo'c'sle and washing clothes.

H. Leonard is still laid up with a sprained ankle and the other man on the port watch has a badly injured hand and can't do much but steer. Leonard gets very little sympathy as sailors are very unsympathetic people and do not believe in a man laying up unless it is absolutely impossible for him to stand his watch. Sighted several steamers, mostly oil tankers heading north.

Got a light air from the south about 8 P.M. Slacked off the sheets and the vessel is heading on the course N × E½E almost dead before the wind. Wind shifted around to west-southwest about 9 P.M. The watch on deck gybed the vessel over on the port tack.

June 12, 1933

Set the main topsail while both watches were on deck at midnight. Wind west-southwest, course N × E½E, clear, cool, sea smooth. The mate, a powerful young Norwegian American (called whitewashed Yankee by sailors) loosened, shifted, and set the fore and mizzen topsails by himself in about 45 minutes and all by hand. The wind was light and the sails were dry. It was the mate's watch on deck but both of his men were injured, one had a sprained ankle and could not walk, the other had an injured hand and could not pull a rope but could hold the wheel. Made 15 miles by log on the middle watch.

The wind freshened to a strong breeze in the forenoon watch, kicking up a choppy sea. This is the first real sailing we have done on the passage north. Painted the yawl boat. Barnegat Lightship abeam at noon about three miles off the port side.

Called out the watch below at 2 P.M. to take in sail. Lowered and tied up the spanker. Clewed up the mizzen topsail and tied it up. The New Jersey coast in sight off to windward, the first land we have seen since we left the South Carolina coast.

The weather moderated rapidly in the afternoon and by 5 P.M. we were in a calm. The sky off to northwest looked very threatening and thunder squalls off to the westward. Clewed up the fore and main topsails, hauled down the outer jib, and tied them up. Hauled down all the head sails, put the wheel down, and when the vessel came into the wind let go the starboard anchor. Twenty-five fathoms of chain out. Flat calm. We are anchored about 3 miles off Sea Girt, New Jersey. Lowered the fore, main, and mizzen sails but did not tie them up. Set anchor watch at 8 P.M. Calm and cloudy with thunder squalls around.

June 13, 1933

Called all hands at 6 A.M. Light northwest breeze, sky clear, sea smooth. Set the main and mizzen sails. Hove up the anchor. Set the forestaysail, jib, foresail, flying jib, and spanker. Stood off on the port tack by the wind to beat up the coast. Worked in the rigging putting in new sheer ratlines, seizings, etc. Tacked ship at 10 A.M. and stood inshore. Tacked ship again at noon and stood offshore. Tacked ship at 1:30 P.M., inshore.

At 2 P.M. lowered the spanker, hauled down the headsails, and let go the starboard anchor off Atlantic Highlands, New Jersey. Thirty fathoms of chain out. Lowered the fore, main, and mizzen sails. All hands knocked off. Turned to after supper. Put a harbor furl on the outer jib and a peak stop on the spanker. Secured the rest of the sails for the night and knocked off. Set anchor watch at 8 P.M.

June 14, 1933

2 A.M. to 4 A.M. stood anchor watch. 6 A.M., wind from the north. All hands turned to. Set mizzen, main, and foresail. Hove up anchor. Set forestaysail, jib, and flying jib. Got under weigh on starboard tack, inshore. 7 A.M. wore ship, set spanker and mizzen topsail. 9 A.M. clewed up topsail and tacked ship on starboard tack again. Set mizzen topsail. Light breeze from the northwest. 11 A.M. sighted towboat standing toward us. Towboat *Relief* came alongside and after bargaining with the skipper a little while, took our towline. Clewed up and tied up mizzen topsail. Rounded Scotland Lightship at noon.

Lowered spanker, unrove the sheet, and put on sail cover. Let go the deck cargo lashings. In the Narrows lowered the sails, unrove the sheets, etc., and put on the sail covers. A Coast Guard cutter came alongside and boarded us and made the customary search, that is looked down into the cabin, lazarette, and into the wheel box.

Came into the Nelson Lumber Company dock in South Brooklyn

but could not get alongside the dock on account of low tide. 8 P.M. tied up the vessel as best we could and knocked off.

June 15, 1933

2 A.M. all hands heave vessel in alongside the dock. 3 A.M. vessel secure alongside dock. 6 A.M. All hands turn to. Cleared up the deck, stowed deck cargo lashings below, hove up the booms clear of the deck load, coiled down gear and mooring lines fore and aft, swept down, and knocked off.

End of the voyage, 15 days out of Georgetown.

Schooner *Albert F. Paul* laying at Todd's Shipyard, Brooklyn, New York

July 23, 1933

Came aboard the vessel in the evening to be ready to turn to in the morning.

July 24, 1933

8 A.M. Turned to. Signed on. Broke out towing hawser from after lazarette and coiled it down on fo'c'sle head ready for tug. Took off sail stops and secured dunnage on deck.

Towboat *Relief* came alongside and made fast to the starboard quarter. Cast off mooring lines and got under weigh. Clear of the pier, passed the hawser to the towboat. Coiled the mooring lines down on the hatches. Wind south-southwest, head wind. Came to anchor at 1 P.M. inside Sandy Hook and cast off towboat. Dinner. Spent the afternoon patching forestaysail and mizzensail. Two men suegeeing around the poop deck. 4 P.M. knocked off.

8 P.M. set anchor watch. Starboard watch takes first watch. Have an extra man aboard, Cooper, working his way to Georgetown, South Carolina.

July 25, 1933

Midnight to 2 A.M. stood anchor watch, calm and clear. 8 A.M. turned to. Calm and cloudy. Stowed mooring lines down in hold.

WASHING DOWN. The day after sailing was field day. Both watches turned to, early in the morning, to scrub the paintwork and decks, which had become grimy from the vessel's stay in port. Some vessels had power-operated pumps and wash deck hose, which were great improvements over the more common method of using the bucket and drawrope, sometimes referred to as the "Nova Scotia pump." The drawbucket was made of canvas, with the mouth sewn to an iron ring that held it open and weighted it down. Soogie-moogie, a mixture of salsoda or washing powder and fresh water, was generally used to scrub the paintwork. In warm, dry weather, wooden decks were washed down daily to keep them from drying out.

[Schooner depicted is probably the *Purnell T. White.*] (Drawn by James S. McCullough)

9. A.M. gentle breeze from the east. Set the main, mizzen, and fore sails. Hove up the anchor, set forestaysail, jib, and flying jib, spanker, mizzen topsail, and spanker topsail. Coiled down the towing hawser on the fore hatch. Set fore and main topsails. Wind from south-southeast. 11:30 A.M. Scotland Lightship abeam. Clewed down mizzen topsail to patch it. 2:30 P.M. wind increased to strong breeze with rain squalls. Clewed up mizzen and spanker topsails. Second dogwatch breeze moderated then shifted suddenly to south at 6 bells. Clewed up fore and main topsails. Wind hauled around again to east, light breeze. Cloudy with squalls around. Set main topsail at 8 bells.

July 26, 1933

Midnight, wind from east-southeast, course S½W. Middle watch moderate breeze, rain squalls. Set fore and main topsails. Steamer almost run us down during a squall. 1 A.M., wind light and baffling. Clewed up topsails. 3 A.M., light to moderate to light east-southeast breeze. Set fore, main, and mizzen topsails. Made about 18 miles on the watch by the patent log. Forenoon watch, moderate easterly breeze, cloudy. Set outer jib. Suegeed the white paint. Sighted a large whale on the starboard beam. Afternoon watch, slacked off sheets and changed course at 8 bells. First dogwatch, cloudy and frequent rain squalls. First watch, hauled down outer jib and tied it up. 2 bells, wind light and baffling, clewed up topsails. 6 bells, wind shifted to south, set main and mizzen topsails.

July 27, 1933

Middle watch, cloudy, wind variable, frequent rain squalls. Clewed up the topsails and took in the spanker. Vessel hove to on port tack. Wore ship at 8 bells.

Morning watch, cloudy and heavy rain squalls. 4 bells, shifted and set mizzen topsail, wind north-northwest moderate gale, sea rough. Shifted and set main topsail at 8 bells. Vessel on the starboard tack, course SW. Cleaned inside of boats during the watch.

Afternoon watch. Wind north-northeast, fresh breeze, sea rough. Vessel going about SW. 8 bells, clewed up topsails and wore ship on port tack. Shifted and set fore, main, and mizzen topsails. Vessel going about S × W. Made 15 miles by patent log during the watch.

Second dogwatch, cloudy, wind dead astern, vessel rolling, set up spanker cross tackles. Spliced foretopsail halliards. Setting the foretopsail the halliards carried away. Rove off new halliards. Swayed up main throat halliards and main and mizzen topsail halliards.

July 28, 1933

Midnight, wind from east-southeast, cloudy, sea moderate, heavy swell. Middle watch cloudy with frequent heavy rain squalls. Vessel rolling heavily. 7 bells called all hands to take in sail, heavy squalls. Clewed up topsails, lowered spanker, hauled down flying jib, jib, and forestaysail, let go starboard anchor in 13 fathoms of water. Fifty fathoms of chain out. Lowered the fore, main, and mizzen sails, tied up head sails, and cleared up the deck. Breakfast.

Forenoon watch, tied up topsails to keep them clear of peak halliards. Put a new tumbler in the main gaff.

Afternoon watch, 6 bells, finished repairs to main gaff and knocked off.

Dogwatch, 4 bells, called all hands to get under weigh. Set the mizzen, main, and foresail. Hove up the anchor. Light breeze of fair wind. Loosed the head sails. Calm again, heavy rain squalls around. Let go the anchor and lowered the sails.

First watch, set anchor watch, calm and overcast.

July 29, 1933

Morning watch, 2 bells, called all hands to set sail. Set the mizzen, main, and foresail. Hove up the anchor. Set forestaysail, jib, and flying jib. Set spanker, outer jib, and main topsail. Coiled down gear clear for running and knocked off for breakfast.

Forenoon watch, wind west-northwest, light breeze, clear, sea smooth with moderate swell. Vessel on starboard tack. First day the sun has shown since we left New York. All our clothing is wet, beds and blankets as well. Deck head in forward house, our quarters, leaks badly.

Afternoon watch, light westerly breeze, vessel steering south-southeast making about half a knot. Wind hauled around to south-

Clewing up the Main Topsail. Tack, sheet, and halliard have been let go, and the watch is manning the clew line. While one sailor holds a turn under the belaying pin, the other one is breaking down on the line. When the topsail was wet and heavy or the wind was fresh, it was too much of a job for two men, and the watch below had to be called out. This often happened in case of a sudden squall or if the vessel had to be put on the other tack. Under ordinary conditions, whenever this task had to be performed, it was left until eight bells, when both watches were on deck. Many large schooners had a steam donkey engine, and steam was kept up all the time at sea. On those vessels, clewing up topsails was not a backbreaking job; it was only necessary to lead the clew line to the gypsyhead, take a couple of turns, give the engineer one bell, and heave away.

[Schooner depicted is unidentified.] (Drawn by James S. McCullough)

east at 4 bells. Clewed up the main topsail and wore ship. Hauled down the outer jib. Vessel going by the wind heading about east northeast. Painted inside of yawl boat.

Second dogwatch, swayed up the spanker, mizzen, and fore throat halliards. Clewed up the main topsail and tied it up. Tied up outer jib.

July 30, 1933

Middle watch, light southwest breeze, vessel by the wind heading about southeast. Wore ship at 4 bells, vessel heading about west-northwest on new tack (port tack). Wore ship at 8 bells, vessel by the wind heading about south-southeast.

Morning watch, light southwest breeze. Wore ship at noon. Vessel back to port tack steering by the wind heading about W × N. Set the outer jib but had to haul it down again to repair roping in the clew. Took off hatch covers, spread out extra foresail to dry, it having been stowed on the main hatch, faked the hawser down on deck to dry it out. Wheel in the beckets, everybody working. 8 bells, clewed up the topsail and wore ship, starboard tack.

First dogwatch, wind fresh still from the southwest. 4 bells, wore ship, port tack.

Second dogwatch, 7 bells all hands stand by to anchor. Hauled down the outer jib, lowered spanker and foresail, hauled down flying jib, jib, and staysail. Let go the anchor. Lowered the main and mizzen sails and secured everything for the night. Bodie Island Light bearing W½S distant about 6 miles. Set anchor watch at 8 P.M.

Sabbath observed, no unnecessary work done.

July 31, 1933

Morning watch, light southwest wind, clear.

Forenoon watch, all hands turned to. Swept down decks and oiled them with tar oil. Patched mainsail. Painted inside of yawl and gig.

First dogwatch, 2 bells, all hands heave up anchor and set sail. Set mainsail, forestaysail, jib, mizzensail, flying jib, foresail, and spanker. Set mizzen topsail at 8 bells. Wind southwest, head wind. Vessel going by the wind on the starboard tack.

August 1, 1933

Middle watch, vessel going by the wind heading south, moderate breeze, heavy swell. Clewed up topsails and wore ship at 8 bells. Port tack. Shifted and set mizzen topsail.

Morning watch, wind south by west, moderate breeze, course by the wind. 2 bells, wind hauled to northward. Clewed up mizzen topsail and wore ship, starboard tack. Shifted and set mizzen and spanker topsail. Set main topsail but tore a hole along the luff and had to clew it down again and patch it. Set it at 8 bells.

First dogwatch, clewed up topsails and wore ship, port tack. Shifted and set mizzen topsail, tied up spanker topsail. Strong wind about southwest by south. Vessel going by the wind heading W½N. Swept down the decks.

First watch, strong southwest breeze. Clewed up the mizzen topsail and wore ship, starboard tack. Vessel going by the wind heading S × E½E. Tied up main and mizzen topsails. Flashing light off to westward, Cape Hatteras, distance 15 miles. Wore ship at 8 bells, port tack.

August 2, 1933

4 A.M., wind from the southwest, sailing by the wind.

Morning watch, strong southwest breeze. Wore ship at 8 bells, starboard tack. Suegeed white paint around poop deck. 4 bells, wore ship, port tack. Vessel heading about NW × W½W. 8 bells, wore ship again, starboard tack. Sailing like hell but getting nowhere.

Forenoon watch, 5 bells, wore ship, port tack.

Afternoon watch, 1 bell, wore ship, starboard tack, fresh southwest wind, sea rough. Lighthouse on Cape Hatteras bearing southwest about 3 miles off. Vessel going by the wind, heading about SSE. Lighthouse abeam 1:45 P.M. Scraped hatch coaming, ready for painting. Painted inside of gig, second coat.

Second dogwatch, vessel still going by the wind heading about S × E½E. Diamond Shoals Lightship bearing south southwest. Cape Hatteras Light bearing west.

First watch, wore ship, port tack.

TIEING UP THE SPANKER TOPSAIL. The lad on the crosstrees has the topsail neatly stowed against the masthead and is passing the gasket. The clew cringle is clear and the topsail sheet hooked onto a topmast shroud. After he has the gasket passed and secured, he will haul up the tack, bight it over a ratline in the topmast rigging, and make it fast. On his way to the deck, he will carry the topsail sheet down to the gaff and hook it into a link at the throat halliard block, not forgetting to put the leather thong through the hole in the sister hook. Tieing up a topsail was not an easy job. Often the sail was wet and heavy, and sometimes it was frozen. If the schooner was running off before a fresh breeze, the sail bellied out between the topmast rigging, and it was difficult to spill.

[Schooner depicted is unidentified.] (Drawn by James S. McCullough)

August 3, 1933

Middle watch, 8 bells, wore ship, starboard tack. Fresh wind, southwest by west, sea rough, course by the wind heading about S × E. 4 bells, wore ship, starboard tack. 7 bells, wore ship again, port tack.

Forenoon watch, painted mizzen hatch and coaming, varnished bright work on poop deck. 5 bells, wore ship, starboard tack. Set spanker topsail. Looks as if we lost some distance during the night. Cape Hatteras Lighthouse is just visible on the horizon.

First dogwatch, fresh southwest wind, rough sea, clear. 8 bells, wore ship, port tack. Skipper caught a fifteen pound dolphin.

Second dogwatch, 5 bells, wore ship, starboard tack.

First watch, wind southwest and increasing, mackerel sky, full moon, heavy sea running. Vessel lifting her forefoot clear of the sea at times, pitching heavily. 4 bells, wore ship, port tack. Blowing a gale. Captain came on deck and called all hands to take in the spanker. Vessel rolling and pitching heavily. Water boiling up through the lee scuppers. Shipping plenty of spray. Part of our Georgetown crew seasick and perhaps a little scared. Diamond Shoals Lightship dead to windward. We gain a little on one tack only to lose it on the next tack. 1 bell, wore ship, starboard tack.

August 4, 1933

Morning watch, 8 bells, wore ship, port tack. Weather moderating, vessel still rolling heavily. Brilliant sunrise forecasting dirty weather. Suegeed white paint on the poop deck. 8 bells, hauled down the flying jib and wore ship, starboard tack. Tied up flying jib and wore ship, starboard tack. Tied up flying jib and mended a bad place in the clew. We are well out in the Gulf Stream now and practically hove to, vessel heading about NW × N.

Forenoon watch, 5 bells, wore ship, port tack. 6 bells, called out the watch below, heavy squall to windward. Squall hit us shortly afterward, heavy rain and blowing a gale. Could do nothing until rain eased up a little then wore ship, starboard tack. Foresail started to go in several places, lowered it and let it hang in the lazyjacks. Port fore boom topping lift block broke and jammed the fall. Wind moderating. Knocked off for dinner. After dinner went to

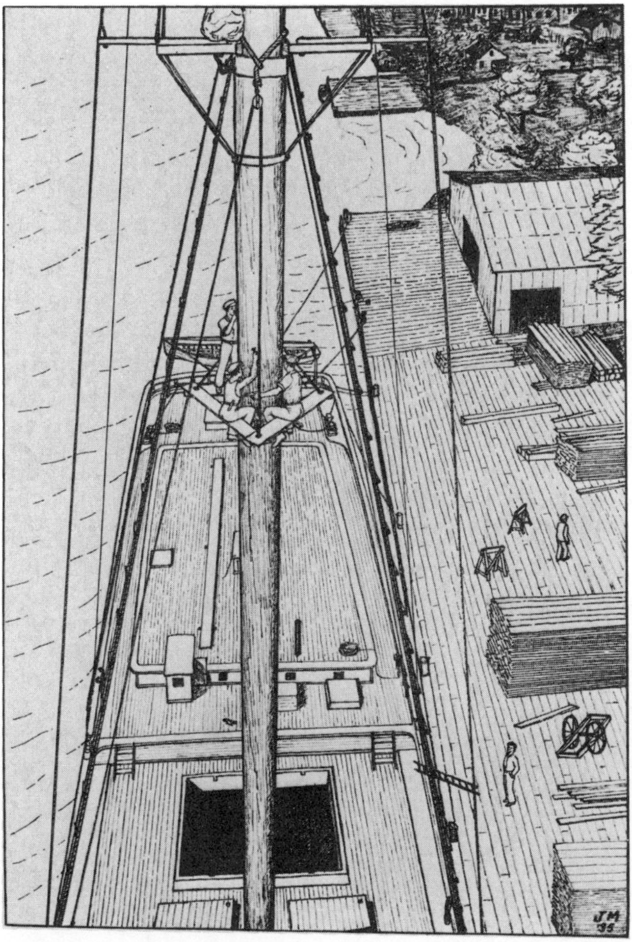

Scraping Down the Mast. Nicely grained Oregon-pine masts, newly scraped and slushed, made a striking picture shining in the sun. Scraping down was a job for warm, dry weather. The topmasts were scraped first, one man to each mast, riding a bosun's chair and lowering himself. The lower masts were scraped from a triangle. Three men usually rode it down, while the mate and one man stood by on deck to lower away. The three men ordinarily scraped down an eighty-foot mast in a day's time. Sheath knives, and scrapers, often made from worn-out hacksaw blades, sharpened and set into handles made of old mast hoops, were used to scrape the darkened wood and old slush off the masts.

After the masts had been scraped, they were slushed with grease or a specially prepared petroleum product similar to vaseline. The slush acted as a preservative for the wood and allowed the mast hoops to slide easily up and down the masts when the sail was being hoisted or lowered.

[Schooner depicted unidentified.] (Drawn by James S. McCullough)

work patching the foresail and sending up another topping lift block.

Afternoon watch, 3 bells, wore ship, port tack. Wind about west, vessel rolling heavily. 4 bells, watch below went below. 8 bells, foresail fixed and topping lift rove off, Wore ship, starboard tack, and set foresail. Wind back to west-southwest.

Second dogwatch, 4 bells, wore ship, port tack. Dark, heavy cloud bank came up from northwest. Heavy thunder and lightning. 5 bells, squall hit us. Gybed over the sails on starboard tack just before it started to rain. Rain came down in torrents for half an hour, decks flooded, not much wind. The heavy rain beat down the sea. Wind light and baffling. Vessel heading E × S. 8 bells, turned in, all standing ready for a call.

First watch, wind light and baffling. Gybed over the sail. Rain squalls, calm, vessel rolling heavily in the swell. Fore boom tackle carried away. Rove it off as a gun tackle.

August 5, 1933

Middle watch, spliced standing part of fore boom tackle. Vessel rolling heavily. Boom tackle carried away again just as we were about to reeve the spliced part. Got a turn around the boom with the messenger. Spliced the fall again and rove it off. 8 bells, wore ship, port tack, wind north-northwest, light breeze. Fair wind at last.

Morning watch, set main topsail and flying jib.

Forenoon watch, wind north, fresh breeze, cloudy. Set fore and mizzen topsails. Shell of main sheet lead block broke. Unrove and fixed it. Took soundings with the deep sea lead, 35 fathoms and no bottom. Don't know where we are except that we are well offshore and in the Gulf Stream. Painted the main hatch coamings and covers. 6 bells, wore ship, starboard tack heading about W × S. Shifted and set the fore and main topsails. Main topsail tack carried away. Spliced it. The vessel looks very good on deck, all cleaned and painted, but aloft she is rotten. Something seems to carry away every watch, good or bad.

Afternoon watch, 3 bells, Diamond Shoals Lightship bearing northwest about 10 miles off. Tied up mizzen topsail. Painted fore hatch.

LOADING LUMBER. This sketch was made from the deck of the four-masted schooner *Emerett* of Seaford, Delaware, Parker Knowlton, Master, while loading lumber at the Palmetto Lumber Company mill near Savannah, Georgia, in 1924.

The negro longshoremen received seven to nine cents an hour at that time, and worked a ten-hour day. During unfavorable weather they had to knock off work, and, of course, their pay stopped. Some large mills had live rollers or conveyors to assist in loading, but at the smaller mills the lumber was loaded entirely by hand.

The *Emerett* loaded about 600,000 board feet of yellow pine lumber. The hold was filled to capacity, and a deck load about seven feet high was put on board to bring the vessel down to her marks. (Drawn by James S. McCullough)

First dogwatch, strong northeast wind, vessel making about 8 knots.

First watch, set the outer jib. 3 bells, Cape Lookout Lighthouse abeam, light vessel off the lee bow. Shifted and set the mizzen topsail. 4 bells, lightship abeam. Made 33 miles this watch.

August 6, 1933

Morning watch, wind northeast, moderate gale, course SW × S. 8 bells, clewed up the topsails and wore ship. Shifted and set the three topsails with the aid of a lot of shouting and swearing. The skipper cursing the mate and the mate cursing the crew. Vessel making better than 9 knots. Greased the main and mizzen gaff jaws. 8 bells, hauled down the standing jib to put a patch on it.

Forenoon watch, 3 bells, called out the watch below. Clewed up the topsails and gybed ship, starboard tack. Shifted and set the fore and main topsails and tied up the mizzen topsail. Course WSW, heavy following sea. 7 bells, called out the watch below. Hauled down the outer jib, clewed up the topsails and gybed ship, port tack. Flattened the fore, main, and mizzen sheets. Changed the course to W × S at 11 A.M. Fresh breeze from northeast sprung up at 5 P.M. Anchored 8 P.M., North Island Light bearing west northwest about 6 miles off. Blowing with storm force.

Schooner *Albert F. Paul* July 25 to August 6, 1933

1,013 miles sailed
249 sailing hours
Average speed 4.06 miles per hour
164 miles best day's run
33 miles best run in one watch
11.5 miles best run in one hour

McCullough failed to keep his notes going during his stay in Georgetown. Or he may have made a rough record with the thought of transferring them into a more readable state but lost that record before he could rewrite it. However, he did write a two-page account in pencil of his return passage to New York, probably after he reached port. And that trip was fraught with heavy weather, descriptions of which would have made his journal more exciting than his earlier accounts of passages in the *Paul*. A few days after he reached New York, news reporters visited the *Paul* as she lay at her dock and interviewed McCullough to gain a story about the stormy passage of the schooner. From that tale, which appeared in the September 29, 1933, issue of the *New York Herald*, and from McCullough's pencil draft we can get an idea of his last trip in the *Albert F. Paul*.

On August 29 the *Paul* shipped a crew and left Georgetown with 529,080 feet of green pine lumber, bound for Brooklyn, New York. The ship was towed out into Winyah Bay to await a fair wind. While laying at anchor, the *Paul* rode out a hurricane on September 6–7 without any difficulty. On September 8 the wind went around to south by west, the tugboat came out of Georgetown with the pilot, and the *Paul* continued on her voyage north. Outside the Georgetown jetties the schooner filled away on the starboard tack for Diamond Shoals Lightship.

The fair wind lasted for two days, carrying the *Paul* around Cape Hatteras, where a calm was encountered. Then a light breeze from the northeast picked up, and the schooner continued on her way, sailing by the wind, for Scotland Lightship.

McCullough's account then continues in his own words.

On September 13 we were still going by the wind and were within 17 miles of Winter Quarter Lightship and about 177 miles from Scotland Lightship. The sky looked bad to windward and the glass was going down so the 'old Man' wore ship and headed for Cape Charles Lightship 50 miles to the southwest.

We anchored off Cape Henry on September 14. The next day the northeast storm signal was run up on Cape Henry. The Coast Guard cutter *Mascoutin* came alongside and told us the worst northeaster in years was heading for Cape Henry and we had better run for shelter. It was too late for us to get under weigh without assistance as we could not heave up our anchor in the heavy head sea. The cutter gave us a hawser and hauled us up into the wind until we got our anchor up and then she towed us into Hampton Roads. There we anchored and rode out the second hurricane of the trip, September 15 to 17.

The storm passed and as the wind came out of the west we hove up the anchors and set some sail. We had sailed about half a mile when the vessel grounded off Sewalls Point, on the eastern side of the entrance to Elizabeth River, Norfolk. We lowered sail and waited for high water, the cutter *Mascoutin* standing by. The schooner floated at high water. The tugboat *Peerless* came off and towed us out clear of Sewalls Point.

Three days later, September 20, after having more or less fair wind, we anchored off Scotland Lightship at 10 P.M. We were out of tobacco and our stores were running low. Beans and salt horse were about all we had to eat. The next morning the pilot boat *Sandy Hook* came alongside and gave us some potatoes and newspapers. The tugboat *Relief* picked us up about noon and towed us into an anchorage off Red Hook.

The next morning the towboat took us to the Cross, Austin and Ireland Lumber Company dock in Newtown Creek, Brooklyn, and we were paid off, thus ending the voyage of 24 days out of Georgetown, dock to dock.

Our best day's run on the voyage north was 163 miles, the best hour's run was 11 knots. We sailed 655 miles by the log in 207 sailing hours for an average of 3.16 miles per hour. The actual distance sailed was considerable more than was shown on the log as we had a favorable current, the Gulf Stream, part of the way.

Menu for one week aboard the four-masted schooner *Albert F. Paul*

1933

Sunday

Breakfast
- Oatmeal
- Ham and eggs (one egg apiece)
- Boiled potatoes
- Bread, butter, and coffee

Dinner
- Vegetable soup
- Boiled beef with tomato sauce
- Boiled potatoes, string beans

TOWING OUT TO SEA. This sketch of the *Albert F. Paul* of Baltimore, Maryland, Robert O. Jones, Master, was made in 1933, as she was being towed to sea from Georgetown, South Carolina, by the old steam tug *W. H. Andrews.* She was loaded with 539,080 feet of green southern pine lumber. Inbound for cargo, Captain Jones and other schooner skippers often sailed the seventeen miles up Winyah Bay from the breakwater to the loading dock in Georgetown, provided that wind and tide were favorable. As an additional aid, they used the vessel's power yawl boat, made fast to the quarter. Towboats usually met loaded sailing vessels off headlands of the ports to which they were bound and bargained with the skippers as to the fees for towing the vessels into the harbor. Sometimes when business was slack, two or more towboats went after the same vessel, and the bargaining was keen. (Drawn by James S. McCullough)

Bread and butter
Apple pie and coffee

Supper
Sardines
Cold corned beef (very bad)
Fried potatoes
Bread and butter
Dried apricots, cookies, and tea

Monday

Breakfast
Cream of wheat
Beef stew
Bacon
Bread and butter
Coffee

Dinner
Vegetable soup
Roast beef
Boiled potatoes, cabbage
Bread
Apple pudding, coffee

Supper
Hungarian goulash (or something)
Cold corned beef (rotten)
Fried potatoes
Beans (half baked—poor draft on Shipmate range)
Cookies (good)
Tea (No sugar or butter)

Tuesday

Breakfast
Oatmeal
Tripe dipped in egg batter and fried (good)

Bacon
Boiled potatoes
Bread and butter, coffee

Dinner
Vegetable soup (with flies in it)
Roast Beef
Boiled potatoes, turnips
Bread and butter
Apricot pie and coffee

Supper
Cold sliced beef (did not smell very good but tasted all right)
Macaroni and tomatoes
Fried potatoes
Gingerbread, stewed apples (dried)
Bread, butter, and tea

Wednesday

Breakfast
Cream of wheat
Cod tongues and sounds
Boiled potatoes
Bread and butter
Milk and coffee

Dinner
Vegetable soup
Roast beef and gravy
Boiled potatoes
Bread and butter
Cornstarch pudding, coffee

Supper
Hamburger steak and onions
Cold sliced corned beef (the rotten stuff)
Fried potatoes
Gingerbread and tea

Thursday

Breakfast
- Oatmeal
- Fried ham
- Bread and butter, coffee

Dinner
- Vegetable soup
- Roast beef
- Boiled potatoes, turnips
- Bread and butter
- Mince pie and coffee

Supper
- Cold sliced roast beef
- Fried potatoes
- Bread and catsup
- Gingerbread, baked apple, and tea

Friday

Breakfast
- Cream of wheat
- Salt mackeral
- Boiled potatoes
- Bread, butter, and coffee

Dinner
- Clam chowder
- Dried codfish
- Boiled potatoes, canned corn, beets
- Bread and butter
- Pudding (cream of wheat, apples, and raisins)
- Coffee

Supper
- Macaroni cooked with beef
- Mash potatoes, canned corn (left over from dinner)
- Buns, butter, cheese, and tea

Saturday

Breakfast
Corn flakes
Rice and curry
Boiled potatoes
White bread and butter
Coffee, sugar, condensed milk

Dinner
Vegetable soup
Roast beef
Boiled potatoes, carrots
White bread and butter
Bread pudding and coffee

Supper
Frankfurters
Fried potatoes
Bread and butter
Prunes and tea

(Plate of cold beef for night lunch, this night)

(Observation made by James S. McCullough)

Appendixes
Index

Appendix A

Voyages Made by the Four-Masted Schooner *Albert F. Paul,* 1917-41

Vessel left Baltimore, October 4, 1917, in tow for Norfolk, Virginia. Detained in Norfolk on account of government taking her cargo for Navy collier. Loaded 1,129 tons of coal, at $26.50 per ton, for Pernambuco, Brazil.

October	28	Sailed from Norfolk for Pernambuco
December	24	Arrived at Pernambuco

1918

January	*	Sailed from Pernambuco for Mobile, Alabama
January	31	Arrived at Mobile for dry-docking
		Sailed from Mobile for Moss Point, Mississippi
		Arrived at Moss Point
		Sailed from Moss Point for Georgetown, Demerara
		Arrived at Georgetown
		Sailed from Georgetown for Port au Prince, Haiti
		Arrived at Port au Prince
		Sailed from Port au Prince for Camden, New Jersey
		Arrived at Camden
		Sailed from Camden for Norfolk
		Arrived at Norfolk
August		Sailed from Norfolk for Bermuda
		Arrived at Bermuda
		Sailed from Bermuda for Brunswick, Georgia
		Arrived at Brunswick

1919

		Sailed from Brunswick for Portland, Maine
		Arrived at Portland
		Sailed from Portland for Norfolk
		Arrived at Norfolk

**Baltimore Sun* January 10, 1918, reported the *Albert F. Paul* had sailed for the Gulf to load lumber.

January	16	Sailed from Norfolk for Para, Brazil
		Arrived at Para
March	21	Sailed from Para for New York
		Arrived at New York
April	18	Hauled out at Perth Amboy Dry Dock
June	9	Sailed from Norfolk for Rio Grande do Sul, Brazil
September	6	Cable of arrival at Rio Grande do Sul
September	13	Sailed from Rio Grande do Sul for Buenos Aires
September	22	Cable of arrival at Buenos Aires
October	9	Sailed from Buenos Aires for Delaware Breakwater
December	7	Arrived at Delaware Breakwater—ordered to Philadelphia
		After discharging cargo, vessel repaired at Philadelphia and towed to Norfolk

1920

March	7	Left Philadelphia for Norfolk
March	9	Arrived Norfolk—dry-docked March 10 and towed to Newport News
March	26	Sailed from Newport News for Guadeloupe
April	27	Cable announcing arrival at Guadeloupe
May	11	Cable announcing sailing from Guadeloupe for Miragoane, Haiti
May	19	Arrived at Miragoane
June	16	Cable announcing sailing from Miragoane for Camden, New Jersey
June	25	Arrived at Delaware Breakwater
July	31	Sailed from Philadelphia for Halifax, Nova Scotia
August	13	Arrived at Halifax
September	4	Sailed from Halifax for Havana, Cuba
September	29	Cable announcing arrival at Havana
October	26	Sailed from Havana for Mobile
October	31	Arrived at Mobile—hauled out
November	5	Left Mobile in tow for Gulfport, Mississippi
November	6	Arrived at Gulfport
November	16	Left Gulfport with coal for Havana
November	23	Arrived at Havana
December	4	Sailed from Havana for Mobile
December	11	Arrived at Mobile

1921

January	5	Sailed from Mobile for San Juan, Puerto Rico Capt. G. U. Fletcher in command
February	7	Cable from San Juan announcing arrival
March	1	Cable from San Juan, sailing for St. Marc, Haiti
March	15	Cable from St. Marc announcing arrival
March	29	Sailed from St. Marc for Baltimore
April	21	Arrived in Baltimore in tow of tug *John G. Chandler*. After discharging logwood, dry-docked at Woodall and Company. Caulked from keel up, including decks.
May	19	Sailed for Savannah, Georgia
June	1	Arrived at Savannah
June	11	Sailed for New York
June	20	Arrived at New York
July	12	Sailed light for Savannah
July	26	Arrived at Savannah
August	15	Sailed for New York
August	25	Arrived at New York—new mainsail
September	19	Sailed for Port Royal, South Carolina
October	2	Arrived at Port Royal
October	19	Sailed for New York
November	8	Arrived at New York
December	9	Sailed for Georgetown, South Carolina
December	16	Arrived at Georgetown

1922

January	5	Sailed for New York—new fore topsail. Loaded to 17½ feet, could not get out, necessary to wait for change of wind to make higher tide. Sailed January 20.
February	3	Arrived at New York—part of deck load lost and minor damages
February	24	Sailed for Jacksonville, Florida, Capt. Richard Copsey in command
March	5	Arrived at Jacksonville—new forestaysail at Jacksonville
March	18	Sailed for Philadelphia
March	27	Arrived at Philadelphia. Hauled out in Philadelphia. Loaded pipe at Florence, N.J.

April	28	Sailed for Ponce, Puerto Rico, in command of Capt. B. A. Warren
May	24	Cable announcing arrival at Ponce
May	31	Sailed for Cap Haitien, Haiti
June	4	Arrived at Cap Haitien
June	27	Cable, sailing for Newport News
July	9	Arrived at Newport News
July	30	Sailed for Cap Haitien—telegram from mate, August 19, stating Captain Warren very sick, send captain. Capt. George G. Carlson left Baltimore August 23 to join vessel at Charleston. Vessel released of charter and chartered for Georgetown, South Carolina.
August	31	Sailed from Charleston for Georgetown
September	4	Arrived at Georgetown
October	8	Sailed for New York
October	12	Arrived at New York
November	9	Sailed for Philadelphia
November	11	Arrived at Philadelphia
November	16	Sailed for Fort-de-France, Martinique
December	4	Cable, arrived at Fort-de-France
		Sailed for Turks Island, Bahamas

1923

January	6	Arrived at Turks Island
January	11	Sailed for Baltimore
February	1	Arrived at Baltimore
March	8	Sailed from Baltimore for Georgetown, South Carolina. Stopped at Norfolk March 15, rudder head sprung.
March	27	Sailed from Norfolk for Georgetown
April	3	Arrived at Georgetown—passed out of Virginia Capes March 31, 1 A.M.; anchored sea buoy, Georgetown, April 1, 5 P.M.—41 hours
April	23	Sailed for New York from Georgetown
May	2	Arrived at New York
June	5	Sailed from New York for Georgetown
June	18	Arrived at Georgetown
July	7	Sailed for New York
July	19	Arrived at New York—dry-docked at Perth Amboy, New Jersey

August	21	Sailed from Perth Amboy for Georgetown, South Carolina
August	31	Arrived at Georgetown
September	19	Sailed for New York
September	27	Arrived at New York
October	27	Sailed from New York for Miragoane, Haiti
November	18	Arrived at Miragoane
December	7	Sailed for New York
December	25	Arrived at New York

1924

January	15	Sailed for Georgetown, South Carolina, Capt. Alonzo S. Wallace
January	23	Arrived at Georgetown
February	10	Sailed for Baltimore
February	24	Arrived at Baltimore
March	14	Sailed for Georgetown
March	20	Arrived at Georgetown
April	9	Sailed for Baltimore
April	17	At Baltimore
May	10	Sailed for Savannah
May	24	At Savannah
June	9	Sailed for Fall River, Massachusetts
June	22	At Fall River–dry-docked at Fall River
August	26	Sailed for Baltimore–in command of Capt. Robert O. Jones
September	9	At Baltimore
September	17	Sailed for Charleston, South Carolina
September	25	At Charleston
October	12	Sailed for New York
November	3	At New York
November	29	Sailed for Georgetown, South Carolina
December	12	At Georgetown
December	25	Sailed for New York

1925

January	8	At New York
January	30	Sailed for Georgetown
February	5	At Georgetown

February	15	Sailed for Baltimore
March	2	At Baltimore
March	21	Sailed for Georgetown
March	31	At Georgetown
April	11	Sailed for Baltimore
April	21	At Baltimore
June	18	Sailed for Turks Island
July	1	At Turks Island
July	8	Sailed for Portland, Maine
July	21	At Portland
August	2	Sailed for Halifax, Nova Scotia
August	6	At Halifax
August	29	Sailed for New York
September	11	At New York
October	28	Sailed for Georgetown, South Carolina
November	2	At Georgetown
November	15	Sailed for Baltimore
November	24	At Baltimore
December	16	Sailed for Charleston

1926

January	7	Arrived at Charleston
February	7	Sailed for New York
February	17	Arrived at New York
March	24	Sailed for Turks Island
April	12	Arrived at Turks Island
April	28	Sailed for Portland, Maine
May	20	Arrived at Portland
June	12	Sailed for Halifax, Nova Scotia
June	19	Arrived at Halifax
July	4	Sailed for New York
July	16	Arrived at New York
September	3	Sailed for Norfolk
September	12	Arrived at Norfolk
September		Sailed for San Juan, Puerto Rico
October	21	Arrived at San Juan
November	3	Sailed for St. Marc, Haiti
November	15	Arrived at St. Marc
December	7	Sailed for Baltimore

1927

January	8	Arrived at Baltimore
January	30	Sailed for Georgetown
February	27	Arrived at Georgetown
March	18	Sailed for New York
April	1	Arrived at New York
May	7	Sailed for Georgetown
May	27	Arrived at Georgetown
June	9	Sailed for New York
June	18	Arrived at New York
July	14	Sailed for Georgetown
August	11	Arrived at Georgetown
August	23	Sailed for New York
September	8	Arrived at New York
October	24	Sailed for Georgetown
October	31	Arrived at Georgetown. Captain Jones shot in knee November 8 and leg taken off November 9. Capt. Charles Nicklas in charge, November 16.
November	23	Sailed for New York and Stamford, Connecticut
December	1	Arrived at New York
December	12	Towed from New York for Stamford
December	13	Arrived at Stamford. Captain Nicklas left Stamford December 17 for Baltimore and arrived there on the nineteenth. Vessel in charge of mate, John Snelgrove. Captain Jones in charge December 30.

1928

February	1	Towed out of Stamford for Georgetown
February	11	Arrived at Georgetown
February	28	Sailed for Bridgeport, Connecticut
March	15	Arrived at Bridgeport
May	1	Towed from Bridgeport for Perth Amboy, New Jersey
May	2	Arrived at Perth Amboy for hauling out and caulking at Perth Amboy Dry Dock
May	10	Sailed for Georgetown, South Carolina
May	26	Arrived at Georgetown
June	7	Sailed for Bridgeport
June	19	Arrived at Bridgeport
August	15	Sailed for Georgetown

September	8	Arrived at Georgetown
September	22	Sailed for New York
October	11	Arrived at New York
October	20	Towed to Stamford
November	19	Towed from Stamford to Port Reading, New Jersey
November	20	Arrived at Port Reading
November	23	Sailed for Charleston, South Carolina
December	19	Arrived at Charleston

1929

January	9	Sailed for New York
January	19	Arrived at New York
March	19	Sailed for Newport News to load coal for Hamilton, Bermuda
March	27	Arrived at Newport News
March	29	Sailed for Bermuda
April	10	Arrived at Hamilton, Bermuda
April	17	Sailed for Jacksonville and Palatka, Florida
April	28	Arrived at Jacksonville
May	18	Sailed for New York
May	28	Arrived at New York
August	15	Sailed for Newport News
August	19	Arrived at Newport News
September	1	Sailed for Bermuda
September	23	Arrived at Bermuda
October	1	Sailed from Hamilton, Bermuda, for Jacksonville
October	14	Arrived at Mayport, Florida, and Jacksonville
October	25	Sailed from Jacksonville for Harrison, New Jersey. Put in Charleston, South Carolina, because of deck load shifting and getting short of provisions.
November	28	Arrived in Charleston
December	8	Sailed for Harrison, New Jersey
December	31	Diverted to New York and arriving this date

1930

February	5	Libeled and sold at U.S. Marshal sale, March 4, 1 P.M.
March	29	Sailed from New York for Georgetown, South Carolina
April	7	Arrived at Georgetown

April	15	Sailed for Norfolk
April	22	Arrived at Norfolk
May	3	Sailed for Georgetown
May	14	Arrived at Georgetown
May	23	Sailed for Norfolk
May	28	Arrived at Norfolk
June	6	Towed from Norfolk to Baltimore
June	7	Arrived at Baltimore
June	18	Towed from Baltimore for Norfolk
June	22	Sailed for St. George, Bermuda
July	3	Arrived at Bermuda
July	12	Sailed from St. George, Bermuda, for Georgetown, South Carolina
August	3	Arrived at Georgetown
August	28	Sailed for Baltimore
September	5	Arrived at Baltimore
October	13	Sailed for Georgetown
October	23	Arrived at Georgetown
November	16	Sailed for Baltimore
November	26	Arrived at Baltimore
December	12	Sailed for Georgetown
December	17	Arrived at Georgetown

1931

January	5	Sailed from Georgetown for Baltimore
January	20	Arrived at Baltimore
February	5	Sailed for Newport News
February	7	Arrived at Newport News
February	10	Sailed for St. George, Bermuda
February	20	Arrived at Bermuda
March	7	Sailed from Bermuda for Georgetown, South Carolina
March	26	Arrived at Georgetown
April	22	Sailed for Baltimore
April	29	Arrived at Baltimore
May	15	Discharged cargo at Back Basin, Baltimore
September	1	Towed from Back Basin and sailed for Georgetown. Passed out of Cape Henry, Virginia, September 4, 3 P.M., wind north 12 miles.
September	9	Arrived at Georgetown

September	26	Sailed for Baltimore
October	14	Arrived at Baltimore. Discharged at Back Basin, October 23. Towed to Booz Railway the twenty-fourth, hauled out. Launched October 27 and towed to Redman-Vane Shipyard. Towed to Union Shipbuilding Company, Baltimore, October 30, to load boiler for Darrell and Meyer, St. George, Bermuda.
October	30	Sailed for Newport News to load coal
November	4	Arrived at Newport News 2 P.M.
November	6	Sailed for St. George, Bermuda
December	6	Arrived at St. George
December	22	Sailed from St. George for Georgetown, South Carolina

1932

January	4	Arrived at Georgetown
January	23	Sailed for Baltimore
February	2	Arrived at Baltimore
February	22	Sailed for Newport News
February	26	Sailed from Newport News for St. George, Bermuda
March	22	Arrived at St. George
March	29	Sailed from St. George for Georgetown, South Carolina
April	9	Arrived off bar, Georgetown; at Georgetown on the tenth
May	12	Sailed for Baltimore
May	17	Arrived at Baltimore; discharged June 4
November	22	Sailed for Wilmington, North Carolina
December	12	Arrived at Wilmington

1933

January	6	Sailed for New York
January	13	Arrived at New York
February	9	Sailed for Wilmington, North Carolina; reported by Coast Guard on the eleventh anchored 10 miles southwest of Winter Quarter Lightship
January	17	Arrived at Wilmington
March	20	Sailed for New York

April	3	Arrived at New York
May	4	Sailed for Georgetown, South Carolina
May	18	Arrived at Georgetown
June	4	Sailed for New York
June	14	Arrived at New York
June	27	Left New York for Stamford, Connecticut, and arrived same day
July	1	Arrived at Bridgeport, Connecticut, from Stamford; later left Bridgeport for New Haven
July	20	Towed from New Haven to New York
July	25	Sailed from New York for Georgetown
August	7	Arrived at Georgetown
September	8	Sailed for New York
September	21	Arrived at New York
October	13	Sailed for Georgetown
October	18	Arrived at Georgetown
November	8	Sailed for New York
November	20	Arrived at New York
December	6	Sailed for Georgetown
December	14	Arrived at Georgetown
December	26	Sailed for New York

1934

January	9	Put in Cape Henry, Virginia, because of gasoline shortage
January	11	Passed out of Cape Henry, 9 A.M. for New York
January	17	Arrived at New York
February	23	Sailed for Georgetown
March	1	Arrived at Georgetown
March	16	Sailed for New York. Put in Lynnhaven Bay, Virginia, on the thirty-first. All well.
April	4	Arrived at New York
April	28	Sailed for Charleston, South Carolina
May	12	Arrived at Charleston. Towed from Charleston on the eighteenth
May	19	Arrived at Georgetown
June	11	Sailed for New York
June	18	Arrived at New York
July	10	Sailed for Georgetown
July	25	Arrived at Georgetown

September	5	Sailed for New York
September	20	Arrived at New York
October	7	Sailed from Port Reading, New Jersey, for Charleston
October	14	Arrived at Charleston
October	19	Towed from Charleston for Georgetown, arriving on the twentieth
October	31	Sailed for New York
November	13	Arrived at New York
December	2	Sailed for Charleston
December	10	Arrived at Charleston
December	15	Towed to Georgetown, arriving on the seventeenth
December	26	Sailed for New York

1935

January	3	Arrived at New York
February	5	Sailed for Georgetown; anchored on Red Hook, but passed out Sandy Hook on the sixth
February	15	Arrived at Georgetown
February	28	Sailed for New York
March	13	Arrived at New York
April	4	Sailed for Georgetown. Passed out Sandy Hook, 10:30 A.M. Anchored off Beach Haven, New Jersey, on the seventh. Unable to get anchor up. Cutter *Comanche* helped get anchor and sailed 3:30 P.M. on the seventh for Georgetown.
April	12	Arrived at Georgetown
May	3	Sailed for New York
May	10	Arrived at New York
June	1	Sailed for Georgetown; arrived at Charleston June 16, then left Charleston for Georgetown
		Arrived at Georgetown
July	16	Sailed for New York
July	29	Arrived at New York
August	27	Sailed for Georgetown
September	2	Arrived at Georgetown
October	19	Sailed for New York. Reported in *Journal of Commerce* of November 1 as passing in Virginia Capes to Hampton Roads October 31 and advised by Boston Insurance Co. as sailing November 4.

November	10	Arrived at New York
November	29	Sailed for Georgetown
December	4	Arrived at Georgetown
December	14	Sailed for New York
December	21	Arrived at New York

1936

January	25	Sailed for Georgetown
February	1	Arrived at Georgetown
February	18	Sailed for New York
March	2	Arrived at New York
March	28	Sailed for Charleston
April	9	Arrived at Charleston. Left Charleston for Georgetown.
April	17	Arrived at Georgetown
April	26	Sailed for New York
May	18	Arrived at New York
June	4	Sailed for Jekyll Island, Georgia
June	28	Arrived at Jekyll Island
July	7	Sailed for Georgetown
July	13	Arrived at Georgetown
July	25	Sailed for New York
August	4	Arrived at New York
August	27	Sailed for Georgetown
September	8	Arrived at Georgetown
September	29	Sailed for New York
October	13	Arrived at New York
November	4	Sailed for Wilmington
November	16	Arrived at Wilmington
November	27	Sailed for New York
December	22	Arrived at New York

1937

March	3	Sailed for Jacksonville, Florida
March	17	Arrived at Jacksonville
April	14	Sailed for Portland, Maine
May	5	Arrived at Portland; towed from Portland to New York
June	4	Sailed from New York for Hamilton, Bermuda

June	14	Arrived at Bermuda
June	20	Sailed for Jacksonville
July	12	Arrived at Jacksonville
July	21	Sailed for Portland
August	5	Arrived at Portland
September	18	Left Portland Dock on the eleventh and sailed on the eighteenth for Jacksonville
October	1	Arrived at Jacksonville
October	23	Sailed for Providence, Rhode Island. Picked up by Coast Guard cutter and taken into Lynnhaven Bay, Virginia, October 28, because of Capt. Robert Jones having pleurisy. Sailed November 2 with Capt. Robert Jones's wife and Capt. George Jones as additional man due to master's illness.
November	8	Arrived at Providence
December	12	Sailed for Jacksonville
December	23	Arrived at Jacksonville

1938

January	8	Sailed for Baltimore. Taken in tow by Coast Guard cutter *George M. Bibb* 390 miles southeast of Cape Hatteras, disabled and leaking, on January 16. Taken over by cutter *Sebago* and towed to Hampton Roads, Virginia.
January	24	Arrived in Baltimore in tow of Wood Towing Co. tug
February	19	Sailed for Jacksonville
February	28	Arrived at Jacksonville
March	15	Sailed for Portland
March	28	Arrived at Portland
April	13	Sailed for Jacksonville
April	25	Arrived at Jacksonville
May	18	Sailed for Portland
June	3	Arrived at Portland. Completed discharging June 17, Bill of Lading May 17. Chartered under charter party dated August 29.
September	2	Sailed for Sheet Harbor, Nova Scotia
September	5	Arrived at Sheet Harbor
September	25	Sailed for New York
October	3	Arrived at New York. Went to Perth Amboy Dry Dock, hauled and painted.

October	27	Sailed light for Savannah
November	3	Arrived at Savannah
November	19	Sailed for New York
December	2	Arrived at New York; discharged December 23

1939

January	20	Sailed for Turks Island, Bahamas
February	3	Arrived at Turks Island
February	9	Sailed for Fernandina, Florida, (advice by cable). Second cable received February 15, sailing February 12 for Fernandina.
February	20	Arrived at Fernandina; discharged March 3
March	13	Left Fernandina in tow of Quinn's fish boat for Jacksonville, arriving Jacksonville Bar same day and anchored. Towed to Jacksonville and docked the fourteenth.
April	20	Sailed for Providence, Rhode Island
May	5	Arrived at Providence; discharged May 22
June	6	Sailed for Perth Amboy Dry Dock (N.J.) for hauling and painting
June	12	Arrived at Perth Amboy. Towed to Port Reading to load coal on June 19.
June	20	Sailed for Jacksonville
July	4	Arrived at Jacksonville
July	16	Towed out from Jacksonville and sailed for Sapelo Sound, Georgia
July	17	Arrived At Sapelo Sound
July	30	Sailed for Providence
August	9	Arrived at Providence; discharged August 25. Chartered October 3 to load coal at Newport News for Bermuda.
October	7	Sailed from Providence for Newport News
October	13	Arrived at Newport News
October	17	Sailed for St. George, Bermuda
October	28	Arrived at St. George
November	3	Sailed for Jacksonville
November	11	Arrived at Jacksonville
November	29	Sailed for Providence
December	9	Arrived at Providence
December	26	Sailed for Newport News

1940

January	9	Arrived at Newport News
January	15	Sailed for Bermuda
January	22	Arrived at Bermuda
February	1	Sailed for Cap Haitien, Haiti
February	10	Arrived at Cap Haitien
February	29	Sailed for Baltimore
March	20	Arrived at Baltimore
April	28	Towed from Baltimore for Norfolk for hauling. Hauled and towed to Newport News, May 3.
May	5	Sailed from Newport News for Bermuda
May	12	Arrived at Bermuda
May	18	Sailed for Jacksonville
June	3	Arrived at Jacksonville
June	15	Sailed for Portland
June	26	Arrived at Portland
July	15	Sailed for Cap Haitien
August	12	Arrived at Cap Haitien
August	25	Sailed for Baltimore
September	16	Arrived at Baltimore
October	1	Sailed for Jacksonville
October	9	Arrived at Jacksonville
October	24	Sailed for Portland
November	6	Arrived at Portland
November	25	Sailed for Newport News
December	6	Arrived at Newport News
December	10	Sailed for St. George, Bermuda
December	19	Arrived at St. George
December	24	Sailed for Newport News

1941

January	18	Arrived at Newport News
January	29	Sailed for St. George, Bermuda
February	9	Arrived at St. George
February	21	Sailed for Cap Haitien
March	6	Arrived at Cap Haitien
March	20	Sailed for Baltimore
April	11	Arrived at Baltimore
May	14	Towed to Norfolk
May	21	Sailed for St. George, Bermuda

May	25	Arrived at Bermuda
June	10	Sailed for Cap Haitien
June	21	Arrived at Cap Haitien
July	6	Sailed for Baltimore
July	19	Arrived at Baltimore
August	8	Sailed for Cap Haitien. Returned to Lynnhaven Roads, Virginia, August 13, by Coast Guard cutter because sails and windlass damaged. Passed out of Cape Henry, Virginia, sixteenth or seventeenth.
September	9	Arrived at Cap Haitien
September	28	Sailed for Baltimore
October	10	Arrived at Baltimore; discharged the twenty-second
October	26	Towed to Norfolk for hauling at Norfolk Shipbuilding & Dry Dock Co. Towed back to Baltimore.
November	4	Arrived at Baltimore
		Vessel sold latter part of November 1941 to Albert Shipping Co. Inc., of New York, New York. Loaded coal for new owners at Hampton Roads for Bermuda. Then sailed from Bermuda to Turks Island to load salt. Never reported after sailing from Turks Island.

Appendix B

Trip Book

Earnings and Expenditures of the *Paul,* 1917–41

Trip #1 October 1917

Schooner *Albert F. Paul,* Captain C. F. Southard

Coal from Norfolk, Va., to Pernambuco, Brazil 1,129 tons @ $26.50		29,918.50
Springer furnishing crews, etc.	42.50	
C. M. Struven & Co. Provisions	977.13	
A. J. Harper Towing to Norfolk	235.00	
Water	10.00	
Capt. Primage* on freight 5%	1,495.93	
War Risk Insurance $80,000 2%	1,600.00	
Commission on charter	1,495.93	
Trimming coal	107.26	
Docking and undocking at Lambert Pt.	18.00	
Custom House at Norfolk	2.70	
Brazilian Consul fees	48.13	
Clearing at Custom House and Consulate	10.00	
Cash to Capt. a/c Expense at Norfolk	222.00	
Captain's letter of credit (Alex. Brown & Sons)	1,000.00	7,264.58
		22,653.92

Dividends

42/180	C. M. Struven	4,620.00	
42/180	G. N. Reed	4,620.00	
37/180	C. C. Paul & Co.	4,070.00	
28/180	R. W. Tunnell	3,080.00	
12/180	C. F. Southard	1,320.00	
6/180	A. W. McNeal	660.00	
4/180	W. H. Edwards	440.00	
3/180	G. H. McNeal	330.00	
3/180	J. W. McNeal	330.00	
3/180	H. W. Randolph	330.00	19,800.00
			2,853.92

*Primage was a percentage of the freight money paid by shippers to the master of the ship for his care of the goods.

Vessel left Baltimore, October 4, 1917, in tow for Norfolk, Va. Detained in Norfolk on account of Government taking her cargo for naval collier. Sailed from Norfolk October 28, 1917. Arrived at Pernambuco, Brazil, December 24, 1917. Left for dry dock at Mobile January ——, 1918. Arrived at Mobile, January 31, 1918.

Trip #1 October 1917

Revised statement after completion of trip

Coal from Norfolk, Va., to Pernambuco, Brazil 1,129 tons @ 26.50		29,918.50
Towing to Norfolk	235.00	
Commission	1,495.93	
Trimming Coal at Norfolk	107.26	
Docking and undocking at Lambert Point	18.00	
Custom House fee at Norfolk	2.70	
Brazilian Consul fee	48.13	
Clearance at Norfolk	10.00	
Pilotage	72.00	
Cables and cabling money	32.70	
Sundry paid by Capt. at Norfolk	.72	
		27,896.06
War Risk $80,000 2%	1,600.00	
Sundries paid by Capt. at Norfolk	15.45	
Pilotage, towing, stores etc. at Pernambuco	540.30	2,155.75
		25,740.31
Springer shipping crew	20.00	
C. M. Struven & Co. Stores	977.13	
Water	10.00	
Captain's Primage	1,495.93	
Crew's wages from Balto. to Pernambuco and return to Norfolk	1,861.34	
T. C. Hurst, Groceries at Norfolk	58.50	
Shipping seamen at Norfolk	10.00	
Capt. wages to Jan. 31–4 mos. 85	340.00	
Comm. on letter of credit–Alex. Brown & Sons	5.00	4,777.90
		20,962.41
Dividends paid as shown on page 108		19,800.00
		1,162.41

Trip #2 June 1918

Mobile to Moss Point Light thence to Georgetown, Demerara, with lumber

Balance in hand from trip #1		2,853.92
Letter of credit given Captain trip #1		1,000.00
Credit a/c Mianus Company		145.19
		3,999.11
Captain and crew wages to Pernambuco and return to Mobile including Expenses at Pernambuco		2,691.51
		1,307.60
55,638 ft. lumber @ 30.00		16,691.55
		17,999.15
Sundry bills paid by Capt. at Moss Point	101.50	
Capt. Primage	834.58	
Commission	834.58	
Railway bill at Mobile	2,539.22	
Provisions at Mobile	823.79	
Chandlery at Mobile	144.82	
Provisions, C. H. Alley Co., Pascagoula, Miss.	195.50	
Loading	695.47	
Towages, Pilotages, Custom House fees and other sundry expenses paid by Capt.	863.78	
Port charges etc. at Demerara	859.65	
Capt. wages to June 1/18 4 mos. 85	340.00	
Annual freight insurance	400.00	
War Risk on full for trip $80,000	200.00	
Insurance on advances	123.24	8,956.13
		9,043.02
42/180 Chas. M. Struven	2,110.04	
42/180 Geo. N. Reed	2,110.04	
37/180 C. C. Paul & Co.	1,858.84	
28/180 R. W. Tunnell	1,406.69	
12/180 Chas. F. Southard	602.87	
6/180 A. W. McNeal	301.43	
4/180 W. H. Edwards	200.95	
3/180 G. H. McNeal	150.72	
3/180 J. W. McNeal	150.72	
3/180 H. W. Randolph	150.72	9,043.02

Trip #3 July 1918

Logwood from Port au Prince, Haiti, to Camden, New Jersey

987.7+ tons logwood @ 13.50		13,333.96
Expenses at Port au Prince	424.13	
Wharfage at Phila.	85.93	
Towage and Pilotage at Phila.	597.00	
Crew's wages for voyage	1,889.63	
Discharging at Phila.	881.53	
Sundry expenses at Phila.	159.68	
War Risk	345.09	
Commission	666.70	
Captain Primage	666.70	
Capt. wages to Aug. 1st 2 mos.	170.00	5,886.39
		7,447.57
Held in hand to pay Railway Bill, etc.		1,447.57
		6,000.00

42/180	Chas. M. Struven	1,400.00	
42/180	Geo. N. Reed	1,400.00	
37/180	C. C. Paul & Co.	1,233.34	
28/180	Raymond W. Tunnell	933.33	
12/180	Chas. F. Southard	400.00	
6/180	A. W. McNeal	200.00	
4/180	W. H. Edwards	133.33	
3/180	G. H. McNeal	100.00	
3/180	J. W. McNeal	100.00	
3/180	H. Ward Randolph	100.00	6,000.00
Held in hand to pay Railway Bill, etc.			1,447.57

Trip #4 August 1918

Coal from Hampton Roads to Bermuda

Balance retained from trip #3		1,447.57
1,085 tons of coal @ 7.50		8,137.50
		9,585.07
Trimming coal at Norfolk	128.52	
Virginia pilot	74.25	
Towage	225.00	
Sundry expenses at Norfolk	425.20	852.97
		8,732.10

	Forward		8,732.10
Railway Bill and sundry exp. at Phila.		1,300.04	
Letter of credit to Captain		750.00	
Towage to sea trip #3		45.00	
War Risk Insurance for voyage		850.00	
Stores and chandlery		1,028.70	
Commission		406.87	
Primage		406.87	
Capt. wages to Sept. 1st		85.00	4,872.48
			3,859.62

September 7, 1918			
42/180	Chas. M. Struven	900.58	
42/180	Geo. N. Reed	900.58	
37/180	C. C. Paul & Co.	793.35	
28/180	R. W. Tunnell	600.39	
12/180	C. F. Southard	257.31	
6/180	A. W. McNeal	128.65	
4/180	W. H. Edwards	85.77	
3/180	G. H. McNeal	64.33	
3/180	J. W. McNeal	64.33	
3/180	H. W. Randolph	64.33	3,859.62

Trip #5 January 1919

Letter of Credit to Capt. Trip#4		750.00
Error in Capt. statement last trip		24.00
Allowance for engineer hoisting cargo		56.00
Interest on Letter of Credit		1.15
Cash for stores sold to schr. *Louise Richards*		30.50
520,388 ft. lumber, Brunswick to Portland @ 20.00		10,407.76
Demurrage*		200.00
		11,469.41
Crew insurance	4.35	
War Risk Insurance on freight	100.00	
Pictures of schooner	78.00	
Expense to Washington—A. F. Paul and C. F. Southard	2.50	
Commission	530.38	
Capt. Primage	530.38	
Capt. Primage discharging coal	35.26	
Capt. Primage loading lumber	44.10	

*Demurrage was the money paid to the vessel for detention in loading or unloading. Demurrage starts at the end of the "lay days," allotted time for the loading or discharging of a ship.

Capt. Primage discharging lumber	32.52	
Capt. wages to Jan. 1, 1919	340.00	
Blacksmith bill, stores, and sundries, Bermuda	264.98	
Custom House fee at Brunswick	16.65	
Expense a/c examination of damage to SS *Coyote*	15.80	
Pilotage in and out of Brunswick	117.25	
Towage in and out of Brunswick	171.58	
Stores, marketing, sundries at Brunswick	143.28	
Docking at Portland	20.00	
Stores 53.08, Oil 2.00, Dish, Lamp, Sundries—28.33	83.41	
Noting protest†	11.00	
Crew's wages for trip	2,341.57	
Portland Shipbldg. Co.	470.51	
Flitner-Atwood Co.—Stores	312.96	
Flitner-Atwood Co.—Chandlery	259.15	
Towage to and from railway	40.00	
Telegrams 1.80, Shipping fee, 30.10	31.90	
Rigging work 15.75 and 16.12	31.87	
Cook 4 days	14.00	
Stove pipe and shovel 10.65 Water .50	11.15	
Rating chronometer and charts	6.75	
Marketing	3.72	6,065.02
		5,404.39

Trip #6 January 1919

Coal Hampton Roads to Para, Brazil Sailed Jan. 16—Capt. Southard

1,207½ tons @ 15.50	18,716.25
Discount on bills T. C. Hurst & Son	15.00
	18,731.25

Crew insurance	.31	
Towage City Island to West Bank (Cahill)	200.00	
War Risk insurance—Johnston & Co.	170.00	
Cash a/c crew	70.00	Paid Jan. 11/19 Capt. a/c at Norfolk 141.82
Water	5.00	
Boat hire	5.00	
Marketing	61.82	
Letter of Credit to Capt.	1,000.00	
Cost of Letter of Credit (A. Brown & Sons)	5.00	

†Noting protest—A document sworn to before a notary or consul declaring that the weather conditions encountered on the voyage were such that if the ship or cargo reveals damage, it was caused by wind and weather.

Trip #6 (cont.)

Chandlery T. C. Hurst & Son, Norfolk	297.62	Draft 657.82
Stores T. C. Hurst & Son, Norfolk	124.45	
Towage Jos. M Clark & Bro.	230.00	
Water 3.75 Telegrams 2.00	5.75	
C. M. Struven & Co. Stores 1,088.33 Chandlery 770.26	1,858.59	
C. M. Struven & Co. Stores 6.25 Freight 24.17	30.42	
Towage at Portland	18.00	
Commission	935.81	
Capt. Primage	935.81	
2% extra for insurance endorsement	1,600.00	
Norfolk Shpbldg. & D. D. Co.	1,631.90	9,185.48
		9,545.77
Trip #5 Lumber		5,404.39
		14,950.16

54/180	C. C. Paul & Co.	4,485.04	
42/180	C. M. Struven	3,488.36	
42/180	Geo. N. Reed	3,488.36	
12/180	C. F. Southard	996.70	
8/180	W. H. Edwards	664.45	
6/180	A. W. McNeal	498.34	
3/180	G. H. McNeal	249.17	
3/180	J. W. McNeal	249.17	
3/180	H. W. Randolph	249.17	
3/180	Nina Coleman	249.17	
2/180	C. Howard Paul	166.11	
1/180	Adele B. Struven	83.06	
1/180	Meta L. Koop	83.06	14,950.16

Settled January 25, 1919

Trips #7 and #8 June 1919

Hampton Roads, Va., to Rio Grande do Sul, Brazil

1,092 tons of coal @ 20.50 per ton	22,386.00	
Towage allowance last trip	3,018.75	
Disc. on railway bill	32.64	
Interest on letter of credit	17.19	
Cash at Para	32.43	
Board for two workaways	50.00	
Letter of credit	1,000.00	
		26,537.01
Cash to mate's wife	360.00	
Crew wages to Para and return to N.Y.	2,326.00	

Telephone and telegrams		4.50
Expense to New York		17.10
Cable, Gilmartin & Trundy		11.10
War Risk		60.00
Freight insurance		100.00
Expense to New York		19.00
Entry fee	Gilmartin and Trundy 2,375.69	55.16
Phone to Baltimore		7.05
Carfare and ferry		.45
Lamp		3.90
Watchman and phone		47.90
Towage, Stapleton to 8th St., East River		75.00
Pilotage in		49.01
Towage sea to Staten Island		216.50
Stevedore Jno. McKenna		314.72
Wharfage 8 days		1,600.00
Telegram		.50
Doctor bill, crew		5.50
Southard, Primage and towage last trip		150.94
Southard, wages to May 1st		340.00
Water bill	Capt. Statement	3.24
Cook 20.00, Mate 18.33		38.33
Marketing at New York		40.23
Marketing and boat hire at Para		232.57
Wharfage 1½ days	Gilmartin and Trundy 1,822.46	300.00
Telephone and electric lights		18.00
Watchman		132.00
Clerk and tallyman		117.00
Port Warden, New York		15.00
Stevedore, Carney & Son		1,036.49
Stevedore, Jno. McKenna		140.00
Labor while shifting		2.00
Bond and stamp at Custom House		1.50
Immigration fine		60.00
Telegram to Baltimore		.47
Towage 34th Street to Perth Amboy, N.J.		100.00
Towage 8th Street to 34th Street		38.23
Shipping fee		20.62
Telephone		.75
Rat guards		7.40
Letter of credit, cost of same 1500.00, 7.50		1,507.50
Marketing at Norfolk	Capt. a/c at Norfolk 69.76	24.25
Batteries		6.80
Fumigating fee		13.78
Railroad fare and meals		14.73
Cash to Cook		10.00

Trips #7 and 8 (cont.)

Thirty meals for stowaway		9.00	
Head tax for two workaways		16.00	
Perth Amboy railway bill		1,051.58	
Taulane's Sons, sails		1,145.50	
Shipping Cook	Elliott 684.75	4.00	
Store bill New York		106.87	
Towage Perth Amboy to sea		75.00	
Chronometer bill		12.20	
Sail bill		304.42	
Store bill		181.73	
Telegram		.53	
Commission		1,119.30	
Primage		1,119.30	
Insurance		2,000.00	
Struven & Co. Stores 1,903.62 Chandlery 132.25		2,635.87	
Commission a/c towage		150.94	
Docking etc. at Norfolk		20.86	
T. C. Hurst & Sons Drayage		115.00	
T. C. Hurst & Sons 156.03 119.76		275.79	
Jos. M. Clark & Sons Towage 50.00 55.00		105.00	
Jos. M. Clark & Sons Water		4.00	20,098.31
			6,438.70
Paid owners			5,000.00
	Due vessel		1,438.70

Share	Owner	Amount	Total
1/180	Meta Koop	27.78	
1/180	Adele B. Struven	27.78	
2/180	C. Howard Paul	55.56	
3/180	Nina Coleman	83.34	
3/180	H. W. Randolph	83.34	
3/180	J. W. McNeal	83.34	
3/180	G. H. McNeal	83.34	
6/180	A. M. McNeal	166.68	
8/180	W. H. Edwards	222.22	
12/180	C. F. Southard	333.32	
42/180	Geo. N. Reed	1,166.65	
42/180	C. M. Struven	1,166.65	
54/180	C. C. Paul & Co.	1,500.000	
	Settled June 9, 1919		5,000.00

Trip #9 January 1920

Linseed from Buenos Aires to Phila.

$941\frac{575}{2240}$ tons @ 24.00	22,597.80

In hand from last settlement		1,438.70	
Refund from Immigration Commission		60.00	
Letter of Credit		1,500.00	
Interest on Letter of Credit		29.53	
Demurrage at Rio Grande do Sul		375.00	
Cash for supplies sold sailor (Slop* chest)		93.32	26,094.35
Cash a/c stowaway		9.45	
Cash a/c stowaway to Gilmartin Co. 11.00 12.38		23.38	
Struven & Co. Extra stores and freight		143.72	
Telephones, telegrams, cables 36.54 3.10 24.74		64.38	
Capt. wages 8 mos. 680.00 Primage 1,148.64		1,828.64	
War Risk insurance round trip		80.00	
Freight insurance		150.00	
Stray & Co. cable		3.36	
Watchman at Phila.		31.22	
MacFarland, Taylor & Costello lawyer's fee		500.00	
Commission		1,148.64	
Crew wages round trip		4,944.51	
Expense at Rio Grande do Sul		581.98	
Expense at Norfolk, Va.		5.00	
Expense at Buenos Aires		3,384.89	
Exchange in money		32.69	
Custom House entering at Phila.	A. D. Cummins & Co.	45.16	
Inward pilotage		77.50	
Towage Breakwater to Phila.		450.00	
Towage at Phila.		100.00	
Telegram Cummins & Co.		.46	
Discharging Loveland & Co.		,489.61	
Surveyor report		1.50	
Weight certificate .30 Pilot's agent 5.00		5.30	
Noting protest 1.50 Survey of hatches and cargo	15.00	16.50	
Bond and permit		5.00	
Stores, launch hire etc. at Breakwater		73.95	
Fumigation		13.58	15,160.42
Due vessel			10,933.93

1/180	Meta L. Koop	50.00
1/180	Adele B. Struven	50.00
2/180	C. Howard Paul	100.00
3/180	Nina Coleman	150.00
3/180	H. W. Randolph	150.00
3/180	J. W. McNeal	150.00
3/180	G. H. McNeal	150.00

*Slops was the merchandise kept on board ship for sale to the crew, such as clothing, tobacco, etc.

Trip #9 (cont.)

6/180	A. W. McNeal		300.00	
		Settled Jan. 22, 1920		
8/180	W. H. Edwards		400.00	
12/180	C. F. Southard		600.00	
42/180	Geo. N. Reed		2,100.00	
42/180	Chas. M. Struven		2,100.00	
54/180	C. C. Paul & Co.		2,700.00	9,000.00
		Hold for bills		1,933.93

Trips #10 and #11 — August 1920 — Captain Wm. M. Martino

Coal from Hampton Roads to Guadeloupe		
1,095 tons @ 9.50	10,402.50	
In hand from last settlement	1,933.33	
Old burlap sold	12.00	
Allowance a/c Armed Guard Dec. 1918	54.00	
Slop Chest a/c	11.85	
Logwood Miragoane, Haiti, to Camden		
847.017 tons @ 12.00	10,164.20	22,578.48

Cook's fare to Phila.	5.00
Shipping fee Springer	5.00
One octant C. F. Southard	25.00
Expense to Phila. A. F. Paul	7.50
Affadavit	.50
Towage Phila. to Norfolk McNally	897.00
Geo. Taulane's Sons, sails	1,300.00
Jonathan May & Sons 180.55 98.28	278.83
C. M. Struven & Co. Stores	750.64
C. M. Struven & Co. Chandlery	345.74
C. M. Struven & Co. Engine	275.00
Marketing at Phila. C. F. Southard	67.09
C. F. Southard wages Jan. 1 to Feb. 10, 1920	113.33
Colonna Railway Co.	459.96
Jos. M. Clark & Co. towage	120.00
Insurance on crew's wages G. R. Johnston Co.	52.50
John E. Hand & Sons Co. Nautical supplies	6.05
Globe Ship Supply Co. 438.83 .80	439.63
Phila. Ship Repair Co.	905.21
Telegrams Cummins	2.78
Water P. F. Martin	25.00
Attendance fee	25.00

(John E. Hand & Sons Co. through Attendance fee, bracketed: A. D. Cummins & Co. 200.00 to Capt.)

Commission on coal	Berwind White & Co.	520.12	
Shipping fee Norfolk	Berwind White & Co.	50.00	
Trimming coal Norfolk	Berwind White & Co.	255.65	
Shifting towage Norfolk	Berwind White & Co.	25.75	
Stores Norfolk	Berwind White & Co.	172.33	
Chandlery Norfolk	Berwind White & Co.	50.10	
Va. pilotage	Berwind White & Co.	76.50	
Custom House and French Consul fees	Berwind White & Co.	21.08	
Sundry Expense at Phila. Capt.		57.95	
Sundry Expense at Newport News Capt.		47.00	
Discharging coal at Point à Pitre		547.50	
Sundry expense at Point à Pitre		66.90	
Loading logwood at Miragoane 50¢		422.50	
Sundry expense at Miragoane		43.20	
Crew wages		3,306.34	
Capt. wages 4 mos. 6 days 400.00		1,680.00	
Gratuity shipping commissioner		10.00	
Shipping fee Neal 5.50 Nick 38.36		43.86	
C. M. Struven & Co. Stores and chandlery		781.33	
Cash to Cook's wife		50.00	
Commission on logwood		508.21	
Telephone		2.55	
Shifting vessel		20.00	
Discharging logwood		1,236.22	
Towage in and out of Phila.		721.50	
Pilotage in and out of Phila.		111.00	
Tug boat Capt.		5.00	
Cummins a/c		57.97	
Custom House fee at Phila.		46.07	
Water and handling stores		108.50	
Jonathan May & Sons Stores, etc.		210.21	17,362.10
			5,216.38

1/180	Meta L. Koop	28.98	
1/180	Adele B. Struven	28.98	
2/180	C. Howard Paul	57.96	
3/180	Nina Coleman	86.94	
3/180	H. W. Randolph	86.94	
3/180	J. W. McNeal	86.94	
3/180	G. H. McNeal Settled 8/16/20	86.94	
6/180	A. W. McNeal	173.88	
8/180	W. H. Edwards	231.84	
12/180	C. F. Southard	347.76	
42/180	Geo. N. Reed	1,217.16	
42/180	Chas. M. Struven	1,217.16	
54/180	C. C. Paul & Co.	1,564.90	5,216.38

Trips #12 and #13 December 1920

Halifax, Nova Scotia, to Havana, Cuba		
748 M ft. spruce @ 18.00	13,481.96	
Coal, Gulfport, Miss., to Havana @ 7.50	8,625.00	
Old spanker	115.00	22,221.96
Mac Andrews	18.68	
Geo. Taulane Sons Jib topsail	215.00	
Croswell Bros. Bunting 2.27—2.02	4.29	
Telegrams and cost of cabling money	29.72	
Commission on lumber	674.10	
Primage on lumber	674.10	
Charges at Halifax, paid by F. K. Warren	371.21	
Charges at Halifax, paid by Captain	150.26	
Loading spruce	1,011.15	
Crew at Halifax	265.53	
Pilotage and towage at Havana	643.70	
Fumigation and Custom House fee at Havana	213.30	
Discharging lumber at Havana	1,460.55	
Marketing, water, and sundry at Havana	536.62	
Crew wages at Mobile	2,469.11	
Custom house fee at Mobile	16.49	
Shipping fee at Mobile	20.00	
Pilotage at Mobile	45.00	
Towage at Mobile	372.00	
Towage to Gulfport	350.00	
Railway at Mobile	611.59	
Telegram from Mobile	12.50	
Harbor fee and running lines	20.00	
Pilotage at Gulfport	68.00	
Custom house fee at Gulfport	22.20	
Shipping fee at Gulfport	50.00	
Sundries at Gulfport	46.00	
Stores and provisions at Gulfport	1,134.62	
Commission on coal	431.25	
Primage on coal	431.25	
Towage out of Gulfport	256.55	
Cash to Captain Havana	1,200.00	
Capt. wages to November 28—5 mos.	425.00	14,249.77
		7,972.19
Dividends to owners 1/90—$70		6,300.00
In hand		1,672.19
Net		7,972.19

1/180	Meta L. Koop	35.00	
1/180	Adele B. Struven	35.00	
1/180	Lillian N. Hinton	35.00	
1/180	Elizabeth R. Hinton	35.00	
1/180	Agnes R. Randolph, Richmond, Va.	35.00	
1/180	Ward Reed Randolph " "	35.00	
1/180	Henry G. Randolph " "	35.00	
2/180	C. Howard Paul	70.00	
3/180	Nina Coleman	105.00	
3/180	H. W. Randolph	105.00	
3/180	J. W. McNeal	105.00	
3/180	G. H. McNeal	105.00	
6/180	A. W. McNeal	210.00	
8/180	W. H. Edwards	280.00	
12/180	C. F. Southard	420.00	
37/180	Geo. N. Reed	1,295.00	
42/180	Chas. M. Struven	1,470.00	
54/180	C. C. Paul & Co.	1,890.00	6,300.00
	Dec. 7, 1920 In hand		1,672.19

Trips #14 and #15 June 1921

Balance in hand last settlement	1,672.10	
Mobile to San Juan Lumber		
652,430 ft. @ 16.00 per M	10,438.88	
Logwood, St. Marc, Haiti, to Balto.		
848 tons @ 5.00	4,240.00	
Sale of old junk	15.00	
Rebate on bills at Havana	98.00	
Rebate on Jonathan May & Sons bill	14.45	
Rebate on bills at Mobile	70.00	
Discount on Woodall & Co. bill	83.14	
1 rat guard sold	2.00	
Cash in Capt.'s hands last settlement	1,200.00	17,833.66

Alexander Brown & Sons a/c cable	1.00
Sergeant Corp. a/c. chg. at Guadeloupe	25.00
Tonnage tax	66.10
Fumigation 12.60 80.98	93.58
Towage in and out and dockage	586.40
Groceries and meats	64.67
American Bureau of Shipping	27.00
Custom House fees	22.00
Pilotage	54.00

Capt. Statement Dec. 1920

Trips #14 and 15 (cont.)

Broker's fees at Havana		50.00	
Capt. Primage on coal last trip		86.20	
Hardware, lamp, etc.		16.60	
Crew's wages at Mobile		922.82	
Custom House fee		16.49	
Pilotage		107.50	
State Harbor Commission		5.00	
Towage from sea to Mobile and return		346.50	
A. H. McLeod & Co. sails		230.86	
Rating chronometer		3.00	
Loading lumber		1,631.08	
Supplies for crew, deducted from pay		190.65	
Shipping fee		50.00	
Mobile Ship Chandlery Co.		603.14	
Water		10.00	
Exchange on draft and telegrams		18.92	
Commission on lumber		521.94	
Freight insurance		100.00	
Cables and telegram		18.73	5,869.18
Capt. primage on lumber		521.94	
Sundry expense at Mobile		40.57	
Capt. expense from Mobile to Balto.		58.85	
Discharging lumber		913.40	
Towage	Capt. Statement San Juan	42.43	
Exchange 8.00 8.00	Capt. Statement San Juan	16.00	
Marketing, water, etc.	Capt. Statement San Juan	87.67	
Notary protest and lawyer fee	Capt. Statement San Juan	70.00	
Standard Grocery Co.	Capt. Statement San Juan	124.83	
Towage	Capt. Statement San Juan	103.05	
Agent's fee	Capt. Statement San Juan	50.00	
Consul fee	Capt. Statement San Juan	10.00	
Pilotage	Capt. Statement San Juan	9.00	
Cable	Capt. Statement San Juan	3.60	
Capt's. expense	Capt. Statement San Juan	9.00	
Expense getting man to hospital	Capt. Statement San Juan	9.00	
Crew wages at San Juan	Capt. Statement San Juan	551.86	
Doctor's fee		3.00	
Pilotage		21.25	
Expense at Port au Prince		7.00	
Marketing		73.60	
Loading logwood		406.62	
Groceries		58.88	
Labor		3.00	
Water		15.00	
Polish		2.50	

Crew at St. Marc	220.95	
Crew wages at Balto. including Capt. Fletcher	2,340.53	
Towage Cape Henry to Baltimore	300.00	
Noting protest	1.00	
Expense at Port au Prince (paid by Young)	23.68	
Repairing stove	8.60	
Discharging logwood @ 1.00	848.00	
A. F. Paul and C. F. Southard—3 days at N.Y.	75.00	
Capt. Southard to May 28—6 mos.	510.00	
Custom House fee Balto.	19.89	
Vane Bros. spark plug	1.00	
Adjusting chronometer and charts	3.75	
Loane Eng. Co.	10.67	
Docking and shifting towages	48.00	13,492.30
Outward towage	45.00	
Capt. primage	212.00	
Commission on logwood	212.00	
American Bureau of Shipping	25.50	
Shipping fee Nick	16.50	
Woodall Co. Caulking, etc.	4,157.22	18,160.52
Receipts from page 121		17,833.66
Due C. C. Paul & Co.		326.86

Trip #16 July 1921

Savannah to New York Lumber		
573,245 ft. @ 7.25 free loaded	4,156.03	
Sale of old junk	50.00	
		4,206.03

Marketing, etc. 33.80 12.23		46.03
Paint and varnish		6.70
Cabin furnishings		31.60
Labor hauling vessel		3.00
Inward pilotage 40.00 Outward 108.75	Savannah, Georgia Capt. Statement 6/10/21	148.75
Dockage		25.00
Towage to sea		183.75
Stores and chandlery 81.50 11.13		92.63
Meats		20.70
Harbor master		4.00
Rating chronometer		5.00
Boat hire and laundry		3.47
Marketing		6.20
Exchange on draft		1.77

Trip #16 (cont.)

Crew's wages for trip	Gilmartin's Statement N.Y., 7/11/21	513.50	
Expense shipping crew		22.60	
Marketing		6.68	
Primage on discharging lumber		36.07	
Towage Sandy Hook to Red Hook		75.00	
Discharging lumber		766.56	
Watchman		17.00	
Towage Red Hook to Harlem River		65.00	
Telegram		1.60	
Watchman		3.00	
Towage Newtown Creek to West Bank		60.00	
Water		10.00	
Telephone and telegrams		6.95	
Gulfport Shipbuilding Co.		11.60	
Commission		207.80	
Stores and chandlery Struven & Co.		748.71	
Sailor		.50	
Capt. Primage		207.80	3,338.97
			867.06

Trip #17 September 1921

Savannah to New York Lumber			
534,966 ft. @ 8.75		4,680.95	
Overcharge in stores at Savannah		13.68	4,694.63
Hardware 2.45, Postage .98, Coal 17.10	Capt. Statement Savannah	20.53	
Marketing 11.69, Stores 12.73, Vegetables 24.18		48.60	
Harbor master 4.00 Marketing 6.68		10.68	
Telegram. 75 Wharfage 27		27.75	
Loading lumber		666.71	
Extra to stevedore		11.55	
Pilotage in and out of Savannah		141.85	
Towage and dockage		208.75	
Provisions at Savannah		129.60	
Chandlery		15.40	
Exchange on draft		.54	
a/c crew at Savannah		119.68	
Provisions		6.60	
Provisions and chandlery		285.50	
Balance crew wages at N.Y.	Capt. Statement N.Y.	618.46	
Capt. expenses at New York		20.62	
Marketing		13.27	
Mate's board in N.Y.		11.57	

Boat hire		2.00	
Shipping fee and expense		17.00	
Watchman	Gilmartin's Statement	14.00	
Discharging @ 1.55	Gilmartin's Statement	829.20	
Towage sea to Red Hook	Gilmartin's Statement	75.00	
Repairs to tank	Gilmartin's Statement	73.57	
Towage Red Hook to Oak Point		50.00	
Towage Oak Point to Red Hook		35.00	
Towage Red Hook to West Bank		60.00	
Capt. wages 4 mos. to Sept. 28		340.00	
Capt. Primage		234.04	
Commission		234.04	
Telegram		.41	4,321.92
			372.71

Trip #18 December 1921

Port Royal, S. C., to New York Lumber		
509,168 ft. @ 5.12½ L & D*	2,609.49	
142,731 ft. @ 5.12½	731.50	
Tobacco	3.70	
Sale of old canvas	12.00	
		3,356.69

Shipping fee and transportation 13.00 4.00	Capt. Statement Port Royal	17.00
Chart .50, batteries 1.70, tinware 2.32	Capt. Statement Port Royal	4.52
Pilotage Tybee Bar	Capt. Statement Port Royal	20.65
Ice	Capt. Statement Port Royal	2.40
Blacksmith, carpenter, transportation	Capt. Statement Port Royal	172.65
Lumber	Capt. Statement Port Royal	20.00
Crew at Port Royal	Capt. Statement Port Royal	79.06
Marketing 24.00 70.24 23.35	Capt. Statement Port Royal	116.59
Towage in and out	Capt. Statement Port Royal	375.00
Outward pilotage	Capt. Statement Port Royal	71.00
Cash to sailor	Capt. Statement Port Royal	1.00
Protest	Capt. Statement N.Y.	1.00
Stores at Cape Lookout	Capt. Statement N.Y.	13.10
Marketing New York	Capt. Statement N.Y.	19.19
Coal	Capt. Statement N.Y.	13.30
Crew wages	Capt. Statement N.Y.	574.93
Mate and cook wages in port to Nov. 14	Capt. Statement N.Y.	29.79
Marketing	Capt. Statement N.Y.	4.23

*Load and discharge.

Trip #18 (cont.)

Charts .50 1.00	Elliott's Statement	1.50	
Telegram	Elliott's Statement	.41	
Towage sea to Red Hook	Elliott's Statement	75.00	
Towage Red Hook to Ganseford St.	Elliott's Statement	60.00	
Towage Newtown Creek to West Bank	Elliott's Statement	50.00	
Watchman bill 8.00 13.00	Elliott's Statement	21.00	
Shipping crew	Elliott's Statement	18.00	
Mate's wages in port	Elliott's Statement	46.50	
Repairs to stove	Elliott's Statement	7.95	
Repairs to chronometer	Elliott's Statement	44.00	
Freight insurance Boston Ins. Co.		70.00	
Telegrams .82 .44		1.26	
Capt. wages 2 mos. 170 Primage 248.58		418.58	
Commission		167.05	
Stores Pendleton 164.03 Struven 224.58		388.61	
Taulane mainsail 230.00 fore topsail 96.86		326.86	
Repair to foresail A. Mill & Sons		86.33	3,318.46
			38.23

Trip #19 February 1922 Capt. B. A. Warren

Georgetown, S.C., to New York Lumber			
545,810 ft. @ 6.50 per M free loaded		3,547.77	
Demurrage last trip		162.50	
Sale of old sail		30.00	
Refund a/c towage		4.14	
			3,744.41

Stores 278.25 chandlery 166.51 Struven			444.76
Stores and chandlery Pendleton			192.78
Towage in and out of Georgetown	Capt. Statement N.Y. March 4, 1922	Georgetown, S.C.	168.00
Pilotage	Capt. Statement N.Y. March 4, 1922	Georgetown, S.C.	155.00
Marketing and stores	Capt. Statement N.Y. March 4, 1922	Georgetown, S.C.	109.25
Stores etc. C. L. Ford	Capt. Statement N.Y. March 4, 1922	Georgetown, S.C.	46.51
Blacksmith bill	Capt. Statement N.Y. March 4, 1922	Georgetown, S.C.	5.25
Laundry	Capt. Statement N.Y. March 4, 1922	Georgetown, S.C.	1.66
Coal and ice	Capt. Statement N.Y. March 4, 1922	Georgetown, S.C.	22.50
Water	Capt. Statement N.Y. March 4, 1922	Georgetown, S.C.	10.00
Exchange on draft	Capt. Statement N.Y. March 4, 1922	Georgetown, S.C.	.59
C. L. Ford groceries	Capt. Statement N.Y. March 4, 1922	Georgetown, S.C.	99.15
Crew's wages at New York	Capt. Statement N.Y. March 4, 1922		617.00
Market bill	Capt. Statement N.Y. March 4, 1922		5.54
Capt. expense	Capt. Statement N.Y. March 4, 1922		2.45
Capt. wages Dec. 7, 1921, to Feb. 18, 1922	Capt. Statement N.Y. March 4, 1922		120.00
Primage	Capt. Statement N.Y. March 4, 1922		177.38

Discharging lumber @ 1.25		682.26	
Primage and commission on demurrage		16.24	
Plumber Daggert		1.25	
Telegrams and telephone	Elliott's Statement	4.02	
Noting protest	Elliott's Statement	2.00	
Watchman bill	Elliott's Statement	17.00	
Blankets	Elliott's Statement	18.00	
Towage sea to Staten Island	Elliott's Statement	75.00	
Towage Staten Island to Oak Point	Elliott's Statement	50.00	
Towage Oak Point to Red Hook	Elliott's Statement	35.00	
Shipping Crew	Elliott's Statement	24.00	
Water bill	Elliott's Statement	10.00	
Commission		177.38	3,289.97
			454.44

Trip #20 April 1922 Capt. Richard Copsey

Jacksonville to Phila. Lumber			
582,681 ft. @ 6.00 per loaded and disch.			3,496.09
Towage New York last trip	Jax. draft	25.00	
Port fee 3.00 Pilotage in 18.75, out 49.18	Jax. draft	70.93	
Caulk ports	Jax. draft	8.00	
Towage in 110.25 Outward 132.30	Jax. draft	242.55	
Stores and chandlery	Jax. draft	169.50	
Exchange in draft	Jax. draft	2.85	
Charts and logbook	Capt. Statement 3/28/22	3.30	
Packing and screws	Capt. Statement 3/28/22	1.60	
Welding and casting	Capt. Statement 3/28/22	2.95	
Knives, forks and kettles	Capt. Statement 3/28/22	2.10	
Batteries 6.00 Bell 1.75 Capt. expense 3.50	Capt. Statement 3/28/22	11.25	
Meats 1.60 Doctor of sailor 3.00	Capt. Statement 3/28/22	4.60	
Capt. expense at Phila. and Jacksonville	Capt. Statement 3/28/22	12.31	
Wages for Capt. Feb. 23 to Mar. 28 @ 150.00	Capt. Statement 3/28/22	180.00	
Crew wages at Phila.	Capt. Statement 3/28/22	426.83	
Telephone and telegrams		7.39	
Repairs to light Fred Busse		11.33	
Stores and chandlery Struven & Co.		370.38	
Stores and chandlery Pendleton		166.68	
Expense to N.Y. A. F. Paul		22.50	
Foresail Taulane		215.00	
Commission		174.80	
Liability insurance		72.80	
Towage Reedy Island to Yellow Pine, N.Y.		170.00	

Trip #20 (cont.)

	Group		
Cash to crew	Capt. Statement 4/27/22	74.66	
Laundry 3.95 Marketing 25.04		28.99	
Capt. expense 13.40 Telephone 1.30		14.70	
Towage Schuylkill to railway		30.00	
Towage to Florence, N.J., and return		70.00	
Shipping crew		33.00	
Lighthouse book and charts.		.80	
Towage Phila. to 14 Ft. Bank		175.00	
Directing movement at Phila.	May & Sons	5.00	
Protest 1.50 Transporting stores etc. 32.00		33.50	
Stores and chandlery May & Sons		187.51	3,027.81
			468.28

Settlement

Trip #16	867.06	
Trip #17	372.71	
Trip #18	38.23	
Trip #19	454.44	
Trip #20	468.28	2,200.72
Less indebtedness Statement June 1921		326.86
		1,873.86

1/180	Meta L. Koop	Baltimore	10.00	
1/180	Adele B. Struven	Baltimore	10.00	
1/180	Lillian N. Hinton	Reedville	10.00	
1/180	Elizabeth R. Hinton	Reedville	10.00	
1/180	Agnes R. Randolph	Richmond	10.00	
1/180	Ward Reed Randolph	Richmond	10.00	
1/180	Henry G. Randolph	Richmond	10.00	
2/180	C. Howard Paul	Baltimore	20.00	
3/180	Nina Coleman	Baltimore	30.00	
3/180	H. W. Randolph	Richmond	30.00	
3/180	J. W. McNeal	Fairport, Va.	30.00	
3/180	G. H. McNeal	Reedville	30.00	
6/180	A. W. McNeal	Reedville	60.00	
8/180	W. H. Edwards	Baltimore	80.00	
12/180	C. F. Southard	Baltimore	120.00	
37/180	Geo. N. Reed	Reedville	370.00	
42/180	Chas. M. Struven	Baltimore	420.00	
54/180	C. C. Paul & Co.	Baltimore	540.00	1,800.00
		In hand		73.86

Settled May 10, 1922

Trips #21 and #22	August 1922	Capt. B. A. Warren	
Balance in hand last settlement		73.86	
Florence, N.J., to Ponce, P.R.			
Cast iron pipe, lump sum, free loaded and disch.		2,600.00	
Logwood Cap Haitien to Newport News			
1,045.8 tons @ 5.50		5,751.90	8,425.76
Railway bill to Phila.		371.75	
Stores and chandlery, Struven 341.02 223.50		564.52	
Commission on pipe		130.00	
Telegram		.41	
Interest and insurance on disbursements at Haiti		46.85	
Pilotage at Ponce	Capt. Statement 7/20/22	9.00	
Custom fee 2.50 Boat hire 2.00	Capt. Statement 7/20/22	4.50	
Clearance 10.00 Water 12.50	Capt. Statement 7/20/22	22.50	
Groceries and marketing 62.40 3.00	Capt. Statement 7/20/22	65.40	
Laundry 5.70 Cables 4.00 4.80	Capt. Statement 7/20/22	14.50	
Blacksmith 4.90 Marketing 39.35	Capt. Statement 7/20/22	44.25	
Loading logwood @ .45	Capt. Statement 7/20/22	472.97	
Groceries, etc. at Cap Haitien 23.72 4.40	Capt. Statement 7/20/22	28.12	
Disinfecting	Capt. Statement 7/20/22	3.85	
Tonnage tax	Capt. Statement 7/20/22	16.39	
Wire	Capt. Statement 7/20/22	5.00	
Crew wages	Capt. Statement 7/20/22	786.40	
Captain expense	Capt. Statement 7/20/22	14.25	
Boat hire 6.00 Ice 2.00	Capt. Statement 7/20/22	8.00	
Captain's wages to July 28th	Capt. Statement 7/20/22	200.00	
Primage on pipe and logwood	Capt. Statement 7/20/22	417.37	
Towage Cape Henry to Newport News		60.00	
Commission on logwood		287.60	
Water Clarke		6.60	
Shipping fee and fare to Hampton Roads		37.92	
Slops		19.40	
Discharging logwood @ .75	Schade Statement	784.35	
Pilotage inward 73.50 Outward 22.50	Schade Statement	96.00	
Dockage	Schade Statement	16.50	
Stores and chandlery, and salt Reyner & Son	Schade Statement	195.86	
Fumigation 39.52 Hospital a/c sailor 22.50	Schade Statement	62.02	
Towage 18.00 Boat hire 20.00	Schade Statement	38.00	
Telegrams .82 Clearance 2.70	Schade Statement	3.52	
Custom officer Sunday boarding	Schade	10.00	
Shipping at Newport News	Schade	12.00	
Inspection quarantine	Schade	10.00	
Attendance fee	Schade	25.00	
Charts, chronometer, hire, etc.	Schade	34.20	
Groceries		1.65	

Trips #21 and 22 (cont.)			
Help at quarantine		4.00	
Cook's wages in port		34.66	
Carfare, meals, etc.		4.35	4,969.66
			3,456.10

1/180	Miss Meta L. Koop 1017 Bennett Place	15.00	
1/180	Adele B. Struven	15.00	
1/180	Lillian N. Hinton	15.00	
1/180	Elizabeth R. Hinton	15.00	
1/180	Agnes R. Randolph	15.00	
1/180	Ward Reed Randolph	15.00	
1/180	Henry G. Randolph	15.00	
2/180	C. Howard Paul	30.00	
3/180	Mrs. Nina Coleman 530 Calhoun Street	45.00	
3/180	H. W. Randolph 2nd and Franklin Street	45.00	
3/180	J. W. McNeal	45.00	
3/180	G. H. McNeal	45.00	
6/180	A. W. McNeal	90.00	
8/180	W. H. Edwards	120.00	
12/180	C. F. Southard	180.00	
37/180	Geo. N. Reed	555.00	
42/180	Chas. M. Struven	630.00	
54/180	C. C. Paul & Co.	810.00	2,700.00
	In hand		756.10

Settled August 22, 1922

Due Capt. 8.54

Trip #23 November 1922

Vessel left Newport News bound for Cap Haitien in command of Capt. B. A. Warren. Vessel put in Charleston, S.C., with Capt. sick. Capt. G. G. Carkow sent to Charleston to take command of vessel. Vessel released of charter and proceeded to Georgetown, S.C., to load lumber for N.Y.

Balance in hand last settlement		756.10	
568,958 ft. lumber, free L & D @ 5.75		3,271.50	
Demurrage		1,200.00	5,227.60
Custom house fee	Capt. Warren Statement	2.50	
Protest		1.50	
Supplies for sailor		7.65	
Capt. Warren's wages to Aug. 21st		40.00	

Capt. Warren expense to N.Y.		26.80
Telephone and telegrams		19.14
Stores put aboard for consignee at Haiti		40.81
Expense at New York A. F. Paul	Statement—Charleston, S.C.	8.00
Marketing 34.05 Repair to lights 6.75		40.80
Laundry 1.32 Mattresses 8.00		9.32
Telegrams		1.83
Inward pilotage 40.00 Towage 10.00		50.00
Outward towage		60.00
Adjusting engine 2.50 telegram .80		3.30
Capt. fare N.Y. to Balto. thence Charleston		40.00
Dishes, spoons, etc.		3.35
Cash to crew		45.12
Inward towage	Statement—Georgteown	35.00
Outward towage		136.00
Inward and outward pilotage		145.00
Shipping crew from Jacksonville		119.55
Telegrams		1.68
Labor 8.00 Water 3.00		11.00
Laundry 1.60 Bolts .75		2.35
Getting crew aboard		1.50
Marketing and chandlery		210.04
Paid crew		298.16
Commission		223.57
Telegrams	N.Y. Statement	.76
Laundry 2.82 Bed covering 15.65		18.47
Marketing 24.38 Ice 7.00		31.38
Captain's expense		16.00
Crew wages		456.51
Watchman 9.00 15.00	Elliott Statement	24.00
Towage Red Hook to Newtown Creek		35.00
Towage Newton Creek to Tebo's		35.00
Towage sea to Red Hook		80.00
Towage Red Hook to West Bank		40.00
Telegram and telephone		2.53
Shipping crew		21.00
Railway bill		382.17
Surveyor bill		15.10
Chronometer		12.00
Stove repair bill		39.14
Attendance fee		50.00
Stores and chandlery Struven		658.38
Annual freight insurance		87.30
Telephone and telegrams		3.30
Capt. wages Aug. 23rd to Oct. 1st		190.00

Trip #23 (cont.)

Letter of Credit to Capt.		800.00	
Cost of Letter of Credit		8.00	4,590.01
	In hand		637.59

Trip #24	March 1923	Capt. Geo. G. Carlson	
In hand last statement		637.59	
Letter of Credit to Captain		800.00	
Phila. to Martinique, Coal			
1,099 tons @ 3.00		3,297.00	
Demurrage		350.00	
Interest on Letter of Credit		3.04	
Salt, Turks Island to Balto. 1,101 tons @ 3.00		3,030.00	
Sale of junk		20.00	
Slops		24.89	
Credit a/c ship laundry (by Capt.)		6.00	
Refund Employee's Liability a/c medical attention		94.50	8,263.02
Stores and chandlery May & Sons	May & Sons	289.78	
Slops for crew	May & Sons	24.89	
Getting stores and water aboard	May & Sons	56.00	
Towage Breakwater to Phila. and return	Warren & Co.	475.00	
Trimming coal @ .15	Warren & Co.	164.85	
Charts and repairs to chronometer	Warren & Co.	11.35	
Clearance 2.50 8.65	Warren & Co.	11.15	
Telephone and telegrams	Warren & Co.	9.47	
Commission Warren & Co.	Warren & Co.	82.42	
Error		.18	
Crew N.Y. and Phila.	Capt. at Phila.	49.00	
Capt. expense N.Y. 6.00 Phila. 12.00	Capt. at Phila.	18.00	
Boat hire 6.00 Watchman 3.00	Capt. at Phila.	9.00	
Meat	Capt. at Phila.	13.75	
Discharging coal Martinique		274.75	
Towage at Martinique		119.39	
Commission C. C. Paul & Co.		82.42	
Commission on Demurrage		17.50	
Telephone and telegraph 4.21 2.80		7.01	
Insurance on disbursements		35.00	
Stores 356.26 Chandlery 204.20 14.55		575.01	
Sails Taulane and Sons		875.00	
Gasoline, stores, repairs to engine, watchman, doctor and sundry expense at Martinique		350.50	
Crew paid off at Martinique		221.03	
Cash to crew aboard		119.25	
	Forwarded		3,891.70

Forward	3,891.70	8,263.02
Master's expense Martinique	26.00	
Light dues	55.08	
Pilotage 32.35 trimming salt 54.30	86.65	
Cables 4.50 Boat hire 2.50	7.00	
Custom fee 1.00 Marketing 37.85	38.85	
Doctor and nurse at sailor 14.00 1.25 5.00	21.25	
168 bu. salt for salting* vessel	15.04	
Cleaning chain	8.00	
Lime 2.25 Flying jib 55.00	57.25	
Getting jib aboard	2.25	
Brooms .75 Fish 2.50	3.25	
Crew at Phila. 33.25 Boat hire 3.00	36.25	
Crew at Balto.	640.42	
Butter .90 Crew by C. C. Paul & Co. 52.80	53.70	
Captain's wages 4 mos. 1 day to Feb. 1st	605.00	
Cash to Geo. Hazel a/c crew	13.70	
Stores and chandlery Struven 35.45 123.00	158.45	
Labor Lewis	10.00	
Entrance fee Masson	22.72	
Quarantine 10.00 Inward pilotage 90.75	100.75	
Marketing Pendleton	51.93	
Chronometer E. Smola Newport News	50.00	
Lewis Martin crew	5.50	
Commission on salt	151.50	
Stove for galley	57.50	
Repairs to engine McCelenshan	207.58	
Fumigation 22.40 Gas and oil 74.51	96.91	
Towage in and out and shifting	214.00	
Shipping fee 16.50 Slops 29.20 Charts 4.70	50.40	
Stove, ice, etc. Captain's Ship Chandlery Co.	65.85	
Repairs to sails Marshall & Godfrey	161.33	
Marketing 45.28, dishes 11.81, wood 9.00 Laundry 3.85	69.94	
Cook 58.17, Labor 11.00, Bedding 7.21 Capt.	76.38	
Knives, forks, spoons 2.10 Laundry 2.37 Balto.	4.47	
Colonna Railway 346.00 American Bureau 42.10	388.10	
Liability Ins. Lawford & McKim	72.80	
Stores and chandlery 57.17 Towage 90.00 Norfolk	147.17	
Marketing 8.07 Crew 80.00 Boat hire 6.00	94.07	
Railway Woodall & Co.	359.90	8,178.64
In hand		84.38

*Salting a vessel was the filling of all open spaces in a wooden ship between frames, from light waterline to plank sheer, with coarse salt as a preservative against decay.

Trip #25	June 1923	Capt. Geo. G. Carlson	
Balance in hand from last trip		84.38	
Georgetown, S.C., to New York Lumber			
713,660 ft. @ 5.00 free L & D		3,568.31	
			3,652.69
Shipping mate		2.50	
Fare to Georgetown for mate		20.75	
Fare to New York for cook		8.70	
Towage at Georgetown In 35.00 Out 178.42		213.42	
Pilotage at Georgetown In 25.00 Out 110.00		135.00	
Chandlery and stores		183.17	
Cash to crew at Georgetown		155.00	
Crew wages at New York		511.46	
Telegrams 1.10 Running lines 2.00		3.10	
Marketing 5.54 Laundry 2.10		7.64	
Broke window in docking		2.50	
Watchman 6.00 6.00 13.00		25.00	
Labor shifting		12.00	
Labor shifting		8.00	
Shipkeeping* 8 days		24.00	
Labor 3.00 Mattress 8.50		11.50	
Marketing 54.58 Laundry 3.60		58.18	
Master expense		22.00	
Master's wages Feb. 1st to June 1st		600.00	
Telegrams and telephone		4.98	
Stores 347.40 Chandlery 162.97 Struven		510.37	
Atlantic Carriers Assn.		14.70	
Commission		178.41	
Towage sea to Red Hook		60.00	
Towage Red Hook to 36th St.		40.00	
Towage Astoria to Red Hook		45.00	
Chronometer bill 3.00 Shipping fee 36.00		39.00	
Slops 12.00 Protest 1.00		13.00	
Towage Red Hook to Sandy Hook		60.00	2,969.38
	In hand		683.31

Trip #26	August 1923	Capt. Geo. G. Carlson
Balance in hand from last trip		683.31
Georgetown, S.C., to New York, Lumber		
590,006 ft. @ 6.00 per M free L & D		3,540.04

*Shipkeeper was a watchman in charge of a vessel in port when there was no crew on board.

Demurrage	141.67	
		4,365.02
Cash to crew 42.67 110.00	152.67	
Boat hire 16.00 Capt. expense 8.00	24.00	
Telegram 1.40 Water 5.00 Fish 1.25	7.65	
Pilotage in 28.00 Out 120.00	148.00	
Towage in and out	174.88	
Laundry 1.72 Blacksmith 4.00	5.72	
Marketing and chandlery 117.16 29.85	147.01	
Lawford & McKim a/c Liability ins.	23.78	
Stores and chandlery Struven	537.03	
Stores and chandlery Pendleton	204.44	
Forestaysail Taulane	105.00	
Affadavit	.50	
Telegrams	1.17	
Watchman 10.00 Paint 60.00	70.00	
Towage Sandy Hook to Red Hook	85.00	
Towage Oak Point to Perth Amboy	80.00	
Crew wages at New York	798.50	
Landing crew 6.00 3.00	9.00	
Labor docking	6.00	
Spring and mattress 29.50 Marketing 26.85	56.35	
Marketing 33.76 Ice 10.85	44.61	
Master's expense	30.00	
Captain's wages June 1st to Aug. 1st	300.00	
Commission 177.00 7.08	184.08	
Shipping crew	24.06	
Railway Perth Amboy D. D. Co.	566.84	3,786.29
In hand		578.73

Trip #27 November 1923 Capt. Geo. G. Carlson

Balance in hand last trip		578.73	
Georgetown, S.C. to New York Lumber			
652,426 ft. @ 5.00 free L & D		3,262.13	
Allowance a/c Part cargo to West End		56.20	3,897.06
Pilotage in and out of Georgetown	Capt.	148.00	
Towage in and out of Georgetown	Capt.	176.83	
Chandlery, marketing and stores	Capt.	108.78	
Repairs to yawl 4.50 Medicine 2.00	Capt.	6.50	
Telegram .70 Boatswain 32.50 Crew 115.00	Capt.	148.20	
Stores and chandlery Pendleton	Capt.	313.16	

Trip #27 (cont.)

Telephone and telegrams	Elliott	1.91	
Towage Perth Amboy through cut	Elliott	30.00	
Shifting vessel 10.00 Watchman 18.00	Elliott	28.00	
Towage lower Bay to Red Hook	Elliott	50.00	
Shifting vessel 18.00 Custom House fees 12.50	Elliott	30.50	
Crew bill 25.60 Chronometer bill 8.25	Elliott	33.85	
Towage Red Hook to Staunton Light	Elliott	40.00	
Towage Red Hook to lower Bay	Elliott	40.00	
Laundry .88 Wharfage at N.Y. 15.00		15.88	
Commission 163.11 Telegram and telephone 2.46		165.57	
Boat hire and message 4.80 Running lines 3.00		7.80	
Crew wages 596.00 Ice 7.00		603.00	
Feed oil caps 5.50 Propeller 15.75		21.25	
Ship laundry 4.13 Marketing 39.60 Master's exp. 36.00		79.73	
Master's wages to Nov. 1st @ 150.00		450.00	
Outward pilotage New York		18.18	2,517.14
In hand			1,379.92
1/180 Meta L. Koop		7.50	
1/180 Adele B. Struven		7.50	
1/180 Lillian N. Hinton		7.50	
1/180 Elizabeth R. Hinton		7.50	
1/180 Agnes R. Randolph		7.50	
1/180 Ward Reed Randolph		7.50	
1/180 Henry G. Randolph		7.50	
2/180 C. Howard Paul		15.00	
3/180 Nina Coleman		22.50	
3/180 H. W. Randolph		22.50	
3/180 J. W. McNeal		22.50	
3/180 G. H. McNeal		22.50	
6/180 A. W. McNeal		45.00	
8/180 W. H. Edwards		60.00	
12/180 C. F. Southard		90.00	
37/180 Geo. N. Reed		277.50	
42/180 Chas. M. Struven		315.00	
54/180 C. C. Paul & Co.		405.00	
Dividend to owners			1,350.00
Cks. sent Jan. 22, 1924 Balance in hand			29.92

Trip #28 January 1924 Captain Geo. G. Carlson

Balance from last statement	29.92
Credit a/c laundry	3.58

Miragoane, Haiti, to New York Logwood		
$822^{415}/_{2240}$ tons @ 6.00 per ton	4,933.11	
		4,966.61
Cables to Baltimore	5.20	
Loading logwood	378.90	
Watchman	32.00	
Marketing 40.01 6.60 8.40	55.01	
Bunting .40 Water 5.00 Repairs to boat 6.00	11.40	
Cash to crew	170.00	
Telegram to Baltimore	.40	
Boat hire	5.00	
Crew wages at New York	836.80	
Marketing	14.96	
Master's expense	6.00	
Capt. wages to Jan. 3, 1924 @ 150.00	315.00	
Stores and chandlery Pendleton	372.01	
Stores and chandlery Struven	362.42	
McFarland, Taylor and Costello for preparing papers for appeal	286.35	
Commission	246.66	
Annual freight insurance	86.30	
Entrance at Custom House	16.39	
Towage Stapleton to Steinway	75.00	
Towage Steinway to Red Hook	50.00	
Slop chest	21.75	
Shipping crew	18.00	
Towage Red Hook to West Bank and water	45.00	
Quarantine service	10.00	
Interest and insurance in disbursements charged by charterers	38.14	
Discharging logwood @ .80	657.75	
Fumigation at New York	37.00	
Coal and water Sullivan	35.00	
Jib and topsail Taulane	230.00	
Error in Capt. statement	8.00	4,426.44
Forwarded		540.17

Trip #29 March 1924 Capt. Alonzo S. Wallace

Balance from last trip	540.17	
Georgetown, S.C., to Balto. Lumber		
511,044 ft. @ 5.50 free L & D	2,810.74	
Allowance a/c use of engine	30.00	3,380.91

Trip #29 (cont.)

Captain's fare to New York	Capt. N.Y. Statement	6.70	
Captain's expense at New York and boat hire	Capt. N.Y. Statement	13.70	
Marketing at New York	Capt. N.Y. Statement	10.99	
Cash to crew	Capt. N.Y. Statement	60.00	
Ship laundry	Capt. N.Y. Statement	6.48	
Telegram .70 Marketing 41.14	Capt. Georgetown	41.84	
Cash to crew	Capt. Georgetown	91.00	
Ship laundry	Capt. Georgetown	1.00	
Blacksmith 3.75 Welding 1.50	Capt. Georgetown	5.25	
Blacksmith 1:25 Coal 17.00	Capt. Georgetown	18.25	
Inward towage 35.00 Outward towage 128.00	Capt. Georgetown	163.00	
Inward and outward pilotage	Capt. Georgetown	158.00	
Crew wages at Balto.		586.08	
Groceries Ford 10.70 Gasoline 11.25		21.95	
Labor 1.50 valve for tank 1.00		2.50	
Schloss Bros.—chain etc.		5.40	
Captain's wages 2 mos. @ 150.00		300.00	
Hauling mate's baggage		1.00	
Water etc. Capt.'s Ship Chandlery Co.		11.00	
Rating chronometer		4.00	
Repairs to sails Marshall & Godfrey		45.90	
Repairs to engine Balto. Machine Works		117.55	
Gas and oil 27.50 3.75		31.25	
Ship's laundry		6.10	
Stores and chandlery Pendleton		204.60	
Stores and chandlery Struven		450.92	
Coal Chapman & Co.		17.25	
Commission		140.54	
Entering protest		1.00	
Inward and outward towages		190.00	
Cook in port 11.00 12.33		23.33	
Marketing 24.22 a/c water tank 2.50		26.72	2,763.30
			617.61

Trip #30 May 1924 Capt. A. S. Wallace

Balance last trip	617.61	
Georgetown, S.C., to Balto. Lumber 522,305 ft. @ 5.25 free L & D	2,742.14	3,359.75
Shipping fee 11.00 Slops 16.45	27.45	
McKim Liability insurance	72.80	
Stores and chandlery Struven 253.06 119.95	373.01	
Carey Machinery .86 Laundry 4.54	5.40	

Mianus Motor Works	12.41	
Flying jib Taulane	105.00	
Telegram .70 Laundry 2.25	2.95	
Cash to crew at Georgetown	124.00	
Blacksmith 4.00 Bracket .25	4.25	
Bit .60 Elec. switch .35 Postage .25	1.20	
Coal 17.00 Machinist bill 16.75	33.75	
Stores and chandlery Ford	82.11	
Pilotage in and out of Georgetown	148.00	
Towage in and out of Georgetown	155.50	
Crew wages in Baltimore	364.55	
Mate's fare from N.Y. to Balto.	6.00	
Telegram .35 Dinner .85	1.20	
Captain's expense 2.10 .75	2.85	
Marketing in Balto.	5.59	
Hose clamps .60 Leather cup .30	.90	
Captain's wages 2 mos. to May 1st	300.00	
Allowance to Captain a/c 2nd mate	25.00	
Wrench .90 Marketing 1.36 27.25	29.51	
Cook 3.00 Beans 3.30	6.30	
Battery .50 Capt. expense 1.22	1.72	
Shipping fee 13.50 Slops 29.44	42.94	
Gasoline Curlett	23.70	
Charts Hand & Son Co.	2.25	
Coal 17.55 Wire 9.80	27.35	
Commission	137.11	
Towage in and out of Balto.	161.10	
Parts for yawl engine	17.54	
Slops	22.20	
Woodall & Co. Railway bill	137.17	2,462.72
Forwarded		897.03

Trip #31 Sept. 1924 Capt. A. S. Wallace

Balance last trip		897.03	
Savannah, Ga., to Fall River, Mass. Lumber			
592,333 ft. @ 5.25 clear		3,405.91	
Sale of junk 6.50 Discount .40		6.90	
Refund a/c gasoline		2.08	4,311.92
Telegram .70 Bunting 3.96	Capt. Stmt. Savannah	4.66	
Captain's expense 1.90 Harbor master 4.00		5.90	
Cash to crew at Savannah		196.56	
Ship laundry 2.00 Stores etc. at Savannah		161.05	
Inward towage 110.25 Outward 147.00		257.25	
Pilotage inward 25.00 Outward 90.00		115.00	

Trip #31 (cont.)			
Crew's wages at Fall River		438.47	
Protest 1.50 Dinner .85		2.35	
Captain's wages to June 28th @ 150.00		290.00	
Allowance a/c second mate		52.50	
Stores 177.42 Chandlery 89.95 C.M.S. & Co.		267.37	
Jib topsail Taulane		126.48	
Bal. Liability Ins. Lawford & McKim		31.21	
Commission		170.26	
Mate's wages to July 23	Capt. Stmt. Fall River	90.00	
Mate's expense vessel laid up 14.05 19.65		33.70	
Railway Crownshield Shipbuilding Co.		343.40	
Capt's. fare to join vessel		6.57	
Dockage at Fall River		30.00	
Towage to railway		40.00	
Shifting at railway		15.00	
Files etc. .50 Telephone and telegrams 2.15		2.65	
Shipping crew		15.50	
Captain's expense at Fall River		4.90	
Labor handling stores		2.40	
Error in lumber freight		.72	2,703.90
			1,608.02
McFarland, Taylor & Costello			
Balance a/c Lawyer's fee and costs			608.39
			999.63
Dividend to owners			900.00
			99.63

December 15, 1924

Checks to owners

1/180	Meta L. Koop	5.00
1/180	Adele B. Struven	5.00
1/180	Lillian N. Hinton	5.00
1/180	Elizabeth R. Hinton	5.00
1/180	Agnes R. Randolph	5.00
1/180	Ward Reed Randolph	5.00
1/180	Henry G. Randolph	5.00
2/180	C. Howard Paul	10.00
3/180	Mrs. Nina Coleman	15.00
3/180	H. W. Randolph	15.00
3/180	J. W. McNeal	15.00
3/180	G. H. McNeal	15.00
6/180	A. W. McNeal	30.00
8/180	W. H. Edwards	40.00
12/180	C. F. Southard	60.00

37/180	Geo. N. Reed	185.00	
42/180	Chas. M. Struven	210.00	
54/180	C. C. Paul & Co.	270.00	900.00

Trip #32 December 1924 Capt. Robert O. Jones

Balance from last settlement		99.63	
Refund in tow bill		24.22	
Balto. to Charleston, S.C. Cocoa meal			
913+ tons @ 1.75 free L & D		1,599.20	
Bags 4 tons @ 2.00		8.00	
Charleston, S.C., to New York Lumber			
577,044 ft @ 5.00 free L & D		2,855.28	
			4,616.33
Towage Fall River	Capts. Statement	20.00	
Repairs to windlass Fall River	Capts. Statement	25.20	
Marketing 11.92 Cutlery, etc. 12.20	Capts. Statement	24.12	
Water bill 1.20 Car fare .60 Marketing 2.70	Capts. Statement	4.50	
Cash to crew 65.00 Cash to mate's wife 100.00	Capts. Statement	165.00	
Stores at Fall River Jno. E. Torphy	Capts. Statement	248.08	
Shifting towage Curtis Bay Towing Co.		28.00	
Towage inward and outward Mullen		100.00	
Boston Iron and Metals Co.		2.50	
Repairs to windlass Balto. Mach. Co.		84.22	
Stores and chandlery Struven & Co.		324.05	
Telephone and telegrams .50 7.60		8.10	
Annual frt. ins. Boston Ins. Co.		87.30	
Captain's expense		2.40	
Commission Meal 80.36 Lumber 144.26		244.62	
Marketing 18.34 57.89 Water 3.00		79.23	Capt. Statement
Harbor master 2.00 Iron Work 3.25 Shipping fee 7.00		12.25	Capt. Statement
Pilotage inward 58.00 Outward 62.00		120.00	Capt. Statement
Towage in and out 154.22 Cash to crew 156.00		310.22	Capt. Statement
Telephone and telegrams .36 140.00 Shipping crew 21.00	Elliott	22.76	
Chronometer bill 4.55 Stove bill 13.50	Elliott	18.05	
Towage sea to Red Hook	Elliott	75.00	
Towage Red Hook to Brooklyn	Elliott	30.00	
Towage Newtown Creek to Red Hook to Lower Bay	Elliott	70.00	
Crew's wages New York		684.00	
Captain's wages to Nov. 30th @ 125.00		537.50	
Coal 14.75 Watchman 9.00 7.50 1.00		32.25	
Crew's wages in port		41.00	
Hardware .60 3.05		3.65	
Laundry 6.89 Repairs .40		7.29	

Trip #32 (cont.)		
Marketing	27.82	
Captain's expense and railroad fare	45.55	
Towage at Read—Factory Charleston	68.00	3,532.66
		1,083.67

Trip #33 February 1925 Captain Robert O. Jones

Balance from last trip	1,083.67	
Georgetown, S.C., to New York Lumber		
610,386 ft. @ 5.00 free L & D	3,051.93	
Refund on gasoline	4.20	
Discount on bills at Georgetown	4.50	4,144.30
Coal 8.00 14.00	22.00	
Hardware 9.45 Shipping fee 5.64	15.09	
Gas and oil 20.85 Capt. expense 5.78	26.63	
Crew's wages 45.00 141.15 Iron work—Georgetown 59.25	245.40	
Marketing, etc. 7.00 54.47	61.47	
Towage in and out, Georgetown	186.56	
Pilotage in and out, Georgetown	128.00	
Blanket 2.00 Eggs 1.80	3.80	
Towage leaving Gravesend Bay	15.00	
Pendleton Jr. & Co. Stores 283.53 Chandlery 184.14	467.67	
Crew's wages at N.Y. 398.85 Mate 27.50 Cook 20.00	446.35	
Coal 21.75 8.00 Gas and oil 10.18 10.93	50.86	
Marketing 38.42 Laundry 5.85	44.27	
Capt's. expense 12.00 Capt's. wages to Jan. 31 350.00	362.00	
Commission 152.60 Telephone and telegrams .36 4.10	156.06	
Noting protest 1.00 Watchman bill 21.00	22.00	
Shipping crew	15.00	
Towage Red Hook to Newtown Creek	35.00	
Towage Newtown Creek to West Bank	80.00	
Towage Sandy Hook to Red Hook	55.00	2,439.16
Due owners		1,705.14

Checks to owners

1/180	Meta L. Koop	7.50
1/180	Adele B. Struven	7.50
1/180	Lillian N. Hinton	7.50
1/180	Elizabeth R. Hinton	7.50
1/180	Agnes R. Randolph	7.50
1/180	Ward Reed Randolph	7.50
1/180	Henry G. Randolph	7.50
2/180	C. Howard Paul	15.00

3/180	Mrs. Nina Coleman	22.50	
3/180	H. W. Randolph	22.50	
3/180	J. W. McNeal	22.50	
3/180	G. H. McNeal	22.50	
6/180	A. W. McNeal	45.00	
8/180	W. H. Edwards	60.00	
12/180	C. F. Southard credited to R. Jones	90.00	
37/180	Geo. N. Reed	277.50	
42/180	Chas. M. Struven	315.00	
54/180	C. C. Paul & Co.	405.00	1,350.00
	In hand		355.14

End 1924 Policy

Trip #34 March 1925 Capt. Robert O. Jones

In hand from last settlement	355.14	
Georgetown, S.C., to Balto. Lumber		
672,260 ft. @ 5.00 free L & D	3,361.30	3,716.44
Towage in and out of Georgetown	203.07	
Pilotage in and out of Georgetown	148.00	
Market bill	63.15	
Lumber for stanchions	9.28	
Blacksmith work	46.80	
Crew's wages at Georgetown 108.45 30.00	138.45	
Fruits and vegetables	7.40	
Stores 106.31 Chandlery 404.12 Struven	510.43	
Stores 155.59 Chandlery 56.97 Pendleton	212.56	
Inward and dockage Cottman	110.00	
Boston Ins. Co. trip insurance	10.00	
Sail bill Taulane	313.00	
Noting protest	1.00	
Telephone and telegrams	5.34	
Commission	168.06	
Shipping fee	2.00	
Crew's wages at Baltimore 364.22 7.50	371.72	
Marketing etc. at Baltimore	44.00	
Fresh meats, ice, and vegetables	28.85	
Engine parts	3.95	
Copper water boiler	8.50	
Captain's wages to March 31st	350.00	2,805.56
In hand		910.88

	Forward		910.88
Checks to owners following trip #35			
1/180	Meta L. Koop	5.00	
1/180	Adele B. Struven	5.00	
1/180	Lillian N. Hinton	5.00	
1/180	Elizabeth R. Hinton	5.00	
1/180	Agnes R. Randolph	5.00	
1/180	Ward Reed Randolph	5.00	
1/180	Henry G. Randolph	5.00	
2/180	C. Howard Paul	10.00	
3/180	Mrs. Nina Coleman	15.00	
3/180	H. W. Randolph	15.00	
3/180	J. W. McNeal	15.00	
3/180	G. H. McNeal	15.00	
6/180	A. W. McNeal	30.00	
8/180	W. H. Edwards	40.00	
12/180	C. F. Southard credited to R. Jones	60.00	
37/180	Geo. N. Reed	185.00	
42/180	Chas. M. Struven	210.00	
54/180	C. C. Paul & Co.	270.00	
		900.00	

Trip #35	June 1925	Capt. Robert Jones	
Balance in hand from last trip		910.88	
Georgetown, S.C., to Balto. Lumber			
689,045 ft. @ 5.00 per M free L & D		3,445.23	
Junk		35.00	4,391.11
Liability insurance Lawford McKim		96.25	
Coal Chapman Co.		31.50	
Outward towage Cottman Co.		60.00	
Chronometer bill Hand & Sons		3.00	
Sail covers Marshall & Godfrey		95.00	
Capt's. Ship Chandlery Co. 22.94 Gas 17.50		40.44	
Stores and chandlery C.M.S. & Co.		247.24	
Inward towage Cottman		100.00	
Carpenter work at Georgetown	Capt. Statement—Georgetown	26.40	
Machinist at Georgetown	Capt. Statement—Georgetown	35.50	
Sailor paid off at Georgetown	Capt. Statement—Georgetown	5.89	
Chains and turnbuckles	Capt. Statement—Georgetown	19.20	
Cash to crew	Capt. Statement—Georgetown	181.90	
Laundry etc.	Capt. Statement—Georgetown	4.81	
Inward 28.00 Outward 120.00 Pilotage	Capt. Statement—Georgetown	148.00	

Inward 35.00 Outward 172.26 Towage	207.26	
Work on yoke	2.26	
Stores 87.17 Interest on advances 2.28	89.45	
Commission	172.26	
Mianus Motor Works	56.68	
Shifting towages at Balto.	45.00	
Chapman & Co. Coal	15.75	
Charts, etc. Hand & Sons Co.	5.10	
Captain's Ship Chandlery Co., Gas, etc.	46.31	
Meats and vegetables Southern Meat Mkt.	61.59	
Rope Frank Loft	47.50	
Fire extinguishers, Laundry etc.	34.50	
Marketing at Balto. 8 weeks	136.00	
Crew's wages and port wages	543.88	
Master's wages to May 31st	350.00	
Part for engine 2.00 Clearance 10.40	12.40	
Outward towage present trip	100.00	
American Bureau 75.00 Ice 8.00	83.00	
Telephone and telegraph 2.60 Trip insurance 30.00	32.60	
Balto. Machine Works	116.29	3,253.32
In hand		1,137.79
Dividend to owners		900.00
		237.79

Trip #36 August 1925 Capt. Robert Jones

Balance in hand from last statement	237.79	
Turks Island to Portland, Me. Salt		
1,134+ tons @ 3.50	3,971.27	
Allowance for use of engine	15.00	4,224.06
Light dues 52.88 Pilotage 32.14	85.02	
Trimming salt 45.35 Cables 3.32	48.67	
Beef 3.75 Salt for vessel 11.20	14.95	
Interest on advances	9.51	
Crew's wages at Portland	509.83	
British consul fee 4.69 Ice 5.40	10.09	
Entrance fee and tonnage tax	18.72	
Public health 10.00 Fumigation 33.70	43.70	
Clearance at Customs	2.50	
Overtime customs a/c discharging	3.06	
Towage in and out of Portland	58.00	
Weight certificate	.20	
Shipping crew in Portland	12.00	

Trip #36 (cont.)		
Custom brokerage	7.00	
Stores and chandlery W. S. Jordan Co.	188.52	
Stores Sweet & Co.	68.12	
Discharging salt @ .85	964.33	
Marketing Sweet & Co.	11.63	
Laundry	4.86	
Expense for crew ashore while fumigating	3.50	
Capt's. expense including gratuity to fumigation officer after hours	15.00	
Captain's wages to July 31st	350.00	
Railway bill Woodall & Co.	578.28	
Commission on salt	198.56	
Stores Struven & Co.	288.90	3,494.95
In hand		729.11

Trip #37	October 1925	Capt. Robert Jones
Balance in hand from last trip	729.11	
Halifax, N.S., and Dartmouth, N.S., to New York		
Lumber 657,786 ft. @ 5.75 per M ft.	3,782.27	
Laths 554,000 @ 1.15 per M	637.10	
Demurrage	700.00	
Refund on gasoline	3.10	5,851.58
Sick mariner fund 13.22 Tax 1.00	14.22	
Wharfage at Dartmouth 8.63 7.50	16.13	
Telegrams 2.68 Pilotage 44.40	47.08	
Harbor master 4.00 Revenue stamps .34	4.34	
Loading lumber and laths	484.16	
Agency fee Warren	25.00	
Exchange	1.25	
Towage out Portland	15.00	
Cash to crew at Halifax 110.40 20.00	130.40	
Marketing at Halifax 13.86 33.40	47.26	
Turnbuckle 5.00 Blacksmith 2.50	7.50	
Wrenches and paint	2.95	
Master's expense Halifax	12.50	
Boston Ins. Co. 10.00 Lawford McKim 40.21	50.21	
Lunches 1.00 Telegram .60	1.60	
Commission on lumber	255.97	
Crew's wages at New York	590.93	
Captain's wages to Oct. 31st	525.00	
Towage at Halifax	120.00	
Watchman 55.50 Marketing 72.50	128.00	

Discharging 483.95 80.00	563.95	
Coal, gas and laundry	37.96	
Mate running engine 10.00 Capt. expense 12.50	22.50	
Entrance Custom 16.39 Protest 1.00 Telegram .36	17.75	
Inward Pilotage 28.88 Wharfage 18.90 50.48	98.26	
Discharging 300.00 147.20 142.80	590.00	
Repairs to stove etc.	7.09	
Chronometer bill	5.00	
Towage Long Island Sound to Newtown Creek	80.00	
Newtown Creek to West Bank	60.00	
Shipping crew	21.00	
Chandlery Struven	296.64	4,279.65
In hand		1,571.93

December 16, 1925

Checks to owners

1/180	Meta L. Koop	7.50	
1/180	Adele B. Struven	7.50	
1/180	Lillian N. Hinton	7.50	
1/180	Elizabeth R. Hinton	7.50	
1/180	Agnes R. Randolph	7.50	
1/180	Ward Reed Randolph	7.50	
2/180	C. Howard Paul	15.00	
3/180	Mrs. Nina Coleman	22.50	
3/180	H. W. Randolph	22.50	
3/180	J. W. McNeal	22.50	
3/180	G. H. McNeal	22.50	
6/180	A. W. McNeal	45.00	
8/180	W. H. Edwards	60.00	
12/180	C. F. Southard credited to R. Jones	90.00	
37/180	Geo. N. Reed	277.50	
42/180	Chas. M. Struven	315.00	
54/180	C. C. Paul & Co.	405.00	
1/180	Henry G. Randolph	7.50	1,350.00

In hand as above	1,571.93
Less dividends to owners as above	1,350.00
Balance on hand	221.93

Trip #38 December 1925 Capt. Robert Jones

Balance in hand from last statement	221.93	
Georgetown, S.C., to Balto., Lumber		
684,908 ft. @ 5.00 per M free L & D	3,424.54	3,646.47

Trip #38 (cont.)

Captain to crew at Georgetown	Atlantic Coast Capt. Statement, Georgetown	59.00	
Shipping fee at Georgetown	Atlantic Coast Capt. Statement, Georgetown	15.28	
Coal and ice 21.80 Telephone 1.00	Atlantic Coast Capt. Statement, Georgetown	22.20	
Carpenter 21.80 Canvas 15.00	Atlantic Coast Capt. Statement, Georgetown	36.80	
Machinist 3.00 Laundry 1.50	Atlantic Coast Capt. Statement, Georgetown	4.50	
Oak .32 Interest on advances 1.17	Atlantic Coast Capt. Statement	1.49	
Inward pilotage 28.00 Outward 130.00	Atlantic Coast Capt. Statement	158.00	
Inward towage 35.00 Outward 171.23	Atlantic Coast Capt. Statement	206.23	
Stores	Atlantic Coast Capt. Statement	70.71	
Annual insurance Boston		87.30	
Coal Chapman 8.00 Meat 18.60		26.60	
Shipping fee Chas. Johnson		52.00	
Shipping fee Nick		2.00	
Inward towage Baltimore Mullen		80.00	
Shifting 15.00 Outward towage 50.00		65.00	
Stores 239.45, Chandlery 231.23 } Pendleton		470.68	
Coal, water, ice, etc. Capt. Ship Chandlery Co.		57.45	
Slops for sailors Saperstein		45.50	
Commission on lumber		171.23	
Crew's wages at Balto. 434.00 45.00		479.00	
Repairs to lamps 17.85 Laundry 3.00		20.85	
Rug for cabin		14.00	
Marketing, etc.		28.50	
Capt's. wages to November 30th		175.00	
Capt's. expense at Balto.		5.00	2,354.32
In hand			1,292.15

End of 1925 policy

Trip #39 April 12, 1926 Capt. Robert Jones

Balance in hand from last statement		1,292.15
Charleston, S.C., to New York Lumber		
694,747 ft. @ 6.50	4,515.86	
Slops a/c crew	45.30	
Refund a/c gas	1.70	
Refund a/c towage at Charleston	50.00	
		5,905.01
Wages 4 sailors at Charleston	200.00	
Wages of cook in full	98.75	
Cash to Mate	50.00	
Towing at Charleston 50.00 154.32	204.32	

Repairing iron work on vessel	Capt. Statement—Charleston	11.25	
Pilotage in and out at Charleston		99.00	
1 Galv. comb. for sheave for block		1.45	
Fresh water		3.00	
Stores 138.65 Chandlery 49.00 Frt. on sail 4.73		192.38	
Harbor master 2.00 1 12″ sheet block 5.15		7.15	
Flashlight batteries		1.50	
Expense getting new sail on board		1.50	
Boat hire at Baltimore		2.50	
Master's expense at Charleston		5.50	
Shipping crew, etc.		41.42	
Meat chopper		3.25	
Wages of seaman to Charleston		8.00	
Master's expense and marketing		7.20	
Crew's wages at New York	Capt. Statement—New York	303.37	
Cook's and mate's wages at New York		187.28	
2 tons coal 31.50 Padlocks 1.20		32.70	
Laundry 4.55 Marketing 68.20 Master's exp. 10.00		82.75	
Hardware for galley and cabin		12.72	
Night watchmen 13.50 12.00 5.00 7.00		37.50	
Master's wages Dec. 1, 1925, to March 31, 1926		700.00	
Gas and oil		31.60	
Wages to cook at April 21, 1926		50.00	
Telegrams and telephone 1.20 1.59		2.79	
Stores 218.21 Chandlery 213.21		431.42	
Liability insurance		96.25	
2/3 commission (C. C. Paul) Lumber to N.Y.		150.53	
Telegram to Balto.		.36	
Services of watchman		7.50	
Clearance at Custom House		2.50	
British Bill of Health		4.70	
Shipping crew		20.00	
Towing sea to Red Hook McCarren		80.00	
Fresh water McCarren		10.00	
Towing Red Hook to Elevator slip		50.00	
Towing mouth of Newtown Creek to Robbins Reef—McCarren		35.00	
Outward pilotage		23.19	
Chronometer, parallel rule, etc.		5.15	
Repair bill Tietjen & Lang		52.95	
1/3 commission (Gilmartin) Lumber Charleston to N.Y.		75.26	3,423.69
In hand			2,481.32

1/180	Meta L. Koop	7.50
1/180	Adele B. Struven	7.50
1/180	Lillian N. Hinton	7.50

Trip #39 (cont.)

1/180	Elizabeth R. Hinton		7.50	
1/180	Agnes R. Randolph		7.50	
1/180	Ward Reed Randolph		7.50	
1/180	Henry G. Randolph		7.50	
2/180	C. Howard Paul		15.00	
3/180	Mrs. Nina Coleman		22.50	
3/180	H. W. Randolph		22.50	
3/180	J. W. McNeal		22.50	
3/180	G. H. McNeal		22.50	
6/180	A. W. McNeal		45.00	
8/180	W. H. Edwards		60.00	
12/180	C. F. Southard	credited to R. Jones	90.00	
37/180	Geo. N. Reed		277.50	
42/180	Chas. M. Struven		315.00	
54/180	C. C. Paul & Co.		405.00	
		Dividends to owners 4/12/26		1,350.00
		In hand		1,131.32

Trip #40 Sept. 8, 1926 Capt. Robert Jones

Balance in hand from last statement		1,131.32
Turks Island to Portland, Me. Salt		
$1{,}121\frac{1809}{2240}$ tons @ 3.75 per ton	4.206.78	
Dartmouth and Halifax, Nova Scotia, to New York, Laths		
4,151,100 laths @ 41.20 M	4,981.32	
Rebate a/c piling laths	97.50	
Deducted from crew wages a/c shore	62.25	9,347.85
		10,347.85

Vessel expense at Turks Island	Capt's. Statement—Portland, Me.	216.80
Crew's wages at Portland		804.00
Discharging salt at Portland 1,122 tons @ .85		953.70
Entry, tonnage tax, etc. Portland		18.72
Inspection 10.00 Fumigation 32.70		42.70
Fuel 20.00 Ice 5.40 Fish .80		26.20
Towing at Portland		98.00
Paints, oils, etc. 62.60 Water 7.50		70.10
Laundry 1.49 Provisions 62.62		64.11
Shipping fee 25.00 Clearance 2.50		27.50
Wages of cook and mate Portland		75.96
Captain's wages 4/1/26 to 5/31/26		350.00
Master's expense Portland		12.00
New mainsail Taulane		320.27

Stores 352.98 Chandlery 206.32 Pendleton		559.30	
Stores 201.42 Chandlery 39.44 Jordan		240.86	
Telephone and telegrams		2.55	
Sick Mariners Fund Halifax	McDonald's Statement	13.22	
Signal tax 1.00 Telegrams 1.26		2.26	
Inward and outward pilotage		44.40	
Harbor fee 4.00 Ice 3.00 Wharfage 9.00		16.00	
Checking laths 16.20 Stowing laths 491.65		507.85	
Commission Laths Halifax to N.Y.		249.06	
Premium collection etc. on draft		7.91	
Marketing 13.75 Chandlery 2.20 Stores 4.49	Capt's. Statement Halifax	30.44	
Painting vessel outside 24.00 Coal 10.75		34.75	
Mate's wages to June 30, 1926		60.00	
Detention of deserters at Halifax 31.50 7.00		38.50	
Checking laths 15.00 Medical attn.–mate 10.00		25.00	
Master's expense at Halifax		15.00	
Commission on salt to Portland		210.34	
Discharging laths at New York .25 per M	Capt's. Statement at N.Y.	1,037.75	
Crew's wages at New York		702.00	
Towing at Halifax 100.00 Water 4.00		104.00	
Gasoline a/c discharging laths		30.10	
Laundry 6.00 Night watchman 37.50		43.52	
Engine parts 12.85 Marketing 84.20		87.05	
Telegram .92 Cooking utensils, etc. 4.38		5.30	
Master's expense at New York		15.00	
Master's wages 6/1/26 to 8/31/26		525.00	
Entrance fee at New York	Gilmartin's Statement	16.39	
Noting protest 1.00 Telegram .72		1.72	
Inward pilotage 28.00 Repairs to rigging 50.00		78.00	
Shipping crew 18.50 Repairs to vessel 755.21		773.71	
Towing City Island to Oak Point		60.00	
Towing Oak Point to Dry Dock to West Bank		100.00	
Fresh water 10.00 Chronometer bill 5.10		15.10	
Attendance fee at N.Y. Gilmartin		25.00	
Wharfage 378.30 Piling laths 332.09		710.39	
Insurance on freight Halifax to New York–Boston		15.00	9,482.53
In hand			996.64

End 1926 Policy

Trip #41 February 10, 1927 Capt. Robert Jones

In hand from last statement		996.64
Hampton Roads to San Juan, P.R. Coal		
1,097½ tons @ 2.75 per ton	3,018.13	

Trip #41 (cont.)
St. Marc, Haiti, to Baltimore Logwood

834 tons @ 5.75 per ton	4,795.50		
Refund a/c gasoline	4.50	7,818.13	
		8,814.77	
Coal 5.75 Water .71 Wheeling coal 6.75	13.21		C. G. Blake & Co. Statement
Towing, docking, undocking, running lines	40.50		
Dumping and trimming coal	153.79		
Stores 57.95 Chandlery 24.12	82.07		
Gasoline 23.50 Agency fees 25.00	48.50		
Phone call 1.45 Watchman 5.00	6.45		
Towing Sewalls Point to Newport News	30.00		
Additional premium liability insurance	34.51		
Telegrams	1.73		
Stores 336.43 Chandlery 385.72 Pendleton	722.15		
Discharging coal @ .45 per ton	493.88		Capts. Statement—San Juan
Water 10.00 Chandlery 68.55 Stores 108.31	186.86		
Rental of hoister 35.00 70.00	105.00		
Towing in 60.00 Out 78.00 Docking 42.00	180.00		
Pilotage in 21.25 Out 10.00	31.25		
Cleaning 2.50 Cablegram 1.60	4.10		
Dunnage* 4.00 Bolts for blocks 5.25	9.25		
French Consul Bill of Health	10.00		
Master's expense at San Juan	7.50		
Exchange 3.20 Watchman at Coal Dock 6.50	9.70		
Master's expense at Newport News	5.00		
Sundries	1.80		
Commission Coal to San Juan	150.91		
Loading logwood @ .47½ per ton	430.35		Capts. Statement—San Juan
Canvas for sails 28.00 Repairing pump 5.35	33.35		
Cablegram 2.37 Medical treatment a/c sailor 5.00	7.37		
Running lines ashore	14.25		
Stores 23.75 7.25 3.50 Marketing 12.85 16.65	63.60		
Master's expense	3.00		
Insurance Hampton Roads to San Juan to Baltimore	50.00		
Telegram .60 Towing to Balto. Enterprise 110.00	110.60		
Fumigation 10.00 Radio 90.00	100.00		
Coal 8.25 Stove pipe, Hardware, etc. 15.50	23.75		Capt. Statement
Radio tubes 1.90 Laundry 4.60	6.50		
Springs for engine 1.60 Compass 5.00	6.60		Capt. Statement at Balto.
Marketing 47.09 Master's expense 5.00	52.09		
Crew's wages at Baltimore	1,778.00		

*Dunnage was wooden planks and blocks used in a vessel's hold to raise the cargo from contact with water, condensation, and chafing and to prevent its getting adrift.

Capt's. wages 9/1/26 to 1/31/27	875.00	
Mate's wages at Balto.	60.00	
Balance to attorneys at New York a/c appeal in case of schooner A. F. PAUL vs. Heard	173.88	
Discharging logwood @ 1.00	834.00	
Annual freight insurance Boston	105.00	
Inward pilotage 50.00 Inspector's service 4.25	54.25	
Entrance Tonnage Tax Customs etc.	20.39	
Commission on logwood St. Marc to Balto.	239.78	
Spanker 115.00 Topsail and rope 10.11	125.11	7,495.03
In hand		1,319.74

Trip #42 May 12, 1927 Capt. Robert Jones

Amount in hand last statement		1,319.74	
Georgetown, S.C., to New York Lumber			
728,849 ft. @ 5.00 per M	3,644.26		
Refund a/c gas tax	1.50		
Sale of old junk	7.00	3,652.76	
		4,972.50	
Shipping sailor at Balto.	2.50		
Outward towage Enterprise to Baltimore Light	60.00		
Chronometer bill 4.65 Shipping fee 12.50	17.15		
Oil and gas 25.20 Coal, Water, etc. 36.00	61.20		
Towing Kent Island to Tolley's Pt. Mullen	25.00		
Pilotage in and out Georgetown	148.00		Capts. Statement at Georgetown
Towage in 35.00 Out 182.21	217.21		
Phone call at Charleston	.50		
Marketing Sea Stores Hardware	120.98		
Vessel and engine repairs 34.21 Gasoline 2.30	36.51		
Coal 23.00 Ice 12.60 2 sailors from Charleston 21.32	56.92		
Sailor's wages at Georgetown 1 sick 1 deserted	90.00		
Material a/c repairing keelson and stanchions	5.00		
Master's expense at Georgetown	.75		
Rigging bill Brooklyn Ship Rig Co.	75.00		
Towing sea to Red Hook	80.00		Gilmartin's Statement
Towing Red Hook to Erie R.R.	50.00		
Watchman 6.00 New trestletree 40.00 Crosstrees 25.00	71.00		
Phone call to Balto. 1.40 Water 10.00	11.40		
Towing Tisdale Lmbr. Yd #2 to Red Hook	45.00		
Towing anchor Red Hook to West Bank	40.00		
Shipping 4 sailors and cook	15.00		
Stores 440.50 Chandlery 514.24	954.74		
Liability insurance	96.25		

Trip #42 (cont.)

Telegrams and telephone calls	1.20		
Gasoline 10.50 2.20 Meats 3.65 Igniters for engine 11.50	27.85		
Crew's wages at New York	712.98	Capt. Statement at N.Y.	
Mate's wages at New York to 5/4/27	99.00		
Cook's wages at New York to 5/4/27	87.83		
Capt's. wages Feb. Mar. and April 1927	525.00		
Marketing 78.20 Laundry 7.05	85.25		
Master's expense at N.Y. 15.00 at Red Hook 10.00	25.00		
Night watchman 13 nights	13.00		
Insurance on freight 18.75 Bills Boston 15.00	33.75		
Commission on lumber	182.21		4,073.18
Amount in hand			899.32

Trip #43 July 15, 1927 Capt. Robert Jones

Amount in hand from last statement			899.32
Georgetown, S.C., to New York Lumber 787,804 ft. @ 5.00 M			3,939.02
Towing in 25.00 Out 196.95 Georgetown	221.95	Capts. Statement Georgetown	
Pilotage in 28.00 Out 130.00	158.00		
Stores 44.77 47.08 Gas and oil 23.80	115.65		
Repairs to vessel and motor boat	25.00		
Ice 12.60 Coal 18.00 Beeswax 1.00	31.60		
Gratuity to stevedores 10.00 Misc. 3.80	13.80		
Stores 284.76 Chandlery 102.22 Pendleton	386.98	Gilmartin's Statement	
Towing Point of Hook to Stapleton S. G. Kennedy	50.00		
Towing Poor House Flats to Pt. Richmond	50.00		
Towing Port Richmond to Cadell D. D.	25.00		
Towing Cadell's D. D. to West Bank	50.00		
Shipping fee	12.00		
Dry-docking, cleaning, painting Cadell's	250.00		
Vessel repairs Cadell D. D.	389.78		
Night watchman 10.00 4.00 7.00 Ice 4.00 Cabin table 3.00	28.00	Capts. Statement at N.Y.	
Ship's laundry 5.60 Gasoline 9.69	15.29		
Marketing 57.30 Provisions 25.83	83.13		
Master's expense at New York	15.00		
Crew's wages at New York 600.67 68.00 72.00	740.67		
Master's wages 5/1/27 to 6/30/27	350.00		
Commission Lumber Georgetown to New York	196.95		
Freight insurance Georgetown to New York	18.00		3,226.80
Amount in hand			1,611.54

Trip #44 October 1927 Capt. Robert Jones

Item	Statement	Amount	Total
Georgetown, S.C., to New York Lumber			
759.898 ft. @ 5.00 M			3,799.49
Survey at New York, American Bureau		25.26	
Towage in and out, Georgetown	Capt's. Statement—Georgetown	217.72	
Pilotage in and out, Georgetown		148.00	
Stores 59.57 66.31 2.45		128.33	
Crew's wages at Georgetown		191.00	
Gasoline and kerosene 17.60 Cyl. oil 3.15		20.75	
Iron work, etc. 21.65 on a/c water tank 100.00		121.65	
Marketing 1.50 Coal and ice 24.60 Misc. 10.00		36.10	
Telephone calls and telegrams		2.40	
Crew's wages at New York	Capt's. Statement—New York	603.33	
Mate's wages at New York to 10/23/27		132.00	
Master's wages 7/1/27 to 10/31/27 4 mos. @ 175.00		700.00	
Watchman at New York 5.00 20.00		25.00	
Ship's laundry 3.44 Ice 3.00		6.44	
Table cloth and dish towels		2.00	
Misc. supplies for galley		6.50	
Sulphur candles 1.80 Marketing 81.35		83.15	
Boat hire on Red Hook Flats		26.00	
Master's expense in port		15.00	
Stores 198.35 Chandlery 187.33 Pendleton	Statement—Gilmartin	386.18	
Towing sea to Red Hook		85.00	
Towing Red Hook to Stanton St.		40.00	
Towing Newtown Creek to Red Hook 35.00 Water 10.00		45.00	
Towing Red Hook to West Bank		40.00	
Telegrams .36 Shipping fee 15.00		15.36	
Commission Lumber Georgetown to N.Y.		189.97	3,292.14
			507.35
Amount in hand from last Statement			1,611.54
			2,118.89

End 1927 Policy

Trip #45 January 31, 1928 Capt. Robert Jones

Georgetown, S.C., to New York and Stamford, Conn. Lumber		
331,624 ft. to New York @ 5.00	1,658.13	
466,103 ft. to Stamford, Conn. @ 5.00	2,330.52	3,988.65

Trip #45 (cont.)

Item	Amount	Account	Total
Phone calls and telegrams .50 11.71	12.21	Wm. H. Whiting	
1 Babbitt A. B. Test Anchor 3,350 lbs @ .08¼	292.88	Wm. H. Whiting	
1 1¾ A.B. Test Anchor Shackle	15.00	Wm. H. Whiting	
Certificate of test	5.00	Wm. H. Whiting	
Annual Freight insurance Boston	135.00	Wm. H. Whiting	
Freight insurance Georgetown to New York Boston	10.50		
Stores 269.20 Chandlery 351.55 Struven	620.75		
Awning Taulane	141.60		
Stores 99.03 Chandlery 87.22 Swan	186.75		
Fare and exp. Capt. Nicklas Balto. to Georgetown	29.40	Statement at Stamford Capt. Nicklas	
Interest on advances 2.51 Spark plug 1.50	4.01	Statement at Stamford Capt. Nicklas	
Stores 4.10 72.08 Chandlery 8.20 3.90	88.28	Statement at Stamford Capt. Nicklas	
Final payment on water tank (cost 200.00)	100.00	Statement at Stamford Capt. Nicklas	
Towing in and out Georgetown 25.00 199.43	224.43	Statement at Stamford Capt. Nicklas	
Pilotage in and out Georgetown 28.00 130.00	158.00	Statement at Stamford Capt. Nicklas	
Irons for tank and iron for dragging for anchor	26.85	Statement at Stamford Capt. Nicklas	
Gasoline 2.00 10.00 Coal 11.00 Ice 6.00 Cotton duck 13.00	42.00	Statement at Stamford Capt. Nicklas	
Mate's fare and expense to Florence, S.C.	10.00	Statement at Stamford Capt. Nicklas	
Flashlight 5.20 Battery etc. Freight on anchor 18.31	23.51	Statement at Stamford Capt. Nicklas	
Placing anchor on board 3.00 Gratuity for stevedores 10.00	13.00	Statement at Stamford Capt. Nicklas	
Watchman 10.00 Marketing 24.00	34.00	Statement at Stamford Capt. Nicklas	
Crew's wages at Stamford 542.84 17.00 47.50	607.34	Statement at Stamford Capt. Nicklas	
Master's expense at New York	7.50	Statement at Stamford Capt. Nicklas	
Capt. Nicklas wages 11/16/27 to 12/16/27 Inc.	206.67	Statement at Stamford Capt. Nicklas	
Fare and exp. Capt. Nicklas Stamford to Balto.	20.00	Statement at Stamford Capt. Nicklas	
Telegrams .36 .54. .36 Watchman 6.00	7.26	Gilmartin	
Towing sea to Red Hook 80.00 to Pier 36 E. R. 55.65	135.65	Gilmartin	
Gasoline 9.95 Coal 37.50 Phone call .30	47.75	Gilmartin	
Mooring ship 4.00 Laundry 8.76 Stores 10.75	23.51	Gilmartin	
Stores 214.77 Ice 9.00 Gas, Oil, etc. 19.58	243.35	Capt. Jones—Stamford	
Coffee pots and bed spread for cook's room	2.98	Capt. Jones—Stamford	
Shifting in dock 3.00 Marketing 64.85	67.85	Capt. Jones—Stamford	
Mate's wages 12/18/27 to 1/31/28	139.38	Capt. Jones—Stamford	
Capt's. wages 11/1/27 to 11/7/27 at Georgetown	40.60	Capt. Jones—Stamford	
Capt's. wages 1/1/28 to 1/31/28 at Stamford	175.00	Capt. Jones—Stamford	
Commission Lumber to New York and Stamford	199.43		4,097.44
			108.79
In hand from last statement			2,118.89
In hand			2,010.10

Trip #46 May 15, 1928 Capt. Robert Jones

Item	Amount	Account	Total
Georgetown, S.C., to Bridgeport, Conn. Lumber 729,342 ft. @ 5.00			3,646.71
Add't'l. premium Liab. Ins. (1927) 37.99 (1928) 96.25	134.24		
Telegrams 1.72 Engine parts 7.50 13.00 Loane	22.22		
Shipping crew 25.35 Stores 74.42 Pendleton 46.56	146.33		
Tow Newtown Creek to Stamford, Conn., to W. Bank, water	245.00	Kennedy	
Tow sea to anchor, City Island	160.00	"	
Tow anchor City Island to anchor—Bridgeport	125.00	"	
Pilotage in and out Georgetown	148.00	Atlantic Coast Lmbr. Co.	
Lumber 3.44 1.06 Interest on advances 2.04	6.54		
Towing in and out 35.00 182.34 Georgetown	217.34		
Stores 59.90 Chandlery 4.95	64.85		
Repairing main 2.00 Pumping engines 53.48	55.48	Capts. Statement Georgetown	
Repairing grate and suction pipe	5.25		
Making shackle 1.75 Gratuity to stevedores 10.00	11.75		
Laundry 2.50 Fish 3.00 1½ ton coal 18.00 Ice 9.00	32.50		
Galv. cable 1.48 Turnbuckles 1.20 Bolts. 80 clamps .30	7.10		
Cash to crew 130.00 Gasoline 10.00	140.00		
2 tons coal 29.50 Stores 9.44 adj. pumping engine	41.94	Capt. Statement Bridgeport & Perth Amboy	
Making and fitting wrist pin and bushings	16.00		
Towing anchor off Bridgeport harbor to Burritt Lmbr. Co. Dock Bridgeport Tow Line	145.00		
Telegrams to Balto. 1.69 Express on engine parts .55	2.24		
Cartage on sails from Sta. to vessel	1.00		
3 2nd hand dining room chairs 3.75 Leather for chairs 1.00, Table cloth 1.00	5.75		
4 spark plugs 3.00 Laundry 9.15	12.15		
Marketing Bridgeport 73.60 Perth Amboy 19.25	92.85		
Master's exp. Bridgeport and Perth Amboy	20.00		
Crew's wages Bridgeport	610.62		
Mate's wages in Perth Amboy to 5/3/28	152.08		
Mate's wages in port 5/4/28 to 5/9/28	13.98		
Capt's. wages 2/1/28 to 5/1/28 3 mos. @ 175.00	525.00		
Chandlery A. W. Burritt & Co.	166.12		
Gasoline 9.00 Kerosene 8.00 Cyl. oil 5.00	22.00	Perth Amboy D.D. Co.	
Water 5.00 Ice 9.00 Marketing 171.15	185.15		
Outward towing Perth Amboy D. D. to Orchard Shoals	35.00		
Commission Lumber Georgetown to Bridgeport, Conn.	182.34		3,750.82
			104.11
In hand from trip #45			2,010.10
In hand			1,905.99

Trip #47 August 21, 1928 Capt. Robert Jones

Item	Note	Amount	Total
Georgetown, S.C., to Bridgeport, Conn. Lumber 739,226 ft. @ 4.75 per M			3,511.32
Towing Bridgeport, Conn., to Perth Amboy D.D.— McCarren		225.00	
Survey fee and expense 5/14/28 American Bureau		33.24	
35 Gals. Balto. Copper Paint		88.45	
Shipping crew 23.40 Telephone and telegram 8.34 1.02		32.76	
Freight ins. Perth Amboy to Georgetown to Bridgeport—Boston		20.58	
Insurance Boston Annual bills and adv.		177.39	
Pilotage in and out 28.00 130.00 Georgetown	Capt's. Statement at Georgetown	158.00	
Marketing 17.65 Sea stores 69.41		87.06	
Lumber for stanchions		5.10	
Towing in and out 35.00 184.81 Georgetown		219.81	
Interest on advances 1.17 Gasoline 10.00		11.17	
Coal and ice 13.00 10.80 Iron work 3.55		27.35	
Cash to crew at Georgetown		128.60	
Gratuity to stevedore 10.00 Laundry 3.00		13.00	
Wire lashings for deck load		4.00	
Chandlery 103.75 Cabin stores 240.54 Ice 15.00	Capt's. Statement at Bridgeport	359.29	
Towing in and out Bridgeport		148.00	
Gas and oil 13.75 Laundry 10.13		23.88	
Marketing 107.70 Hardware 3.65		111.35	
Master's expense in port		10.00	
Moving vessel and hoisting sails to dry		12.00	
Telegram .30 Transporting crew to vessel 1.00		1.30	
Crew's wages at Bridgeport		466.36	
Cook's wages in port 1½ months		127.50	
Capt's. wages 5/1/28 to 8/1/28 3 mos. @ 175.00		525.00	
Commission Lumber to Bridgeport		175.57	
Stores and chandlery Swan		82.20	3,273.96
Due vessel			237.36
In hand trip #46			1,905.99
			2,143.35

In hand from trip #47 2,143.35

Expense a/c vessel seized by U.S. Government at Portland, Maine May 25, 1926 Trip #40

Expense at Portland, Maine

Court expense services of U.S. Marshal	
Service of warrant attachment	2.00
Travel 3 miles @ .06	.18

Copy	.30	
Custody—Daykeeper 16 days @ 5.00	80.00	
Custody—Nightkeeper 15 nights @ 5.00	75.00	
Wharfage 16 days @ 1.50	24.00	
Services of Monition	2.00	
Proclamation .30 Advertising 5.43	5.73	
Service of order of restoration	2.00	
Commission on 745.00 amount of settlement on parties 1½ on 500.00 and 1% on 245.00	6.23	197.44
Expense a/c attorneys Nathan W. Thompson & Jacob H. Berman, Portland, Maine		
Fines of Capt. Jones and Mate Howlett	100.00	
Retained for informer	125.00	
Clerk of Court a/c entering and dismissing libel	10.00	
U.S. Customs officials a/c penalty imposed	745.00	
Attorney's fees	1,000.00	1,980.00
Total expense at Portland		2,177.44
Expense at Baltimore		
Expense a/c A. F. Paul and R. B. White to Wash., D.C.	8.49	
Expense A. F. Paul a/c going to Portland, Maine	60.55	
Telephone and telegrams 18.20 3.09	21.29	
Miscellaneous	.90	
Affidavit	.25	
Attorney expense John H. Skeen 300.00		
Phone calls to Portland 14.00		
Telegram to Portland .48	314.48	
Total expense at Baltimore		405.96
Total gross expense		2,583.40
Cash from Mate Howlett		550.00
Net expense to vessel		2,033.40
Cash in hand trip #47		2,143.35
Net expense to vessel		2,033.40
Amount in hand 8/21/28		109.95

Statement sent owners 9/29/28

[Owners the same as at end of Trip #39 except Captain Jones is listed as owning 12/180 shares in place of Captain Southard.]

Trip #48 November 30, 1928 Capt. Robert Jones

In hand from last statement		109.95
Georgetown, S.C., to New York and Stamford, Conn. Lumber		
346,898 ft. @ 4.50 to New York	1,561.04	

Trip #48 (cont.)

Item		Amount	Total
426,290 ft. @ 4.75 to Stamford		2,024.88	3,585.92
Junk sold at New York			4.50
Shipping fee and R.R. a/c shipping crew to Stamford		27.35	
Freight ins. Bridgeport to Georgetown to New York		45.00	
Repairs at Perth Amboy D.D. on a/c Inv. 5/9/28		500.00	
Addtnl. premium Liab. Ins.		48.80	
Telephone calls and telegrams		3.28	
Gum lumber 1.40 Stores 125.92 Chandlery 8.85	Adv. on B/L	136.17	
Pilotage in and out 28.00 130.00 Georgetown	Adv. on B/L	158.00	
Towage in and out 35.00 193.30	Adv. on B/L	228.30	
Gasoline 11.00 Machine and water tank work 36.75	Capt. at Georgetown	47.75	
Ship's laundry 3.00 Stevedore 10.00 Ice and coal 19.30	Capt. at Georgetown	32.30	
Cash to crew at Georgetown	Capt. at Georgetown	128.30	
Marketing 73.80 Coal 23.25 Engine parts 13.00	Capt's. Statement at Port Reading	110.05	
Gas and kerosene 15.00 Work on shackle and pin 3.00	Capt's. Statement at Port Reading	18.00	
American flag Stove brick and pipe Toilet seat	Capt's. Statement at Port Reading	11.15	
Watchman at New York 5.00 Ship's laundry 9.80	Capt's. Statement at Port Reading	14.80	
Addtl. freight on anchor	Capt's. Statement at Port Reading	.30	
Help putting anchor on board	Capt's. Statement at Port Reading	5.00	
Provisions 36.27 Ice 9.90 Port Reading	Capt's. Statement at Port Reading	46.17	
Capts. expense at New York, Stamford, and Port Reading	Capt's. Statement at Port Reading	20.00	
Tow Port Reading to Old Orchard and water	Capt's. Statement at Port Reading	45.00	
Crew's wages on trip	Capt's. Statement at Port Reading	746.03	
Sailor's wages in Stamford 20.00 Railroad fare to N.Y. 1.25	Capt's. Statement at Port Reading	21.25	
Cook's and mate's wages at Stamford	Capt's. Statement at Port Reading	119.50	
Capts. wages 8/1/28 to 12/1/28 4 mos.	Capt's. Statement at Port Reading	700.00	
Towing Sandy Hook to Pier 12 Stapleton	Gilmartin	85.00	
15 fathoms 1¾″ anchor chain and shackle 2,370 lbs. @ .05	Gilmartin	118.50	
1 stockless anchor 3,850 lbs. @ 6.80 F.O.B. factory freight prepaid to Stamford	Gilmartin	261.80	
Tow Newtown Creek to Stamford, Conn.	Gilmartin	125.00	
Tow Stamford, Conn., to Red Hook	Gilmartin	75.00	
Commission Lumber Georgetown to New York and Stamford		179.30	4,056.70
Due C. C. Paul & Co.			356.33

End policy 1928–1929

Trip #49	March 30, 1929	Capt. Robert Jones

Port Reading, N.J., to Charleston, S.C. Coal

956 tons @ 1.10 a ton 1,051.60

Item	Note	Amount	Total
Charleston, S.C., to New York Lumber			
639,405 ft. @ 4.75 M		3,037.19	4,088.79
Cash a/c sale of old spanker and junk			36.00
			4,124.79
Shipping fee 19.50 Tow Red Hook to Pt. Reading coal dock		84.50	
Docking at coal pier 20.00 Trimming coal 86.04	Capt. Statement at Charleston, S.C.	106.04	
Exp. a/c towing Pt. Reading to Old Orchard 5.00		5.00	
Towing sea to Charleston 79.32 Dock Johnson Coal Co. 15.00		94.32	
Pilotage in and out 76.50 76.50 Charleston		153.00	
Harbor fees 2.00 Lumber for spanker gaff 3.75		5.75	
Delivering timber for gaff for vessel		3.00	
Carp. work on gaff 18.00 Water 3.00 Timber .97		21.97	
Wrenches and oil can 1.00 Laundry 3.00		4.00	
Machine and iron work on vessel		75.87	
Cash to crew at Charleston		181.00	
Stores 92.95 Chandlery 40.57 Cherry & Co.		133.52	
Towing Johnson Coal Co. to N. State Lmbr. Co.		25.00	
Towing N. State Lmbr. Co. to anchorage 2 tugs		50.00	
Master's expense at Charleston		10.00	
Exchange on draft 1.05 Freight on sails from Phila 1.18		2.23	
Marketing 82.27 Meat and ice, etc 16.70		98.97	
Coils, plugs, wire, and ether for pump engine		10.75	
Towing City anchorage to sea		75.00	
Annual freight insurance Boston		202.50	
Ins. bills N.Y. to Charleston to N.Y.		54.00	
Crank shaft pinion 5.30 and key Telegraph and telephone 6.21		11.51	
Ins. bills and advances Charleston to N.Y.		22.50	
Commission Coal Pt. Reading to Charleston		52.58	
Noting protest 1.00 Side lights and hangers 55.00	Gilmartin's	56.00	
Towing Sandy Hook to Red Hook Kennedy		75.00	
Towing Red Hook to Van Brunt St. Kennedy		35.00	
Towing Chelsea to Newtown Creek Kennedy		35.00	
2 gaffs 25.00 Water 10.00 Delivery 5.00 Kennedy		40.00	
Towing Newtown Creek to Red Hook		35.00	
Repairs to chronometer		7.25	
Coal 21.75 Laundry 9.95 Watchman 25.70 7.50 10.50	Capt. Statement Gilmartin's	75.20	
Grate bars 2.25 Launch hire 32.00		34.25	
Marketing 88.55 Master's expense 15.00		103.55	
Crew's wages 11/22/28 to 1/21/29 at N.Y.		709.00	
Wages to mate and cook in port 1/22/29 to 3/17/29	Capt. at N.Y.	315.00	
Capts. wages 12/1/28 to 3/1/29 3 mos @ 175.00		525.00	
Stores and chandlery from sch. *Charles M. Struven* Perth Amboy D.D.		104.17	

Trip #49 (cont.)		
Expense delivering to vessel Crating 3.00 Frt. 2.74		
Transport 25.00 Expense 3.50	34.34	
Commission Lumber Charleston to New York	151.86	
Stores 266.32 Chandlery 191.99 Swan	458.31	4,276.84
In debt this trip		152.05
Due C. C. Paul & Co. from previous statement		356.33
Due C. C. Paul & Co.		508.38

End Policy 1928–29

Trip #50 August 15, 1929 Captain Robert O. Jones

Newport News, Virginia, to Hamilton, Bermuda Coal		
1,093 tons @ 3.00 per ton	3,279.00	
Palatka and Jacksonville to New York, N.Y. Cypress		
764.200 ft. @ 8.25 M	6,304.65	9,583.65
Slops from crew		29.08
Cash from consignee a/c gas used in discharging coal		15.00
From captain a/c steamer chair purch. for self and chgd. in Jax		
Ship Chand. Co.'s bill		3.50
Refund from Boston Ins. Co. a/c lay-up time		15.20
		9,646.43

Repairs Perth Amboy D.D. Co. 5/9/28	
Amt. 2,638.90 Chgd. previous statement 500.00	
Docking 110.25 Paint, caulking, etc. 1,289.60	1,250.90
Shipping rudder 475.00 Other repairs 264.05	888.00
Shipping fee 12.00 Tow West Bank from Red Hook	
Kennedy 40.00	52.00
Stores 230.43 Chandlery 245.46 Swan	475.89
Telegraph and telephone 3.65 .36 1.45	5.46
Addtl. premium Law & McKim	40.49
Liability Ins. Law & McKim	96.25
Sail bills Taulane 325.00 110.00 300.00 105.00	840.00
Insurance bills and adv. Boston	195.00
Insurance bills and adv. Annual Boston	177.30
Survey fee at N.Y. 6/29/29	16.62
Paint shipped Balto. to N.Y.	93.86
Towage Little Creek to Newport News	50.00
Watchman 5.20 Towage 38.00	43.20
Dumping and trimming coal @ .14 ton	153.02

Item	Amount	Statement	Total
Running lines 2.50 Fresh water 3.26	5.76	Statement A. R. Hoffman, Newport News	
Marketing, stores and delivery	53.18		
Launch hire 3.00 Gasoline 31.74	34.74		
Clearance 2.50 British consul fee 4.75	7.25		
Tow Newport News to Thimble Light	40.00		
Outward pilotage 54.08 Phone calls 3.95	58.03		
Attendance fee Hoffman	25.00		
Master's expense Newport News 2.50 Bermuda 7.00	9.50	Capt. Jax.	
Fresh meat 14.10 Fish 5.20 Bermuda	19.30		
Laundry 12.00 Fresh water for sea 15.80	27.80		
Labor (carp.) and lumber Repair main gaff	11.07		
Sundries and master's exp. Jacksonville	12.15		
Light dues 39.66 Tow in and out of Hamilton 300.00	339.66	Statement Watlington & Conyers	
Discharging coal Hamilton	524.64		
Running lines 9.60 Wharfage 73.50	83.10		
Pilotage in and out of Hamilton	62.64		
Ice 5.04 Cablegrams 2.28	7.32		
Loading 286,000 ft. cypress at Palatka @ 1.40 M	400.40	Statement Jax. S.C. Co.	
Loading 478,200 ft. cypress at Jacksonville @ 1.50 M	717.30		
Towage sea to Jacksonville to sea	181.91		
Pilotage in and out 17.10 47.35 Jacksonville	64.45		
Entrance tonnage tax Custom's fee	16.39		
Quarantine inspection Jacksonville	10.00		
Stores 131.82 Chandlery 86.68	218.50		
Interest on exchange on draft	6.09		
Discharging 764,200 ft. @ 1.25	955.25		
Commission Coal Newport News to Bermuda	163.95		
Commission Cypress to New York	315.23		
Cypress damaged by coal dust, etc. 3,189 ft. @ 15.00 M	47.83		
Noting protest 1.00 Telegram .36	1.36	Gilmartin	
Tow sea to Red Hook 75.00 to Wallabout 40.00	115.00		
Tow Wallabout to Perth Amboy	70.00		
Paid sailor a/c shifting to Perth Amboy	5.00	Capt. Statement at N.Y.	
Watchman at Wallabout	30.00		
Ship's laundry 4.00 Gas and oil 5.80	9.80		
Ice 6.00 Gratuity to lmbr. inspector 10.00	16.00		
Marketing 126.20 Master's expense in port 25.00	151.20		
Crew's wages in New York 5/29/29	1,014.00		
Cook's wages in port 5/29 to 8/13/29	202.56		
Capts. wages March 1, 1929, to 8/1/29 5 mos. @ 175.00	875.00		11,286.35
Due C. C. Paul & Co.			1,639.92
Due C. C. Paul & Co. from last trip			508.38
Total amount in debt			2,148.30

Statement sent owners 9/30/29

Trip #51 March 1, 1930 Capt. Robert Jones

Refund Boston Ins. Co. a/c no gasoline carried in cargo		15.00
Slops from crew	8.12	
Newport News to Hamilton, Bermuda Coal 986 tons @ 3.00	2,958.00	
Cash for gasoline used running engine disch. coal	30.00	
Jacksonville, Fla., to Harrison, N.J., diverted to Elizabethport, N.J. Lumber 466,990 ft. @ 8.50 M	3,969.41	
Demurrage on lumber cargo 13 days @ 90.00 Shepherd & Morse	1,170.00	
Sale of old junk	6.00	8,141.53
Demurrage a/c lumber—Savannah to Fall River May 1924		300.00
		8,456.53

Shipping crew at N.Y. 16.85 Mate's lunch at N.Y. .50	17.35	Capt. Statement Newport News
Towing Perth Amboy to Old Orchard	45.00	
Six lamp chimneys .75 Stores and chandlery 77.12	77.87	
Repairs to pump engine Newport News	55.37	
Spark plug Battery Wire Tape etc.	2.00	
Launch hire—Motor boat broke down	30.00	
Cash to crew at Newport News	55.22	
Master's expense in port	2.25	
Cash to Mate McClure paid off	24.00	Statement—Hoffman & Co.
Telegrams and telephone calls 1.20 1.15	2.35	
Charts .60 Gas and oil 48.50	49.10	
Testing out Mianus engine	6.03	
Custom's clearance fee	2.50	
Towage 36.00 Running lines 2.50 Water 1.80	40.30	
Trimming 986 tons coal @ .14	138.04	
British consul fee 4.75 Carfare seaman to Norfolk—return	5.45	
Pilotage Norfolk to sea	51.98	
Agency fee Hoffman	25.00	
Expense sending mate from New York to N. News Fare 12.00 Berth 3.75	15.75	
Cash to mate 2.00 Telegram to Newport News .60	2.60	
Telegrams and phone calls 4.04 .60 2.16 .67	7.47	
Cash to crew at Hamilton	91.15	Master's Statement Bermuda
Cash to mate deserted	21.15	
Cash to sailors paid off	62.70	
Cash to sailor running engine discharging coal	10.00	
Meat 16.78 Ice 2.52 Fish 2.70 Vegetables in port 10.44	32.44	
First aid to sailor a/c being burned	3.00	
Master's expense in port to St. George twice for sailors	22.00	

Item	Amount	Account
Light dues 39.66 Cablegrams 1.14 1.14	41.94	Watlington & Conyers
Discharging coal 986 tons	473.28	
Tow in, docking, and out to sea Hamilton	300.00	
Pilotage In and Out Hamilton	61.20	
Running lines for ship at coal dock	9.60	
Wharfage at Hamilton	58.80	
Shipyard work making trestletrees, crosstree legs, outriggers, strongbacks, hatches, and bolsters	153.11	Capt. at Jacksonville
Caulking bow ports 7.00 Fresh water 15.00	22.00	
Bolt canvas 22 inches by 131 yards	47.50	
Two Bermuda sailors paid off	90.00	
Cash to crew at Jacksonville	82.00	
Laundry 2.50 Master's expense 10.00	12.50	
Loading 470,757 ft. lumber @ 1.50	706.13	Capt. Statement Jax. S.C. Co.
Towing sea to Jacksonville to sea 735 tons @ .33 less 25%	181.92	
Pilotage in 17.10 Out 49.55 Jacksonville	66.65	
Shipping two sailors 14.00 Quarantine 10.00	24.00	
Custom fees 16.39 Harbor fees 3.00	19.39	
Stores 135.37 Chandlery 92.59	227.96	
New jib 105.00 Telegrams 1.32	106.32	
Interest and exchange on draft	4.40	
Put into Charleston in distress		
Slops to crew 77.04 Master's expense 2.00	79.04	
Towing sea to Charleston to sea	130.00	Richardson Bros.
Noting protest 2.50 Pilot in Charleston 78.75	81.25	
Stores and chandlery Richardson Bros.	375.75	
Ice and fish 3.60 at Charleston Radiogram 4.76	8.36	Capt. Statement—Perth Amboy
Four tons of coal at Elizabethport 27.50 27.50	55.00	
Marketing in port 12/31/29 to 2/5/30	71.57	
Ship's laundry	4.24	
Balance crew wages on trip	1,346.86	
Paid sailor's fare to Bermuda	34.50	
Cook's wages in port 1 mo. 2 days	75.00	
Capts. wages 8/1/29 to 2/5/30—6 mos. 5 days @ 175.00 mo.	1,079.00	
Services of man helping shift and straighten up decks to Perth Amboy	10.00	
Master's expense in port	28.30	
Noting protest 1.00 Copy protest 1.00	2.00	Gilmartin
Telegraph and telephone 2.77 Docking Perth Amboy 10.00	12.77	
Wharfage Pier 12 S 1/2/30	23.34	
Disch. lumber 466,990 ft. @ 1.50 M	700.49	
Ins. Boston Bills N.Y. to Hampton Roads to Bermuda to Jacksonville, to Harrison, N.J.	122.50	
Insurance Boston Annual Frt.	202.50	

Trip #51 (cont.)

Insurance Boston Advances, Jacksonville to Harrison, N.J.	37.50	
Exp. A. F. Paul Balto. to New York and return	15.50	
Commission Coal Newport News to Bermuda	147.90	
Commission on lumber and demurrage, Jax. to Elizabethport, N.J.	256.97	
Watchman at New York	50.00	
Addtl. premium Liab. Ins.	50.11	
U. S. Ship Comm. a/c wages due sailors	5.25	8,592.47
Due C. C. Paul & Co.		135.94
Due C. C. Paul & Co. from last trip		2,148.30
Due C. C. Paul & Co.		2,284.24

Vessel owes following bills

Invoice date			
8/16/29	Wm. H. Swan & Sons	555.42	
8/15/29	Lewis Martin & Son	55.00	
12/12/29	Kennedy Tow Line	150.00	
1/29/29	George Taulane Sons	465.00	
7/19/29	Perth Amboy Dry Dock	567.33	1,792.75
	Vessel in debt		4,076.99

End 1929–1930 Policy

Schooner *Albert F. Paul* Purchased at U.S. Marshal's Sale March 4, 1930

To U.S. Marshal at sale		1,900.00
Less Marshal's expense		
Marshal's and clerk's fees	107.42	
Lawyer fee—Crowell & Rouse	200.00	
Court clerks, Notary, Commissioner's fee, Carfare, Phone calls, etc.	26.35	333.37
Balance to apply on bills		1,566.23
Check to Wm. H. Swan a/c bills		226.52
To pay outstanding bills		1,792.75

Wm. H. Swan Slops 29.08 Stores 305.19 Chandlery 221.15	555.42	
L. Martin & Son 2 tarpaulins	55.00	
Kennedy Tow Line Tow to dock, Water, Phone calls	150.00	
Taulane Spanker cover	465.00	
Perth Amboy D. D. Repairs	567.33	1,792.75
Expense A. F. Paul to New York a/c sale		17.71
C. P. Runyon		20.00

Recording bill of sale		2.00
Captain R. Jones a/c service aboard		50.00
Wharfage	54.00	
Less a/c overcharge taken from invoice shown below	10.00	44.00
Telephone calls and telegrams 7.21 10.11		17.32
L. Martin & Son Mainsail		310.00
Perth Amboy D. D. Repair bill	1,401.28	
Less damage (includ. in bill) to Gilmartin from McCarren Tow Line and used by Gilmartin as disbursement in leaving N.Y. for Georgetown to load ties for Norfolk	45.00	1,356.28
Expense of Captain Jones		
Water for testing tanks	5.50	
New cabin stove pipe	7.50	
Marketing 3/15 to 3/28/30	14.00	
To engineer of sch. *R. R. Govin* a/c installing new pump etc.	26.65	
Master's expense at Perth Amboy locating topmast etc.	10.00	
1 Jack saw	3.00	66.65
Taulane Flying jib 115.00 Fore-topsail 115.00		230.00
U.S. Marshal's fee etc. shown above		333.77
		4,240.48
In debt to C. C. Paul & Co. at end of Trip #51		2,284.24
Total price after repairing after sale		6,524.72
Assessment C. C. Paul & Co. 27/90	1,957.41	
Assessment C. H. Paul 1/90	72.50	2,029.91
Cost 62/90 after U.S. Marshal sale		4,494.81

Trip #52 May 15, 1930 Capt. Robert Jones

Georgetown, S.C., to Norfolk, Va. Ties			
13,000 Ties @ .20		2,600.00	
Slops from crew Swan bill		15.05	
Slops from crew Georgetown		6.00	
Refund from captain a/c laundry		9.53	2,630.58
Gasoline and kerosene	Perth Amboy Dry Dock	14.00	
Towing Perth Amboy to Old Orchard Light	Perth Amboy Dry Dock	40.00	
Phone calls .60 Rating chronometer 3.00		3.60	
Shipping crew		20.55	
Inward and outward pilotage Georgetown	Draft	168.00	
Towage in and out 35.00 110.50 Georgetown Water 5.00	Draft	150.50	
Stores 35.50 Chandlery 4.95 Slops 6.00	Draft	46.45	
Exchange on draft	Draft	2.32	

Trip #52 (cont.)

Item	Amount	Total	Note
Ship's laundry	2.32		Capt. Statement Georgetown
Ice, coal, meat, etc. for sea	52.78		Capt. Statement Georgetown
Coal at Georgetown	6.00		Capt. Statement Georgetown
Labor sawing up old topmast, gaff, etc.	1.50		Capt. Statement Georgetown
Cash and slops to sailor deserted	14.15		Capt. Statement Georgetown
Inward towage and docking	50.00		Capt. Statement Norfolk
Gas engine parts 2.00 Ship's laundry 2.22	4.22		Capt. Statement Norfolk
Oil can, wrench, and pliers	1.05		Capt. Statement Norfolk
Master's expense in port	10.00		Capt. Statement Norfolk
Crew's wages to 5/2/30 at Norfolk	376.44		Capt. Statement Norfolk
Capt's wages 3/15/30 to 4/30/30 1½ mos. @ 175.00	262.50		Capt. Statement Norfolk
Stores 294.15 Chandlery 214.19 Slops 15.05 Swan	523.39		
Liability insurance Law & McKim	96.25		
Commission on ties Georgetown to Norfolk	130.00	1,976.56	
In hand		654.56	

Trip #53 July 10, 1930 Capt. Robert Jones

Item	Amount	Total
Cash in hand from last trip		654.56
Georgetown, S.C., to Norfolk and Baltimore Ties and lumber		
7,215 ties to Norfolk @ .20	1,443.00	
249,984 ft. lumber to Balto. @ 5.25	1,312.41	2,755.41
		3,409.97

Item	Amount	Note
Norfolk Lighterage Co. Towing from Atl. Creosoting Wks. to Thimble Shoal	50.00	
1,500 gals. water	5.00	Capt. Georgetown
Shipping crew at Norfolk	8.00	Capt. Georgetown
Coal 12.00 Fish 1.20 Gratuity 3.00	16.20	Capt. Georgetown
New Galley Stove, Iron Work, etc.	47.50	Capt. Georgetown
Pilotage in and out 28.00 140.00 Georgetown	168.00	Draft
Towage in and out 35.00 124.50 Water 5.00 Georgetown	164.50	Draft
Chandlery 20.84 Stores 48.88 Exchange draft 2.75	72.47	Draft
N. L. Co. Towing Sewalls Pt. to Atl. Creosoting Co.	50.00	
N. L. Co. Towing Norfolk to Baltimore	150.00	
Crew's wages at Norfolk	359.92	Capt. Statement at Balto.
Conning up and resetting rigging after disch. ties	10.00	Capt. Statement at Balto.
Wages 2 men Norfolk to Balto. and fare back to Norfolk	20.00	Capt. Statement at Balto.
Marketing at Norfolk	12.72	Capt. Statement at Balto.
Master's expense Norfolk and Baltimore	7.15	Capt. Statement at Balto.
Cook's wages in port	47.88	Capt. Statement at Balto.
Parts for engine in Balto.	12.97	Capt. Statement at Balto.
Marketing and fresh meat at Balto.	12.69	Capt. Statement at Balto.

Item	Amount	Total
Ship's laundry 6.08 Door springs .15	6.23	
Expense getting ice aboard, etc.	1.50	
Dishes and enamel ware	.85	
Capt's. wages 5/1/30–6/15/30 1½ mos.	262.50	
Repairing ship's bell and clock	5.30	
Stores 174.70 Chandlery 112.91 Swan	287.61	
Commission on ties and lumber	137.78	1,916.77
In hand		1,493.20

Trip #54 October 31, 1930 Capt. Robert Jones

Item	Amount	Total
Cash in hand from last trip		1,493.20
Newport News to St. George, Bermuda Coal 1,099½ tons @ 3.25 ton	3,573.37	
Georgetown, S.C., to Balto. Lumber 568,575* ft. @ 5.00	2,842.87	6,416.24
Refund gas tax		6.88
		7,916.32

Item	Statement	Amount	Paid by
Towing Balto. to Newport News anchorage		150.00	
Towing Pier 6 to Redman & Vane		20.00	
Hauling, cleaning and painting, paint furnished by owners		195.00	
Extra work, cementing, repairs, etc.		195.72	
Ice 3.15 Repairing sextant 3.00		6.15	
38 gals. copper paint	Hoffman Statement	90.36	
Shipping 3 sailors Norfolk	Hoffman Statement	9.00	
Towage 38.00 Running lines 2.50	Hoffman Statement	40.50	
Dumping and trimming coal @ .14	Hoffman Statement	153.93	
Fresh water 1.58 Launch hire 6.00 Phone .40	Hoffman Statement	7.98	
Custom fee Clearance	Hoffman Statement	2.50	
Pilotage Newport News to sea	Hoffman Statement	55.13	
Agency fee Hoffman	Hoffman Statement	15.00	
Shipping 1 sailor Norfolk		3.00	Capt. at N. News
Expense getting sailor to Newport News .40 and aboard 1.00		1.40	Capt. at N. News
Launch putting master aboard		1.00	Capt. at N. News
Pillow slips for cabin use		3.00	Capt. at N. News
Master's expense Norfolk and Newport News		1.80	Capt. at N. News
Light dues Pilotage, Cable, Provisions	Darrell & Meyer	145.38	
Discharging coal @ .50	Darrell & Meyer	549.75	
Docking Towage in and out	Darrell & Meyer	250.00	
Cash to crew at St. George		145.27	Capt. Bermuda
Fish 2.42 Master's exp. at St. George		7.42	Capt. Bermuda

*Marginal note: "B/L 566,744."

Trip #54 (cont.)

Item	Amount	Total	
Commission on coal to Bermuda	178.67		
Exch. on draft arriving at Georgetown	2.75		
Pilotage in and out 28.00 140.00 Georgetown	168.00		Draft leaving Georgetown
Towage in and out 25.00 141.69 Water 5.00 Georgetown	171.69		
Blacksmith 92.05 Carpenter work 5.60	107.65		
Shipping 4 sailors 30.00 Exch. on draft 3.87	33.87		
Chandlery 25.88 Stores 116.47 Georgetown	142.35		
Telegraph and telephone 4.72 3.98 4.54	13.24		
Stationery .64 Rent of chronometer 18.75	19.39		
Meat and ice at Bermuda 5.82 Kerosene 1.40	7.22		Capt. Statement leaving Georgetown
Custom fees and doctor at Georgetown	26.39		
Crew paid off at Georgetown	479.80		
Lumber 5.70 Chickens 4.80 Fresh fish .65	11.15		
Stevedores shifting vessel and battening hatches after hours	10.00		
Toilet tank 7.50 Laundry 3.45 Master's incidentals 5.32	16.27		
Towing Channel to Atlantic Wharf	75.00		
Chandlery 189.70 Stores 132.37 Vane Bros.	322.07		
Chandlery 90.07 Stores 192.65 Swan	282.72		
Gasoline, oil and cup grease Capt. Ship Chandlery Co.	39.08		
Coal 14.25 Hauling tank 5.00	19.25		
Ship's laundry 6.63 Bed linen etc. 6.65	13.28		Capt. Statement at Balto.
Crew wages at Balto.	249.40		
Cook's wages in port while disch.	52.04		
Cook's wages in port while tied up 12 days	12.00		
Capt's. wages 6/15/30 to 10/1/30 3½ mos. @ 175.00	612.50		
Marketing for 5 weeks	41.50		
Master's exp. in port	5.00		
Commission on lumber	142.14		
1 6″ Plymouth hawser 100 fathoms @ .16 lb.	96.77		
Chronometer bill Hand	26.50		
1 tank for fresh water Boston Iron and Metals	38.00		
2,188 lbs. ice @ 5.00 ton City Ice and Fuel Co.	5.25	5,470.23	
In hand		2,446.09	

1/90 = 27.178+

89/90	C. C. Paul & Co.	2,418.91	
1/90	C. Howard Paul Cr. to a/c	27.18	2,446.09

To owners 12/15/30

Trip #55 Dec. 15, 1930 Capt. Robert O. Jones

Georgetown, S.C., to Balto. Lumber

556,139 ft. @ 5.00 M	2,780.70	
Exchange on draft, paid by Capt.	3.73	2,784.43

Item	Amount	Paid by	Total
Stores 15.21 254.32 Chandlery 33.60 184.56 Vane	487.69		
Towing to channel Mullen	50.00		
30 doz. eggs from Capt. Nicklas*	10.50		
Pilotage in and out 28.00 130.00 Georgetown	158.00	Draft	
Towage in and out 25.00 136.91 Water 5.00 Georgetown	166.91	Draft	
Stores 55.15 Chandlery 53.69 Phone .50 .65	109.99	Draft	
Shipping sailors and fare to Georgetown	11.50	Draft	
Exchange on draft	3.73	Draft	
Cash to crew at Georgetown	76.13	Capt. at Georgetown	
Machine and blacksmith work	45.25	Capt. at Georgetown	
Lumber for stanchions in hold	2.00	Capt. at Georgetown	
1 whole pig 8.16 ½ ton coal 6.00	14.16	Capt. at Georgetown	
Laundry 1.50 Gratuity to stevedores 5.00	6.50	Capt. at Georgetown	
Balance of wages of sailor deserted at Georgetown paid ship comm. at Balto.	23.03	Capt. at Balto.	
Laundry 5.07 Marketing 23.50 1.50 5.75	35.82	Capt. at Balto.	
Crew's wages at Balto.	430.81	Capt. at Balto.	
Cook's wages in port 15 days @ 50.00 per mo.	25.00	Capt. at Balto.	
Capt's. wages 10/1/30 to 12/15/30 3½ mos. @ 175.00	437.50	Capt. at Balto.	
Piling wet lumber in cargo—Myers	10.00		
Towing channel to Pier 6	75.00		
Commission on lumber	139.04		
New maintopsail Taulane	110.00		2,428.56
In hand			355.87

Trip #56 March 2, 1931 Capt. Robt. O. Jones

Item	Amount	Total
Amount in hand from last trip		355.87
Georgetown, S.C., to Balto. Lumber and piling		
Lump sum freight	2,635.25	
Refund of gasoline tax	6.00	
Slops from crew	7.59	
Cash from Capt. a/c telegram	.60	
From stevedore—use of hoisting engine	26.88	
From stevedore—repairs hoisting engine	18.12	2,694.44
		3,050.31
1 2 Horsepower Domestic Spec. Geared pump	190.00	
½ ton bitum. coal 4.50 1½ ton nut coal 21.50	26.00	
Vessel repairs—Redman & Vane	55.91	
Annual freight insur. Boston	210.00	
Telephone calls and telegrams 1.20 1.73 1.45	4.38	

*Captain Nicklas, former master of schooner *Purnell T. White* and substitute for Captain Jones on *Albert F. Paul* for a passage, had retired to raise chickens. Now he sells the fruits of his efforts to the *Paul*.

Trip #56 (cont.)

Item	Amount	Note	Total
Gas and oil 27.45 Ice 5.25 Coal 21.38	54.08		
Towing out Pier 6 to off Curtis Bay	25.00		
Pilotage in 28.00 Out 130.00 Georgetown	158.00	Draft	
Towage in 35.00 Out 123.97 Water 5.00 Georgetown	163.97	Draft	
Stores 64.18 Chandlery 4.90 Carpenter work 10.80	79.88	Draft	
Slops to crew 7.59 Exchange on draft 2.72	10.31	Draft	
Machine and blacksmith work	39.50	Capt. at Georgetown	
½ ton coal 6.00 Laundry 1.50	7.50	Capt. at Georgetown	
1 pig 12.96 Gratuity 7.00 Pliers .25	20.21	Capt. at Georgetown	
Cash to crew at Georgetown	98.54	Capt. at Georgetown	
Cash to crew at Baltimore	355.72	Capt. at Balto.	
Capts. wages 12/15/30 to 1/30/31 1½ mos. @ 175.00	262.50	Capt. at Balto.	
Marketing in port 2 weeks and help with stores and ice	22.20	Capt. at Balto.	
Cook's wages in port 1/21/31 to 2/4/31 15 days @ 60.00 mo.	30.00	Capt. at Balto.	
Ship's laundry 7.57 Master's exp. in port 1.20	8.77	Capt. at Balto.	
Stores 252.48 Chandlery 216.58 Vane Bros.	469.06		
Commission Lumber	131.76		
Towing Off Bloody Point to Canton Hollow Norf. Ltge. Co.	60.00		
Shifting Canton Hollow to Pier 6	20.00		
Repairs to hoisting engine	38.96		2,542.25
Due vessel			508.06

End 1930–1931 Policy

Trip #57	May 31, 1931	Capt. Robert O. Jones

Item	Amount	Total
Amount in hand last statement		508.06
Newport News to St. George, Bermuda Coal 1,090½ tons @ 3.00	3,271.50	
Georgetown, S.C., to Baltimore Lumber 586,305 ft. @ 5.00 M	2,931.52	6,203.02
Refund of gasoline tax		5.12
Slops to crew at Norfolk		11.84
Cash from Capt. a/c telegram		.60
From stevedore a/c item in Vane's bill chgd. to sch. in error		1.70
		6,730.34

1 coil 3½″ 4 str. Plymouth rope	71.97
Chronometer bill Hand	17.95
Stores 200.25 Chandlery 151.37 3.20 Vane	354.82
Gasoline, Oil, and Grease Capts. Ship Chandlery Co.	29.81

Item	Amount	
Towing Balto. to channel	50.00	
Towage 38.00 Running lines 2.50 Water 1.68	42.19	Hoffman—Norfolk
Dumping and trimming coal @ .14	152.67	
Launch hire 10.00 Cleaning, etc. 2.50	12.50	
Repairing windlass Southern Shipyard	28.26	
Telegram .36 Phone calls 2.40 .80	3.56	
Pilotage out 56.93 Agency fee Hoffman 15.00	71.93	
Master's expense Norfolk 5.50 Bermuda 5.00	10.50	Capt. at Bermuda
Expense at Bermuda getting sailor	7.50	
Exp. a/c launch going to sch. *Sally Wren* looking over old material	5.00	
Fish 2.85 Cablegram a/c sailing 1.44	4.29	
Cash to crew at Bermuda	112.65	
Light dues 39.66 Pilotage in and out 64.80	104.46	Capt. Statement Darrell & Meyer
Cablegram 1.44 Provisions 19.50	20.94	
Medical attent. 9.60 Medicine a/c crew 6.12	15.72	
Disch. coal 1,090½ tons @ .50	545.25	
Tow 5 Fathom Hole to St. George, berthing, and towing to sea	250.00	
Bal. crew wages Paid off in Georgetown	484.31	Capt. G.town
Entering Custom House 16.39 Doctor's fee 10.00	26.39	
Exch. on first draft from Georgetown	2.75	
Almanac .30 Ice 5.25 Telephone 1.56 Telegraph 3.25	10.36	
Addtl. premium Liability insur.	29.27	
Commission Coal to Bermuda	163.58	
Railroad fare 18.43 Meals 1.00 Sending mate to Georgetown	19.43	
Liability insurance Law & McKim	96.25	
Carpenter work on rudder, windlass, step ladders, strongbacks, hatches, etc.	43.20	Capt. Georgetown
Sewing sails, cleaning water tank, etc.	11.25	
Ship's laundry 5.47 Lumber for ladders etc.	10.67	
Phone calls Gratuity to stevedores	6.00	
6 day's use of lighter repairing rudder	6.00	
Pilotage in 28.00 Out 130.00 Georgetown	158.00	Draft—Georgetown
Towage in 35.00 Out 148.85 Water 5.00 Georgetown	188.85	
Rudder and windlass repairs Ainsworth	69.60	
Making shaft, fitting etc. for windlass Ainsworth	16.80	
Misc. blacksmith work Ainsworth	32.37	
Stores 83.71 Chandlery 18.24 Hardware 2.44 Ford	104.39	
Shipping 4 sailors Seamen's House	27.30	
Exch. on draft leaving Georgetown	3.56	
Stores 59.98 Chandlery 46.47 Slops 11.84 Swan	118.29	
Jib topsail #5 Duck Taulane	120.00	
Caulking Redman and Vane	39.55	
Telegrams and phone calls	2.55	

Trip #57 (cont.)			
Towing channel to Pier 6	75.00		
Commission Lumber	146.58		
Cash to crew at Balto. to 4/30/31	278.38		
Capt's. wages 2/1/31 to 5/31/31 4 mos. @ 175.00	700.00		
Bacon, beef, and eggs C. L. Ford	8.45		
Marketing 4 weeks, 3 days to 5/31/31	42.73		
Help shifting up dock .50 Brass polish .35	.85		
Hinge .25 Ship's laundry 7.62 Master's exp. 2.00	9.87	4,964.55	
Amount due vessel		1,765.79	

Trip #58 October 31, 1931 Capt. Robt. O. Jones

In hand from last trip		1,765.79	
Georgetown, S.C., to Baltimore Lumber			
575,627 ft. @ 4.37½ M	2,518.37		
Refund gas tax 2.00 3.20	5.20		
Refund Boston Ins. Co. a/c Lay-up Pol. 3484 3664 3143			
13.46 7.60 7.60	28.66		
Cash from Capt. a/c telegram	.60	2,552.83	
		4,318.62	
Hire of chronometer 2½ mos. @ 7.50 Smola	18.75		
Repairing chronometer Smola	14.50		
Gas and coal oil Captain's Ship Chandlery Co.	9.08		
Paint 38.73 21.48 Intl. Paint Co.	60.21		
1 coil 3¼ Manila rope	57.23		
1 ton nut coal Hetz	13.50		
Capt's. marketing June and July	92.46		Capt. Statement—Balto. (from here)
Polish .35 Dishes .65 Glasses .15 Egg beater .15	1.30		
Wash soap .48 Screws for hinges .15	.63		
Sulphur candles a/c roaches	1.20		
Shifting up dock, putting up awning and putting strongback under motor boat	1.75		
Unbending mizzen sail	.75		
Master's wages June and July @ 80.00 cut by Master to 75.00	150.00		
Marketing August 1931	32.70		
Ice 30 days @ .10 3.00 40 gal. bbl. 1.25	4.25		
Oil cloth .29 Getting ice, coal, etc. aboard	1.29		
Fresh meat 173 lbs. @ .12 Cermak	20.76		
Captain's wages August 1931	30.00		Capt. Statement—Balto. (to here)
Rope and repairs to mizzen sail etc.	202.37		
Telegrams 3.20 Chandlery 244.42 42.38 9.90 9.20 Stores 207.10	516.20		

Towing out to channel	50.00		
Pilotage in 28.00 Out 140.00 Georgetown	168.00		
Towage in 35.00 Out 143.55 Georgetown	178.55		
Stores 53.47 Chandlery 20.55 Blacksmith 22.72	96.74		
Exchange on draft Georgetown	3.39		
Cash to crew at Georgetown	62.95		
Caulkers 48 hrs. @ .40 19.20 Fish 2.25	21.45		
Ship's laundry 3.50 Water 5.00 Gratuity to stevedores 5.00	13.50		
New peak halyards 7.00 2 ex. rings 2.88	9.88		
Balance of crew's wages on trip	328.07		Capt. Statement Balto.
Captain's wages 9/1/31 to 11/1/31 2 mos. @ 125.00	250.00		Capt. Statement Balto.
Marketing in port 15 days	22.32		Capt. Statement Balto.
Ship's laundry 11.49 Coal buckets and shovel 1.70	13.19		Capt. Statement Balto.
4 deck brooms 1.40 Cabin broom .50	1.90		Capt. Statement Balto.
Cook's wages in port 10/16 to 10/28	22.00		Capt. Statement Balto.
Rope 22.80 Provisions bought by master 17.90 27.28	67.98		Capt. Statement Balto.
Help lifting limbers, cleaning bilges, putting out anchors and chains, and replacing a/c survey	Capt. Balto. 23.25		
Master's expense in port	Capt. Balto. 2.10		
10 days wharfage on 105,916 ft. lumber	21.18		
Piling wet lumber	5.00		
Towing Sandy Point to Atlantic Wharf	75.00		
Commission	125.92	2,791.30	
Amount due vessel		1,527.32	

1/90 = 16.97

89/90	C. C. Paul & Co.	1,510.35	
1/90	C. Howard Paul Credit to a/c	16.97	1,527.32

To owners 12/31/31

Trip #59 February 29, 1932 Capt. Robert O. Jones

Hampton Roads, Va., to St. George, Bermuda Coal 1,050 tons @ 2.75 ton	2,887.50	
Freight on boiler as agreed	262.50	
Cash from Darrell & Meyer a/c shoring boiler	7.00	
Georgetown, S.C., to Baltimore Lumber 603,381 ft. lump sum	2,400.00	
Refund of gas tax	7.00	
From C. L. Ford exch. on draft	.65	5,564.65

Overhaul sextant etc. Smola	6.10
1 ton nut coal 4.25 Block, fall, etc. 5.80	20.05

Trip #59 (cont.)

Item	Amount	Statement
White and green paint Linseed oil	21.73	
Phone calls and telegrams 5.85 .36	6.21	
1 hatch cover Marshall & Godfrey	16.50	
Towing B/B* to Booz Shipyard to Redman & Vane	30.00	
40 gals. copper paint Captain's Ship Chandlery Co.	88.20	
Hauling, painting, etc.	490.00	
Towing Union Shipbldg. Co. to Seven Foot Knoll	40.00	
Ice 2.10 Marketing 9.44	11.54	Statement—Hoffman N. News
Towage 38.00 Running lines, etc. 2.50	40.50	Statement—Hoffman N. News
Trim coal @ .14 a ton 147.00 Water 2.14	149.14	Statement—Hoffman N. News
British bill of health 4.75 Clearing 2.50	7.25	Statement—Hoffman N. News
Pilotage Newport News to sea	57.20	Statement—Hoffman N. News
Agency fee A. R. Hoffman	15.00	Statement—Hoffman N. News
Light dues Pilotage Cablegram, Provisions, Repair rudder, etc.	148.30	Darrell & Meyer
Discharging coal @ .50 a ton	525.00	Darrell & Meyer
Towing sea to St. George to sea	250.00	Darrell & Meyer
Commission Coal and boiler	157.50	
Launch hire 10.00 Capt. expense at Newport News 1.25	11.25	Capt. Statement—Georgetown
Meat 4.20 Fish 2.25 Bermuda	6.45	Capt. Statement—Georgetown
Master's expense and gratuity Bermuda	6.50	Capt. Statement—Georgetown
Entry tonnage 16.39 Tax and quarantine 10.00 Georgetown	26.39	Capt. Statement—Georgetown
Pilotage in 28.00 Out 140.00 Georgetown	168.00	Capt. Statement—Georgetown
Towage in 28.00 Out 152.56	177.56	Capt. Statement—Georgetown
Kerosene 6.60 Ice 7.00 Pig 13.68	27.28	Capt. Statement—Georgetown
Eggs 4.37 Sausage 1.40 Chickens 2.80	8.57	Capt. Statement—Georgetown
Fish 2.25 Sweet potatoes .50 Gratuity 5.00	7.75	Capt. Statement—Georgetown
Laundry 4.75 Master's exp. to Charleston, rigging wire, etc. 6.00	10.75	Capt. Statement—Georgetown
Phone calls 2.00 a/c sailors Apples 2.00 Rolled oats .60	4.60	Capt. Statement Georgetown
Rigging wire Turnbuckles, etc. Richardson	93.80	Capt. Statement Georgetown
Machinery Iron work Gasoline	121.28	Capt. Statement Georgetown
Shipping 2 sailors and transportation from Charleston to Georgetown	16.95	Capt. Statement Georgetown
Express money order a/c same	.12	Capt. Statement Georgetown
Oak and pine lumber Rankin & Tyson	11.40	Capt. Statement Georgetown
Carpenter work a/c new pin rail, trestle trees, graving pieces	54.00	Capt. Statement Georgetown
Mate paid off in Georgetown	140.00	Capt. Statement Georgetown
Sailor paid off in Georgetown	72.34	Capt. Statement Georgetown
2 sailors paid off in Newport News	21.53	Capt. Statement Georgetown
Cash to boy help cooking cook sick	2.00	Capt. Statement Georgetown

*B/B—Back Basin was a lumber-unloading site in Baltimore.

Stores 82.90 Chandlery 15.95 Exch. draft .65	Ford	99.50	
Iron Wire rope Fittings etc.	Ford	33.03	
Cost of money orders .20 .44 .88 .37 .18		2.07	
Towing channel to Pier 6		70.00	
Annual freight insurance Boston		210.00	
2 tons ice 5.00 5.00		10.00	
Stores 224.54 Chandlery 158.12 Gas 25.38 Oil 9.30		417.34	
Special survey #3 Report 3819		116.00	
Commission Lumber		120.00	
Crew's wages at Balto. to 2/2/32		606.33	
Capt's. wages 11/1/31 to 2/29/32 4 mos. @ 125.00		500.00	
Cook's wages 2/2/32 to 2/22/32		30.00	
Ship's laundry 8.00 Marketing 20 days 17.75		25.75	
Help cleaning up a/c survey, making and placing 2 mast coats		4.50	
Capt. expense to hospital a/c paying man and expense at Baltimore		1.20	5,314.46
Amount due vessel			250.19

End Policy 2/21/31—2/21/32

Trip #60 July 31, 1932 Capt. Robert O. Jones

In hand from previous trip			250.19
Newport News, Va., to St. George, Bermuda Coal 996 tons @ 2.75		2,739.00	
Georgetown to Baltimore Lumber 643,745 ft. Lump sum		2,400.00	
From L. Ford a/c error in bill		1.20	
Refund on gas tax		6.80	5,147.00
			5,397.19
Marketing 23.96 18.90 Telephone and telegraph 4.63 2.82 1.80		52.11	
1 hatch cover 16.50 Canvas, etc. 20.75 3.40		40.65	
Shipping fee 8.90 Cost of money order .20		9.10	
Tow Pier 6 to off Curtis Bay		25.00	
Repair gas line and renew gasket in water line	Statement—A. R. Hoffman	11.12	
Towage 36.00 Running lines 2.50 Water 1.80	Statement—A. R. Hoffman	40.30	
Trimming coal 996 tons @ .14 per ton	Statement—A. R. Hoffman	139.44	
Custom's clearance 2.50 Freight mast hoops .50	Statement—A. R. Hoffman	3.00	
Shipping sailor at Newport News	Statement—A. R. Hoffman	3.00	
Pilotage Newport News to sea 16′11″ @ .3.30	Statement—A. R. Hoffman	55.83	
Customs, brokerage and attendance fee	Statement—A. R. Hoffman	15.00	
Launch hire a/c meeting sailor from Balto.		6.00	
Launch assisting through Newport News Channel		5.00	

Trip #60 (cont.)

Item	Source	Amount	Total
Hardware 1.50 Capt's. expense at Bermuda 7.25 1.75	Capt. Statement Bermuda	10.50	
Fish Bermuda 1.80 Gloves from slops, 1.25, given crew manning pumps in sinking condition		3.05	
Gratuity to launch-transport gear from 4msch. *Sally Wren*		5.00	
Light dues Pilotage Cablegram Provisions Boat hire	Darrell & Meyer	115.11	
Towing sea to St. George to sea		250.00	
Disch. coal 996 tons @ .50 per ton		498.00	
Commission coal		136.95	
Pilotage in and out Georgetown 28.00 140.00	C. L. Ford	168.00	
Towage in 35.00 Out 163.49 Georgetown		198.49	
Chandlery 57.45 Stores 88.89 Ford		146.34	
Exp. a/c sending cash to C. L. Ford		.30	
Entry tonnage tax etc. Georgetown	Capt. Statement	26.89	
Cash 2 sailors paid off Georgetown		116.80	
Carpenter work, repairs Georgetown		92.10	
Gas and oil 13.50 Linoleum Georgetown		21.50	
Lumber 4.41 Water 5.00 Rankin & Tyson		9.41	
Blacksmith and machine works Ainsworth		49.10	
Spruce stick for gaff		10.00	
Painting outside and scraping sides and masts 14½ days @ 1.00	Capt. Statement Georgetown	14.50	
Ship's laundry 3.00 Gratuity to stevedores 4.00		7.00	
Exp. to Charleston Immigration 2 phone calls		4.60	
Eggs 2.10 Fish 3.10 bought by cook		5.20	
Telegram from Georgetown		.60	
Tow Channel to Pier 6		70.00	
Fee and expense a/c load line survey		28.25	
Addtl. premium Liability insurance		7.93	
Stores 224.30 Chandlery 238.36 Vane Bros.		462.66	
Gas 21.25 Oil 4.80 Vane Bros.		26.05	
Liability insurance Law & McKim		72.80	
Crew's wages on trip	Capt. Stmt. Balto.	626.46	
Capt's. wages 3/1 to 6/30/32 4 mos. @ 125.00		500.00	
Cook's wages in port to 7/19/32		35.00	
Ship's laundry on arrival		13.91	
Marketing 22.00 Commission on lumber 120.00		142.00	4,280.05
Due vessel			1,117.14
Tow Jenkins Wharf to Redman & Vane		15.00	
Stick from Rankin & Tyson a/c rudder stock	Capt. Stmt.	40.00	
Help getting stick off deck load		3.00	
Transfer log Gills to Redman & Vane		20.00	
Mate at shipyard helping carpenters and cleaning bilges 26 days @ 1.50		39.00	
Ice in port 2 mos. 10 days		6.00	
Teaspoons, dishes, and glasses		1.40	

Towels 1.00 Charging batteries 1.50	Capt. Statement Georgetown	2.50	
Ship's laundry July 3.82 Locks .50		4.32	
Marketing in port		60.65	
Capt's. wages for July		125.00	
½ ton nut coal 7.65 Log rotator 6.00		13.65	
Manila rope 18.20 Ice 5.00		23.20	
Pipe and ells 23.47 8.23 Hauling iron rods 1.00		32.70	
Loane repairs engine and pump		32.00	
1 piece oak Chesapeake Marine Railway		5.78	
15 gals. raw linseed oil		6.35	
Delivering same		1.00	
Excise tax .04 .07 .03		.14	
Repairs 34.03 7.20 Redman & Vane		41.23	
3 gals. copper paint		6.28	
313 lbs. 1¼ bolt iron @ .10		31.30	
Gasoline 9.30 Chandlery 85.65		94.95	
Marketing Captain 7/20/32–11/19/32		133.45	
Greasing masts, painting mast heads, and scrubbing outside vessel		7.50	
Launch Mr. Sylvester of Darrell & Meyer–Bermuda		.90	
2 bed sheets for cabin		1.50	748.80
			368.34
Refund gas tax		2.40	
1 compass sold to 4msch. *G. A. Kohler* 11/16/32		12.00	14.40
In hand			382.74

Trip #61	February 9, 1933	Capt. Robert O. Jones

In hand from previous trip		382.74
Wilmington, N.C., to New York Lumber lump sum	2,000.00	
Refund gas tax	6.00	2,006.00
		2,388.74

Southern Meat Market		43.17
1½ ton coal 19.88 Chronometer bill 4.90		24.78
Excise tax .06 .10 Telegraph and telephone 4.39 Ice 5.00		9.55
Tow R/V to off seawall		20.00
Vane Bros various bills		
Gas and oil 30.86 11/11/32 Stores 3.80 6/4/32	Vane Bros. $503.21	34.66
Chandlery 10.52 7/22/32 Stores 15.85 7/27/32		26.37
Stores and chandlery August 1932		23.61
Chandlery 14.85 9/7/32 Stores 18.12 10/14/32		32.97
Stores and chandlery September 1932		35.50

Trip #61 (cont.)

Item	Statement	Amount	Total
Stores and chandlery October 18, 1932		10.28	
Stores 206.56 Chandlery 133.26 Trip		339.82	
Tow Wilmington to Southport on a/c		25.00	
Balance tow Wilmington	Captain's Statement—New York	50.00	
Taxi fare at Balto. getting sailor	Captain's Statement—New York	.75	
Medical aid and supplies a/c Captain	Captain's Statement—New York	7.50	
Vessel taking master ashore at Charleston	Captain's Statement—New York	5.00	
Harbor master Wilmington	Captain's Statement—New York	4.00	
Pilotage in 25.00 Out 61.00 Wilmington	Captain's Statement—New York	86.00	
Coal and carpenter work 8.00 5.40 Wilmington	Captain's Statement—New York	13.40	
Docking 15.00 Stores 42.52 Chandlery 8.10	Captain's Statement—New York	65.62	
Phone call 1.55 Taking man to hospital 3.00 Rope 3.00	Captain's Statement—New York	7.55	
Machinist tank and new sprocket chain	Captain's Statement—New York	20.80	
2 sailors paid off Wilmington 44.00 33.00	Captain's Statement—New York	77.00	
Crew's wages at New York 1/14/33	Captain's Statement—New York	380.00	
Capt's. wages 11/16/32–1/15/33 @125.00	Captain's Statement—New York	250.00	
Cook's wages 1/15–2/1/32 17 days @ 1.00	Captain's Statement—New York	17.00	
Mate's wages 1/15–2/1/32 17 days @ 1.00	Captain's Statement—New York	17.00	
Fresh water 5.00 2 men undocking 2.00	Captain's Statement—New York	7.00	
Laundry bloodstained a/c captain	Captain's Statement—New York	3.50	
Marketing in port	Captain's Statement—New York	24.80	
Captain's wages in port 17 days @ 75.00	Captain's Statement—New York	42.50	
Yard watchmen Brooklyn 2.00 Hoboken 2.00	Captain's Statement—New York	4.00	
Master's expense 10.00 Laundry 5.39	Captain's Statement—New York	15.39	
Coal 17.50 Radio battery 7.45 Chg. batteries 2.00	Captain's Statement—New York	26.95	
Meats 30.90 Vegetables and ice 16.95 Gas 6.50 Kerosene 7.50	Captain's Statement—New York	61.85	
Towage Sandy Hook to 20th Street Brooklyn	Gilmartin Statmt.	85.00	
Receipt book	Gilmartin Statmt.	.15	
½ commission Gilmartin	Gilmartin Statmt.	50.00	
½ commission C. C. Paul & Co.		50.00	
Canvas, sail, twine, and needles		37.26	
Telegraph and telephone calls		11.38	2,047.11
Amount in hand			341.63

End of Policy
E 20513
O 120168
Exp. 2/21/33

Trip #62 May 5, 1933 Capt. Robert O. Jones

In hand from last trip		341.63	
Wilmington, N.C., to New York Lumber lump sum		2,000.00	
Slops from crew	33.15		
Deduction on crew wages a/c vessel arriving prior to 2/20/33 per agreement with captain	24.00	57.15	
		2,398.78	
Shipping crew Harris	10.00		Gilmartin
Tow 12th Street, Hoboken to anchor Red Hook and water	35.00		Gilmartin
Tow Red Hook to Narrows	20.00		
Marketing New York February 2–3–4	3.80		Capt. Statement at N.Y. See next statement on trip for balance of Captain's items
Pilotage in 15.00 Out 61.00 Wilmington	76.00		Capt. Statement at N.Y.
Towage in and out Stone Wilmington	150.00		Capt. Statement at N.Y.
Harbor master's fee Wilmington	4.00		Capt. Statement at N.Y.
Marketing and sea stores Wilmington	63.14		Capt. Statement at N.Y.
Paint and chandlery Wilmington	82.35		Capt. Statement at N.Y.
Laundry 4.22 Water 5.00	9.22		Capt. Statement at N.Y.
New jaw fore gaff and lumber	18.18		Capt. Statement at N.Y.
Rethreading pipe and unions Wash deck lines	2.85		Capt. Statement at N.Y.
Chg. batteries 1.50 Captain's expense Wilmington	4.50		Capt. Statement at N.Y.
Crew wages at New York to 4/6/33	506.00		Capt. Statement at N.Y.
Captain's wages 2/2 to 4/6/33 @ 125.00 mo.—2 mos. 5 days	270.75		Capt. Statement at N.Y.
Watchman 20th Street Brooklyn	3.00		Capt. Statement at N.Y.
Watchman Church E. Gates 16 nights @ .75	12.00		Capt. Statement at N.Y.
Help shifting to Church E. Gates	2.00		Capt. Statement at N.Y.
Cook in port 24 days lump sum	15.00		Capt. Statement at N.Y.
Master's wages in port 4/7 to 4/30/33 inclus. 24 days @ 75.00 mo.	60.00		Capt. Statement at N.Y.
Marketing in port 24 days	29.65		Capt. Statement at N.Y.
Master's exp. in port 24 days	12.50		Capt. Statement at N.Y.
Tow Sandy Hook to Red Hook	60.00		Gilmartin
Tow Red Hook to Nelson's Dock 20th Street Brooklyn	25.00		Gilmartin
Noting protest 1.00 Telegram .54	1.54		Gilmartin
½ commission Gilmartin	50.00		Gilmartin
½ commission C. C. Paul & Co.	50.00		
Stores 88.20 Chandlery 166.44 Slops 33.15 Swan	287.79		
Taulane New mizzen on a/c	110.00		
Ins. advances and bills Wilmington to New York	24.00	1,998.27	
Amount in hand		400.51	

Trip #63 July 31, 1933 Capt. Robert O. Jones

In hand from last trip		400.51	
Georgetown, S.C., to New York, Stamford, Bridgeport, & New Haven, Conn.			
792,486 ft @ 3.25 M		2,575.58	
Refund Liab. insur. Law & McKim	22.30 4.21		
Refund Boston Ins. Co. Annual Freight	23.62		
Refund Boston Ins. Co. Annual Freight	31.50	55.12	
		3,057.72	
1 ton nut coal 11.75 Laundry 4.80	16.55		Capt. Statement filed in last trip
Chg. batteries 1.50 1 ton ice 6.50	8.00		
Fresh meats 16.92 Codfish 1.80 2 kits mackerel 3.50	22.22		
5 doz eggs 1.05 Peaches 1.20 Jam 1.80	4.05		
Catsup .60 Brooms 2.70 Water buckets .75	4.05		
½ bus fare Balto. to N.Y. to mate a/c worked for stevedore on ship last week—no pay	2.75		
Shipping crew New York	10.00		Gilmartin 5/4/33
Tow Church E. Gates to Narrows and water	70.00		
Excise tax .10 .09 .06 Telephone and telegraph 1.26	1.51		
Liability insurance Law. & McKim	72.80		
Pilotage in and out 28.00 115.00 Georgetown	143.00		Capt's. statement at New York
Towage in and out Georgetown	233.12		
Meat 23.08 Stores and supplies 35.57	58.65		
Carpenter work Fashion piece, etc.	18.20		
Caulking 4.55 Blacksmith 27.66	32.21		
3 chairs 4.05 Gas and charge batteries 7.28	11.33		
Medicine 1.35 Ice 8.00 Potatoes 1.75 Eggs 3.00	14.10		
Chickens 2.18 Cloth 2.80 Laundry 2.00	6.98		
Gratuity stevedores 7.00 Interest on advances 2.11	9.11		
Watchman N.Y. 13 nights 6.50 Ice 5.00 Chg. battery .75	12.25		
Marketing 6/15–7/19 Leaving New Haven	58.20		
Capt's. expense incl. long distance calls, R.R. fare, etc. a/c ashore and making arrangements	23.40		
Crew's wages 4 sailors 5/1–6/15 @ 30.00	180.00		
Crew's wages mate 4/29–6/15 @ 60.00	96.00		
Crew's wages cook 4/27–6/15 @ 60.00	100.00		
Wages cook in port 6/16–7/17 32 days	32.00		
Wages mate in port 6/23–7/17 25 days	25.00		
3 of crew towing Bridgeport to New York D. D., cleaning hold, washing, painting, etc.	6.00		
Capt's. wages May June July	375.00		
Excise tax .06 .03 .04 Phone calls .63	.76		

Item		Amount	Total
Stores 117.16 Chandlery 106.72 Swan		223.88	
Insurance bills Georgetown to New York		25.00	
Tow sea to Nelson's Dock Brooklyn	Gilmartin	85.00	
Tow Nelson's Dock to Red Hook	Gilmartin	10.00	
Tow Red Hook to Stamford Lmbr. Co.	Gilmartin	115.00	
½ commission Gilmartin		64.39	
½ commission C. C. Paul & Co.		64.39	2,234.90
Amount in hand			822.82

Trip #64 October 23, 1933 Capt. Robert O. Jones

In hand from last statement		822.82	
Georgetown, S.C., to New York Lumber			
Lump sum freight	2,300.00		
Cash from Captain a/c personal telegram	.75	2,300.75	
Laundry 6.35 Marketing 6.19	12.54		Capt. stmt. at N.Y. Filed in trip #63
Deponte Bros. Stores New Haven	90.65		Capt. stmt. at N.Y. Filed in trip #63
Oil can .40 Cups .40 Flashlight batteries .30	110.00		Capt. stmt. at N.Y. Filed in trip #63
Crew knives .10 Fresh meat 12.00 Ice 7.00	19.10		Capt. stmt. at N.Y. Filed in trip #63
Articles and signing on crew	10.00		Capt. stmt. at N.Y. Filed in trip #63
Part cost of towing New Haven to N.Y. D.D. Bridgeport Tow line to stand balance of 56.00	14.00		Capt. stmt. at N.Y. Filed in trip #63
45 gals. brown copper paint Balto. Copper Pt.	86.24		
Washing off, Cleaning bottom, Painting 1 coat up to 13′ mark, not includ. docking, towage, and pilotage	100.00		
Scorching and caulking hull, chg. battery, and water	54.51		
Phone call	3.10		
Towing Tebo's D. D. to West Bank	40.00		
Tow in 35.00 Out 134.77 Georgetown	169.77		Capt's. Statement at N.Y.
Pilotage in 28.00 Out 115.00 Georgetown	143.00		Capt's. Statement at N.Y.
Stores in port Ford Georgetown	58.85		Capt's. Statement at N.Y.
Meat and sea stores and supplies Georgetown A C L	35.01		Capt's. Statement at N.Y.
Lumber Rankin & Tyson	7.78		Capt's. Statement at N.Y.
Blacksmith bill Ainsworth	26.07		Capt's. Statement at N.Y.
Engine oil and charging batteries	6.00		Capt's. Statement at N.Y.
Gas oil 4.36 1½ ton coal 14.50 Ice 10.00	28.86		Capt's. Statement at N.Y.
Carpenter work on vessel 72 hrs. @ .35	25.20		Capt's. Statement at N.Y.
Caulking on vessel 64 hours @ .35	22.40		Capt's. Statement at N.Y.
12 doz eggs 2.40 Gratuity stevedores and putting sails ashore 3.00	5.40		Capt's. Statement at N.Y.
Wages crew trip	511.39		Capt's. Statement at N.Y.
Capt's. wages August and September 2 mos.	250.00		Capt's. Statement at N.Y.
Marketing in port includ. feeding 2 sailors from Georgetown with no charge for shifting vessel	32.30		Capt's. Statement at N.Y.

Trip #64 (cont.)

Cook's wages in port	15.00		
Watchman 21 days	9.50		
Captain's expense, etc.	10.00		
Capt's. wages in port 10/1–10/12/33 @ 60.00 per mo	24.00		
Excise tax .02 .12 .04 Telegraph and telephone 2.02	2.20		
Extra stores C. L. Ford	16.13		
Phone calls to Bridgeport .90 Perth Amboy .25	1.15		Gilmartin & Co. Stmt. 10/16/33
Phone call to Balto.	1.65		
Tow sea to Newtown Creek	85.00		
½ commission Gilmartin	57.50		
½ commission C. C. Paul & Co.	57.50		
Redman & Vane on a/c Inv. 7/29/32	249.16		
Wood Towing Corp. Sewalls Point to Thimble Shoal a/c storm 9/17/33	40.00		
Taulane balance inv. 10/21/31 for new mizzen sail	110.00		
American Bureau Survey fee and exp. a/c grounding coming from Stamford, Conn.	15.20		
Survey a/c annual load line inspection	15.00		
Stores 93.02 Chandlery 95.51 New hawser 114.26	302.79	2,765.05	
Amount in hand		358.52	

Trip #65 — December 8, 1933 — Capt. Robt. O. Jones

In hand from last statement	358.52		
Georgetown, S.C., to New York Lumber lump sum frt.	2,300.00		
Slops from crew	10.20	2,310.20	
		2,668.72	
Laundry under N.R.A.	8.86		Capt. Stat. Last Trip
Ice for sea 7.35 Meat 12.84 Chg. batteries 1.50	21.69		
Shipping crew	10.00		Gilmartin Stat. 10/16/33
Tow Newtown Creek to West Bank and water	50.00		
Telegraph and telephone 1.70 Excise tax .14 .04	1.88		
Pilotage in 28.00 Out 115.00 Georgetown	143.00		Capt. Statement
Towage in 35.00 Out 135.35 Water 3.00 Georgetown	173.00		
Gratuity Stevedores	3.00		
Fore and aft and 4 up and down fenders @ .50	5.00		
Charging 2 batteries @ .75	1.50		
12 doz. fresh eggs @ .25	3.00		
2 chickens 8 lbs. @ .15	1.20		
Phone calls to Charleston	2.25		
Boric acid .25 Adhesive tape .35	.60		
4 small Congoleum rugs for cabin	1.00		

Pans, Coffee pot, and few dishes	2.30		New York 12/4/33
Ice 6.00 Coal 9.50	15.50		
Groceries, deck supplies, wash deck hose	42.24		
Fresh meat for sea use	22.46		
Meat a/c delay in sailing 20 lbs. @ .18	3.60		
Work on wildcat and various work Ainsworth	55.81		
Supplies and machine work	4.25		
Caulk waterways and poop deck 12 hours @ .40	4.80		
Crew wages at New York	310.04		
Captain's wages 10/12–11/30/33 Inclus.	199.88		
Marketing at New York, extra men on sails	23.30		
Night watchman	12.00		
Master's expense in port—New York	10.00		
Exp. in taxi a/c bringing rope for sail aboard	1.45		
Telegrams 1.00 .72 .82 Noting protest 1.00	3.54		Gilmartin
Tow to mouth of Newtown Creek	95.00		
Commission 1⅔% to Gilmartin	38.33		
Commission 3⅓% to C. C. Paul & Co.	76.67		
Stores 164.34 Chandlery 170.01 Stores 10.20	344.55	1,692.05	
In hand		976.67	

Trip #66	February 19, 1934	Capt. Robt. O. Jones

In hand from previous trip	976.67		
Georgetown, S.C., to New York 522,093′ Lumber lump sum freight	2,300.00		
Refund gasoline tax	3.30		
Cash from J. H. Bate Co. a/c Newtown Creek towages	75.00	2,378.30	
Excise tax .02 Telegraph and telephone 3.09	3.11		
1 ton coal 11.50 Gasoline 15.95	27.45		Capts. statement filed in previous trip
Kerosene 3.60 Laundry 4.39 Fresh meat 23.07	31.06		
Potatoes and vegetables 13.95 Ice 5.40	19.35		
Chg. radio batteries 1.00 2 new B batteries 4.50	5.50		
Flashlight 2.25 1—2 bell .69	2.94		
Cook's wages in port—flat rate while discharging	15.00		
Shipping crew at New York	10.00		Gilmartin
Tow to West Bank and water	50.00		
Telephone and telegraph 2.21 1.26 Redman & Vane Shpyd.	203.47		
Affidavit a/c gas tax .25 Excise tax .06	.31		
Tow in 35.00 Out 130.52 Georgetown	165.52		
Pilotage in 28.00 Out 115.00 Georgetown	143.00		
Water 3.00 Gratuity to stevedores 4.00	7.00		

Trip #66 (cont.)

Item	Amount	Total	
Fresh meat 24.84 Stores and supplies 26.60	51.44		Capt. Statement at New York
Turkey for Christmas 3.45 Coal 9.50 Ice 6.00	18.95		Capt. Statement at New York
Blacksmith and machine shop	23.10		Capt. Statement at New York
Oak for after bitt starboard side and installing—J.D. Watts G'town	33.50		Capt. Statement at New York
Chg. 2 radio batteries	1.50		Capt. Statement at New York
30 fathom 5″ mooring line	8.00		Capt. Statement at New York
Gas 9.15 Beef 9.03 F'light batt. .75 Spark coil 3.25	22.18		Capt. Statement at New York
Launch hire at Red Hook anchored	6.00		Capt. Statement at New York
Crew wages—trip to 1/18/34	379.60		Capt. Statement at New York
Cook's wages in port 1/19/ to 2/7/34	20.00		Capt. Statement at New York
Capt's. wages Dec. 1933 and Jan. 1934	250.00		Capt. Statement at New York
Help docking after crew paid off	3.00		Capt. Statement at New York
Marketing in port 33.95 Capt. expenses 10.00	43.95		Capt. Statement at New York
Night watchman per receipt	10.00		
Protest 1.00 Telegrams .35 1.00 .30	2.65		Gilmartin
Towage in 100.00 Creek towage 75.00	175.00		Gilmartin
Commission 1⅔% to Gilmartin	38.33		Gilmartin
Commission 3⅓% to C. C. Paul & Co.	76.67		
Ins. bills and adv. 21.53	21.53		
Stores 95.07 Chandlery 140.01 Swan	235.08	2,104.19	
Amount in hand		1,250.78	

End Policy
E 2052
C 139933 Exp. 2/21/34

Trip #67 April 30, 1934 Capt. Robt. O. Jones

Item	Amount	Total	
In hand from last trip		1,250.78	
Georgetown, S.C., to New York Lumber lump sum freight	2,300.00		
Refund gas tax New York	3.30	2,303.30	
		3,554.08	
Dishes, etc. for cabin 1.65 Gas 15.95 sea	17.60		Capt. Stmt.
Ship's laundry 4.36 Coal 14.25	18.61		Capt. Stmt.
Vegetables 16.95 Meat 25.16 Ice 6.10 Chg. batt. 1.00	49.21		Capt. Stmt.
Shipping crew	12.00		Gilmartin
Tow to lightship and filling water	100.00		Gilmartin
Redman & Vane S. B. Co. on a/c	150.00		
Contact plunger, spring, etc. Loane	2.40		
Excise tax .06 .04 Telephone and telegraph 1.26	1.36		

Item	Amount	Total	Account
Liability insurance—Law & McKim	72.80		
Beef 12.80 1 bag potatoes 3.00 Vegetables 1.70	17.50		Capts. Statement New York
Pilotage in 28.00 Out 115.00 Georgetown	143.00		
Towage in 25.00 Out 130.29	155.29		
Fresh water 3.00 Gratuity—stevedores 2.00	5.00		
Paint 39.75 Chandlery 17.72 Stores 19.76 Ford	77.23		
Meats, Butter, etc. A. C. Lmbr. Co.	27.54		
Eggs 4.40 Sausage 3.60 Shad 2.25 Chg. batts. 1.50	11.75		
Paid 2 sailors from Georgetown 5.00 each to go to G'town to save shipping back	10.00		
Paid sailor off a/c immigration officer	23.00		
1½ ton egg coal 15.00 Ice 6.00	21.00		
Blacksmith and machine bill Ainsworth	66.20		
Caulking sides etc. at Georgetown	19.20		
Call to Charleston, sailor and tug	2.40		
Miscellaneous items Lynnhaven Bay	6.96		
Crew wages on trip	432.00		
Cook's wages in port ½ pay	10.00		
Capt's. wages Feb. March April	375.00		
Sailors sewing sail 5.00 Brooklyn watchman 10.00	15.00		
Marketing 21.20 Padlock .50 Coffee pot. 85 Capt. exp. 12.00	35.05		
Telegraph and telephone .76 .36 2.25 .72 .49 .30	4.88		Gilmartin 4/23/34
Tow to Red Hook 55.00 to 20th St. Brooklyn 35.00	90.00		
2 hatch tarpaulins 4X waterproof @ 23.00 Martin	46.00		
⅓ commission Gilmartin	38.33		
⅔ commission C. C. Paul & Co.	76.67		
Stores 131.15 Chandlery 178.31 Swan	309.46	2,442.44	
In hand		1,111.64	

Trip #68	July 15, 1934	Capt. Robt. O. Jones

Item	Amount	Total	Account
In hand from last trip		1,111.64	
Port Reading, N.J., to Charleston Coal 1,058.19 tons @ 1.10 gr. ton	1,164.85		
Georgetown, S.C., to New York Lumber lump sum frt.	2,300.00		
Gas refund 3.30 Slops from crew 17.20	20.50	3,485.35	
		4,596.99	
Tow Newtown Creek to Port Reading to West Bank and water	140.00		Gilmartin
Shipping crew	12.00		
Gasoline 14.85 Vegetables 17.30 Meats 30.89	63.04		Capt. Statement
Charge batteries 1.00 Ice 5.40 Laundry 4.90	11.30		
Rethread pipes, etc., for water tank	1.00		

Trip #68 (cont.)

Exp. sending sailor to Port Reading		1.15
Canvas for new foresail C.C. Paul & Co.		147.40
Making new foresail Marshall & Godfrey		166.38
Telegram .44 Excise tax .20		.64
45 gals. copper paint N.J. Paint Wks.		82.60
Repairs Redman & Vane S.B. Co. 150.00 39.46		189.46
Trimming and docking Port Reading	Capt. Statement—Charleston	130.31
Meat at Port Reading after delay		5.25
Phone calls to New York a/c sailor and tug		.75
Paid off sailor a/c illness		7.02
Taxi R.R. station to coal pier a/c sailor		1.00
Docking vessel, coal dock Charleston		15.00
Tow Charleston to Georgetown		140.00
Pilotage in 78.75 Out 30.00 Charleston		108.75
Harbor master 2.00 Ice 2.00		4.00
Flashlight 3.08 Knives, forks, etc. 3.00		6.08
Marketing Meat Vegetables		16.42
Solder Cleaning paste .66 Capt. exp. 1.15		1.81
Pilotage in and out Georgetown		143.00
Towage out Georgetown @ .25 M	Capt. Statement—New York	131.91
Water 3.00 Call to Charleston a/c tug .60		3.60
Lumber 1.00 Carpenter 22.75 Caulking 16.80		40.55
Stores 32.23 Chandlery 65.48 Meat 48.06		145.77
Mach. and blacksmith 54.65 Ice 8.00 Dishes 5.25		67.90
Gratuity stevedores 2.50 Eggs 4.00 Chicken 2.10		8.60
Sailor's wages on trip		280.30
Mate and cook wages on trip		250.00
Capt's. wages May and June		250.00
Night watchman		12.75
Cook's wages in port 6/20–7/4 inclus.		15.00
Sailor 2 days drying out sails		3.00
Marketing in port and at drydock—21 days		33.60
Ice in port 4.50 Capt. exp. in port at D.D. 13.25		17.75
Sailor assisting to Dry Dock 2.00 Laundry 5.70		7.70
Vegetables 15.60 Meat 3.00 etc. 40.89		59.49
Ice for sea 5.40 Eggs .81	Capt. N.Y.	6.21
20 fathom mooring line @ .07 lb.		5.25
Telegram Balto. .36 Georgetown .72	Gilmartin 7/10/34	1.08
Phone call to Balto. 1.00 1.18		2.18
Telegram .33 Rating chronometer 2.00		2.33
Tow Red Hook to mouth of Newtown Creek		40.00
Tow mouth Newtown Creek to Tebo's D. D.		40.00
Tow Tebo's D. D. to West Bank		40.00
Shipping crew		13.00

½ commission Lumber	57.50	
½ commission Coal	29.10	
½ commission Coal	29.14	
½ commission Lumber	57.50	
Stores 114.77 Chandlery 18.50 150.55 Slops 17.20	301.02	3,347.59
In hand		1,249.40

Trip #69 October 15, 1934 Capt. Robt. O. Jones

In hand from last trip		1,249.40
Georgetown, S.C., to New York 537,310′ Lumber Lump sum	2,300.00	
Dunnage from Rankin & Tyson	250.00	
		2,550.00
Slops from crew		6.40
		3,805.80

Drydocking, clean and wash bottom, apply one coat copper paint furnished by owners up to 12′6″ mark exclusive of all towages and pilotages—Tender 7/2/34	242.00	
Other repairs Robins D. D.	129.05	
Telephone and telegraph 9.67 3.28 Excise tax .06 .12	13.13	
Towage in 40.00 Pilotage in 28.00 Out 115.00	183.00	Capt. Statement at Georgetown
Towage out Georgetown	134.33	
Water 3.00 Phone call .60 Lumber 1.02	4.62	
Stores 37.77 Chandlery 32.43 Ford	70.20	
27 lbs. Marlin 6.75 Meat in port and for sea 61.15	67.90	
Ice 6.00 Eggs 2.40 Gas and oil 15.32	23.72	
B-batteries and aerial for radio	5.00	
Charge batteries 1.50 Axe handles .25	1.75	
Ice for sea and port	10.50	
Machine, welding and blacksmith	25.03	
Second hand fire extinguisher 2.00 Door spring .45	2.45	
Loading and hauling timber for jib boom 16.00	16.00	
Jib boom timber, 64 ft., from Rankin & Tyson no chg.		
Making jib boom	82.50	
Hoist, jib boom, bobstay chain, turnbuckle	20.85	
Caulking as directed by captain	4.55	
Gas a/c stick for jib boom	1.10	
Help getting stick for jib boom to hoister	1.20	
Wages, sailor paid off at Georgetown	65.42	
Pd. doctor med. attn. etc. taking man to hospital	12.00	
Phone calls to Charleston	1.20	

Trip #69 (cont.)

Getting sailor from Andrews, S.C.	3.00	Capt. Statement—New York	
Crew's wages, trip, at New York	592.79		
Cook's wages in port	15.00		
Capt's. wages July–Aug.–Sept.	375.00		
Watchman—15 nights	12.00		
Charge batteries 1.50 Marketing 25.80	27.30		
Stevedore, help dry and refurl sails	3.00		
Capt's. expense New York and Port Reading	12.00		
Cook pots, pans, and galley utensils	3.10		
Fresh meats, hams, etc.	46.54		
Ice and help 5.90 Gasoline 17.05	22.95		
Laundry 6.21 Meat etc. 4.34	10.55		
Phone calls	.75		
Telegraph and telephone calls .76 2.60 1.60 1.24 1.00	7.20		
Tow sea to mouth of Newtown Creek	100.00		
Tow Newtown Creek to Port Reading to sea and filling water	140.00		
Shipping fee	12.40		
1/3 commission Gilmartin on 2,550.00 Lumber	42.50		
2/3 commission C. C. Paul	85.00		
Stores 97.99 Chandlery 186.04 Slops 6.40	290.43		2,919.01
			886.79

Trip #70 December 10, 1934 Capt. Robert O. Jones

In hand from last trip	886.79	
Port Reading, N.J., to Charleston, S.C. Coal 1,000 tons @ 1.10 gross ton	1,100.00	
529,000 ft. lumber Georgetown to N.Y. Lump sum	2,300.00	3,400.00
		4,286.79

Addtl. premium Liab. Ins. 2.36 .44		2.80
Excise tax .04 .08 Notary fee .25		.37
Pilotage in 76.50 Out 30.00 Charleston	Charleston	106.50
Harbor master 2.00 one cake ice 1.00		3.00
Marketing Charleston		13.35
Cash and slops to 3 sailors deserted		37.40
Tow sea to city anchorage 661 tons @ .12		79.32
Docking vessel Johnson's Wharf		15.00
Tow Charleston to Georgetown		140.00
Sailor cleaning up while towing to Georgetown		5.00
Docking in and out Port Reading		35.00
Trimming coal 1,000 tons @ .09		90.00
2 men at Georgetown, clean hold, no crew		1.00

Laundry a/c changing crew	Capt's. Statement New York	2.75		
Carpenter work around vessel		33.85		
Charge batteries $1.50 Gratuity stevedores 3.00		4.50		
Machine and blacksmith Ainsworth		19.30		
Special bolts .75 Kerosene 4.13		4.88		
Water 3.00 Ice 9.00 Lumber for pumphouse 10.52		22.52		
Stores 50.05 Supplies 35.76 Ford		85.81		
Tow out of Georgetown @ 25 M		132.25		
Pilotage in 28.00 Out 115.00 Georgetown		143.00		
Sailor sick—paid off 4 days @ 35.00 mo.		4.68		
3 men from Wilmington and 15.00 Transportation—1 deserted 10.00		25.00		
1 man from Charleston 7.00 Transp. 5.00 and a/c tug on way		12.00		
Long distance calls, Wilmington & Charleston, a/c sailor and tug		5.30		
Crew wages on trip		336.57		
Capt's. wages Oct. and Nov.		250.00		
Cook's wages in port 15.00 Capt's. exp. in port 12.00		27.00		
Marketing 23.85 Laundry 4.85 Gasoline 16.50		45.20		
Charge batts. 1.00 Dishes, brush, etc. 1.45		2.45		
Meats 37.46 Vegetables 7.50 Ice for sea 5.40		50.36		
Watchman 12.00 Extra fresh meat 4.00		16.00		
Sailor hurt, paid off		4.00		
Taking sailor to hospital		3.00		
Phone call to insur. company and for another sailor		1.00		
Telegrams .33 .33 Phone calls 1.00	Gilmartin Stmt.	1.66		
Repairing mainsail Martin		80.00	4,286.79	
Tow sea to mouth of Newtown Creek—via Red Hook		100.00		Gilmartin's Statement
Tow mouth of Newtown Creek to Port Reading to sea, water		140.00		
Shipping of 4 men and expense of 1 man to Port Reading		13.08		
½ commission coal Gilmartin		27.50		Ledger
⅓ commission lumber Gilmartin		38.33		1,281.90
⅔ commission lumber C. C. Paul & Co.		76.67		276.60 Chgd. to
½ commission coal C. C. Paul & Co.		27.50		10.00 Capt.
				1,571.50
Stores 198.35 Chandlery 223.87 Slops 27.50		449.72		
Excise tax .04 Telephone and telegraph .63		.67	2,715.29	
In hand			1,571.50	

1/90 = 17.46

89.90	C. C. Paul & Co.	1,554.04	
1/90	C. Howard Paul Credit to a/c	17.46	1,571.50
			x x x x

To owners 12/26/34

Trip #71 February 26, 1935 Capt. Robert O. Jones

Item		Amount	Total
Port Reading, N.J., to Charleston, S.C. Coal			
$904\frac{19}{20}$ tons @ 1.10 a ton		995.50	
Georgetown, S.C., to New York Lumber lump sum		2,300.00	
Slops to crew 27.50 20.74		48.24	
Gas refund 3.30 From Captain a/c telegram		4.06	3,347.80
Telegram .38 Tax on cks. .08 Frt., G'town, storm trysail 2.65		3.11	
Trimming and dock at Port Reading		116.45	
Pilotage in 74.25 Out 30.00 Charleston	Capt. at Charleston	104.25	
Tow sea to city 661 tons @ .12	Capt. at Charleston	79.32	
Docking at Johnson's Dock	Capt. at Charleston	15.00	
Harbor master's fee 2.00 Tow Charleston to G'town 140.00	Capt. at Charleston	142.00	
Tar tape .20 Hammer .75 Chg. battery .75	Capt. at Charleston	1.70	
Pump house lock .25 Captain's expense .60	Capt. at Charleston	.85	
Marketing in port 12/10–12/17/34 inclusive	Capt. at Charleston	14.35	
Pilotage in and out Georgetown	Capt. Statement New York	143.00	
Towage out Georgetown	Capt. Statement New York	136.07	
Water 3.00 Trucking sail .65	Capt. Statement New York	3.65	
Carpenter work fore hatch, etc.	Capt. Statement New York	33.80	
Stores 36.39 Chandlery 11.34 Ford	Capt. Statement New York	47.73	
Machine and blacksmith work	Capt. Statement New York	19.95	
Ice 9.00 Kerosene 4.48 Lumber for coaming 1.50	Capt. Statement New York	14.98	
Gratuity to stevedores	Capt. Statement New York	3.00	
Charge batteries 1.50 Misc., mate and cook 1.05	Capt. Statement New York	2.55	
Wages, sailor deserted at Charleston	Capt. Statement New York	20.81	
Phone call to Charleston a/c sailor and tug	Capt. Statement New York	1.80	
Shipping 5.00 and transp. 6.00 sailor from Ch'lston to G'town special auto	Capt. Statement New York	11.00	
Wages of crew—trip	Capt. Statement New York	344.62	
Watchman—Brooklyn 21 nights	Capt. Statement New York	15.00	
Capt's. wages Dec. '34–Jan. '35	Capt. Statement New York	250.00	
Telegram to Georgetown .91 Pay off receipts .45	Capt. Statement New York	1.36	
Labor getting anchor and chain clear for welding wildcat and replacing	Capt. Statement New York	16.00	
Help shifting vessel twice 7.00 charge battery 1.00	Capt. Statement New York	8.00	
Clean snow and ice and overhauling lines to lay-up berth 1/26 & 1/28	Capt. Statement New York	6.00	
Tug placing vessel in berth	Capt. Statement New York	20.00	
Machinist repair engine. Cross Austin's men. No chg. material	Capt. Statement New York	10.00	
Marketing 1/4/35–2/2/35	Capt. Statement New York	37.40	
Cook's wages in port 1/5–1/31/35	Capt. Statement New York	20.00	

Captain extra a/c snowstorm	15.00		
Gasoline 9.26 Fresh meat 48.14	57.40		
Ice 5.40 Laundry 9.18 Coal 12.75	27.33		
3 sailors on pay 1/31–2/1/35	8.32		
Notary .25 Telegraph and telephone 4.45 Excise tax .04	4.74		
Stores 78.51 Chandlery 160.89 Slops 20.74	260.14		
Telegrams to Balto. .40 .79 .45 and G'town .79	2.43		Gilmartin
Notary protest 1.00 Phone calls 1.65 1.65 2.30 1.95	8.55		Gilmartin
Repairs and welding wildcat—windlass	95.00		Gilmartin
Tax—retail relief—New York	1.90		Gilmartin
Tow sea to Red Hook			Gilmartin
Tow Red Hook to mouth Newtown Creek	205.00		Gilmartin
Tow mouth Newtown Creek to Red Hook and filling water			Gilmartin
Telegram to Georgetown .76 Call to Staten Island .75	1.51		Gilmartin
½ commission Coal Gilmartin	24.86		Gilmartin
⅓ commission Lumber Gilmartin	38.33		Gilmartin
Shipping 5 men 15.00 Expense .60	15.60		
½ commission Coal C. C. Paul & Co.	24.92		
⅔ commission Lumber C. C. Paul & Co.	76.67	2,511.45	
In hand		836.35	

End Policy
E—21841
O—143301
Exp. 2/21/35

Trip #72 April 10, 1935 Capt. Robt. O. Jones

Georgetown, S. C., to New York Lumber	2,300.00	
Refund from Captain—tow out of Georgetown	27.80	
Refund gas tax 3.30 City tax on Todd's bill 1.90	5.20	
Slops from crew	27.02	2,360.02

Tow in Georgetown—2 day's work	Capt. Statement—New York	40.00
Tow out of Georgetown @ .25 M ft.	Capt. Statement—New York	127.80
Pilotage In 28.00 Out 115.00 Georgetown	Capt. Statement—New York	143.00
Phone calls to Charleston .80 Water 3.00	Capt. Statement—New York	3.80
To stevedores 3.00 Charge radio batteries 1.50	Capt. Statement—New York	4.50
1 ton coal 10.00 Caulk top sides 11.20	Capt. Statement—New York	21.20
Carpenter work, starboard hatch, etc.	Capt. Statement—New York	18.70
Kerosene 5.31 Ice 9.00	Capt. Statement—New York	14.31
Stores 47.07 Chandlery 6.10 Ford	Capt. Statement—New York	53.17
Machine and blacksmith work	Capt. Statement—New York	10.75
Crew's wages trip	Capt. Statement—New York	394.46
Captain's wages Feb. and March	Capt. Statement—New York	250.00

Trip #72 (cont.)

Laundry 5.50 Gasoline 22.73	28.23		
Night watchman	12.00		
Marketing 31.20 Repairs to governor 1.50	32.70		
Wages—cook in port	15.00		
Fresh meats 47.25 Ice 5.40	52.65		
Master's exp. 12.00 Coal 8.75 Chg. batteries 1.00	21.75		
Telegrams to Balto. .40 .33 and G'town .79 .79	2.31		Gilmartin
Tow—sea to Red Hook			
Tow—Red Hook to Newtown Creek	190.00		
Tow—mouth of Newtown Creek to West Bank and water			
Shipping 4 men 12.00 and expense .50	12.50		
Commission ⅓ Gilmartin	38.33		
Commission ⅔ C. C. Paul & Co.	76.67		
Notary a/c gas refund	.25		
Liab. insur. Lawford & McKim	72.80		
Stores 119.01 Chandlery 175.21 Slops 27.02 Swan	321.24		
1 storm trysail from C. C. Paul & Co.	65.00	2,023.12	
In hand this trip		336.90	
In hand from last trip		836.35	
In hand		1,173.25	

Trip #73 June 6, 1935 Capt. Robt. O. Jones

Georgetown, S. C., to New York Lumber Lump sum		2,300.00	
Slops from crew 14.41 Gas refund 1.65		16.06	
		2,316.06	
Notary Gas tax .25 Telephone and telegraph 7.35	7.60		
Addtl. Premium Liab. Insur.	9.50		
Stores 111.11 Chandlery 178.13 Slops 14.41	303.65		
Tow in 35.00 Out 100.00 Georgetown	135.00		Capt's. Statement—New York
Pilotage in 28.00 Out 115.00	143.00		
Water 3.00 Stevedores 3.00	6.00		
Labor and material Repairs to windlass	127.65		
Elec. weld and material—windlass	8.00		
Stores 47.92 Chandlery 61.70 Ford	110.37		
Kerosene 4.72 Ice 9.00 Brushes .30 Pliers .35	14.37		
4 chickens 2.00 Phone calls 1.20	3.20		
Making and installing two knees, port side; main hatch coamings, 9 pcs. material for fore and aft & vertical fenders	28.75		
Caulking around windlass and tow bitts, few butts on deck .35 hr.	9.45		
Exp. to Charleston a/c coal cargo	2.25		

Item		Amount	Total
Crew wages on trip		392.41	
Capt's. wages April and May		250.00	
Steam lighter cash from quarantine to Red Hook		15.00	
Help shifting to Forrest Box Co.		2.00	
Watchman marketing in port		37.40	
Dishes and screen door spring		1.30	
Couch covers and window curtains		3.75	
Ice in port for sea 10.00 Laundry 7.60		17.60	
Cook's wages in port		15.00	
Capt's. expense New York and Port Reading		12.00	
Taking lines—coal pier		1.00	
Install and adjust new radio 3.00 Phone .50		3.50	
Telegraph .79 .33 Shipping crew and exp. 13.30	Gilmartin	14.42	
Tow Red Hook to Newtown Creek		65.00	
Tow Long Island City to Port Reading			
Tow to sea and water		145.00	
⅓ commission Gilmartin		38.33	
⅔ commission C. C. Paul & Co.		76.67	1,999.17
In hand			316.89
In hand from last statement			1,173.25
Due vessel			1,490.14

Trip #74 Sept. 17, 1935 Capt. Robt. O. Jones

Item		Amount	Total
Port Reading, N.J., to Charleston, S.C.			
970 tons cwt. @ 1.10 a ton		1,067.50	
Georgetown, S.C., to New York Lumber Lump sum		2,300.00	
Refund tax 6.60 Slops crew 16.39 Telegraph .79		23.78	3,391.28
Trimming, docking and undocking, Port Reading		107.30	
Exp. stores at Port Reading		38.89	
Tow into Charleston, docking and tow Charleston to G'town		204.32	
Pilotage In 76.50 Out 30.00 Charleston		106.50	
Harbor master 2.00 Rigging wire, paint 79.31		81.31	
Marketing 34.70 Ice 1.00 4.00 Laundry 3.50 Charleston		43.20	
Towage out Georgetown 110.00 Water 3.00		113.00	
Pilotage in and out Georgetown 143.00 Kerosene 3.54		146.54	
Stevedores 3.00 Caulking on top of after house 6.40		9.40	
Carp. work graving piece in heel of mizzenmast at deck etc.		23.70	Capt. Statement
Stores and extra stores for sea		130.20	
Mach. and blacksmith work Ainsworth		28.35	
Ice 10.00 Eggs and chickens 8.95 Trucking sail .65		19.60	
Crew's wages 636.38 Capt's. wages June—July—Aug. 375.00		1,011.38	

Trip #74 (cont.)

Item		Amount	Total
Marketing at New York 66.40 Watchman 16.50		82.90	
Ice in port 9.00 Laundry 10.15		19.15	
Help shifting vessel 3.00 Capt. exp. 15.00		18.00	
Cook's wages in port—3 weeks		20.00	
Cigars to inspector		3.25	
Telephone and telegraph .79 .90 .46 .30 ship 5 men 15.00 exp. .45	Gilmartin	17.90	
½ commission coal Gilmartin	Gilmartin	26.67	
⅓ commission lumber Gilmartin	Gilmartin	38.33	
Tow Sandy Hook to Newtown Creek	Gilmartin	100.00	
Tow mouth Newtown Creek to Tebo's D. D.	Gilmartin	40.00	
Tow Tebo's D. D. to West Bank	Gilmartin	50.00	
42 gals N.J. copper paint		80.36	Invoice 8/19/35
Robins Dry Dock, clean and paint 242.00, other exp. 334.14		576.14	Invoice 8/23/35
½ commission coal 26.71, ⅔ commission lumber 76.67		103.38	
Stores 172.10 Chandlery 274.73 Slops 11.24		458.07	
Making and shipping mainsail to Georgetown		153.40	
Canvas #10 and #1 for same		174.44	
Telegrams etc. .58 1.26		1.84	4,027.52
	In debt this trip		636.24
	In hand from last statement		1,490.14
	Due vessel		853.90

Trip #75	December 6, 1935	Capt. Robt. O. Jones

Georgetown, S.C., to New York Lumber Lump sum		2,300.00
Slops to crew 10.73 From Capt. phone call .79		11.52
Pilotage in and out Georgetown	Capt. Statement—New York	143.00
Inward towage, sailed part way in	Capt. Statement—New York	20.00
Outward towage	Capt. Statement—New York	127.12
Water 3.00 Belt lacing .90 Lumber for pin rail 1.54	Capt. Statement—New York	5.44
Gratuity stevedores 2.25 Kerosene 3.51	Capt. Statement—New York	5.76
Stores 82.33 Chandlery 26.64 Ford	Capt. Statement—New York	108.97
Additional meat a/c delay 23.32	Capt. Statement—New York	23.32
Ice 9.00 Machine and blacksmith work 17.75	Capt. Statement—New York	26.75
Material and grinding pump valves	Capt. Statement—New York	6.75
Carpenter work 42 hrs. @ .40	Capt. Statement—New York	16.80
Medicines 1.50 second hand blocks 8.00	Capt. Statement—New York	9.50
25 lbs. sugar 1.50 Phone calls 1.00 3.30	Capt. Statement—New York	5.80

Wages sailor paid off sick		55.96	
Crew's wages trip		731.12	
Capt's. wages Sept.–Oct.–Nov.		375.00	
Marketing Georgetown and Red Hook		27.14	
Cook's wages in port, flat rate		15.00	
Laundry 9.70 Watchman 10.50 Help shifting vessel 9.00		29.20	
Captain's expense in port		12.00	
Boat fare at Red Hook		3.00	
Wm. H. Swan & Sons 7.14 Phone calls 3.54		10.68	
Expense getting crew and aboard		4.00	
Tow Sandy Hook to mouth of Newtown Creek	Gilmartin	125.00	
Tow 20th Street Brooklyn to Red Hook		30.00	
Tow Red Hook to West Bank and water		50.00	
1/3 commission Lumber Gilmartin		38.33	
2/3 commission Lumber C. C. Paul & Co.		76.67	
Phone call and telegram		.63	
Shipping crew Saperstein		40.90	
Stores 222.91 Chandlery 218.66 Slops 10.73		452.30	2,576.14
In debt this trip			264.62
In hand from last trip			853.90
Due vessel			589.28

Trip #76 February 5, 1936 Capt. Robt. O. Jones

Georgetown, S.C., to New York Lumber Lump sum		2,400.00	
Slops to crew		20.39	
Cash from Capt. a/c Swan's bill chgd. last trip—Capts. own item		7.14	
1/2 dunnage (from Rankin & Tyson) last trip on a/c		250.00	2,677.53
Telephone and telegraph		9.85	
Exp. trying to get crew, boat hire, etc.		12.50	
Sailor's assistance getting stores aboard		2.00	
Extra marketing	New York	2.45	
Taxi getting sailors from railroad sta. to McCaswns.		3.55	
Launch, sailors and captain awaiting tug		2.30	
Pilotage in and out Georgetown		143.00	
Tow in Georgetown with extra boat a/c wind		40.00	
Towage out of Georgetown		122.10	
Water 3.00 Gratuity stevedores 3.00 Marketing .45		6.45	
Phone calls to Charleston .60 1.40		2.00	
3 pcs. steel A.C.L. Coop		12.45	
Extra gasoline for standby		10.49	

Trip #76 (cont.)

Item		Amount	Total
1 ton Egg—2 bags blacksmith coal	Georgetown—Capt. Statement	11.20	
Marketing C. L. Ford & Sons		29.92	
6 doz. eggs 2.10 Turkey for Xmas 3.00 Pork 6.72		11.82	
Machine work, welding and blacksmith		66.30	
Putting in foremast pieces, etc.		28.00	
Crew's wages on trip		292.96	
Capt's. wages December and January		250.00	
Watchman at Cross Austin's—22 nights		16.50	
Shoveling snow and shifting		17.25	
Marketing 12/23–1/21/36		47.15	
Cook's wages in port and laying up		25.00	
Laundry 8.04 Taxi fare 3.00		11.04	
Exp. Captain arranging tie-up berth		14.25	
Telegrams to Baltimore and Georgetown		1.39	
Ice for sea 5.40 Gas 16.83 Cigars American Bureau Survey 2.30		24.53	
Sailor's taxi 4.00 Meats 14.55 2 tons Nut coal 16.50		35.05	
Telegraph and phone calls .79 .40 1.00	Gilmartin	2.19	
Shipping mate		4.00	
Survey fee and exp. Annual Load Line Ins.		25.20	2,677.53
Tow sea to Red Hook	Gilmartin 1/27/36	85.00	
Tow Red Hook to mouth of Newtown Creek		40.00	
Shifting at Cross Austin's to lay-up berth awaiting orders		20.00	
Tow mouth of Newtown Creek to West Bank and filling water		70.00	
⅓ commission Lumber 2,300.00 Gilmartin		38.33	
Balance commission Lumber C. C. Paul & Co.		81.67	
Commission demurrage		12.50	
Slops 20.39 Stores 270.39 Chandlery 260.82 Swan		551.60	
Shipping crew Saperstein		41.55	2,223.54
In hand this trip			453.99
From previous trip			589.28
Due vessel			1,043.27

Trip #77 April 22, 1936 Capt. Robt. O. Jones

Item	Amount	Total
Georgetown, S.C., to New York Lumber Lump sum	2,350.00	
Slops to crew 10.54 From Captain a/c telegram .79	11.33	
½ balance—demurrage from Rankin & Tyson—Trip #75	250.00	2,611.33
Pilotage in and out Georgetown	143.00	
Tow in 40.00 Out 125.00 Georgetown	165.50	

Water and lumber 3.00 .95 To stevedores 3.00	6.95	
Phone call 2.40 Dry cell and radio battery 7.10	9.50	
Eggs 4.50 Stores 53.88 Chandlery 6.25	64.63	
Ice 7.50 Coal 15.00 Kerosene 6.44	28.94	
Machine and blacksmith work	15.55	
40 fathoms 5½″ 2nd hand mooring line	12.50	
Carpenter work–4 capstan bars, etc.	19.55	
Exp. and shipping fee, sailor from Charleston	6.50	
Wages, sailor deserted–Georgetown	25.55	
Launch going ashore on arrival	2.00	
Crew's wages on trip	373.06	
Bus fare, sailor N.Y. to Charleston	11.40	
Capt's. wages February and March 1936	250.00	
Marketing 29.35 Laundry 8.30 Coal 6.17	43.82	
Cook's wages in port–3 weeks	20.00	
Shifting vessel and cleaning hold	7.50	
Capt's. expense in port	12.00	
Night watchman–Tisdale & Forrest	10.50	
Ice for sea 6.00 Phone call to New York 1.50	7.50	
Exp. getting sailor aboard	2.85	
16 lbs. meat Port Reading 3.52 Ice 7.50	11.02	
To extra expense trimming extra coal	1.75	
Telegraph and telephone .79 .40 .34 1.95 3.45	6.93	
Wharfage at Staten Island Jan. 1934	6.30	
Shipping crew for next trip	12.80	
Tow sea to Red Hook	75.00	
Tow Red Hook to Tisdale Lmbr. Co.	55.00	
Tow Forrest Box to Pt. Reading and return to W. Bank and water	45.00	
⅓ commission Gilmartin	38.33	
⅔ commission C. C. Paul & Co.	79.19	
½ balance demurrage C. C. Paul & Co.	12.50	
Notary .25 Telephone and telegraph 11.74 Liab. Insur. 72.80	84.79	
Stores 128.19 Chandlery 98.95 Slops 10.54	237.68	
Insur. on advance freight	24.50	2,029.57
In hand this trip		581.76
From previous trip		1,043.27
In hand		1,625.03

1/90 = 18.055

89/90 C. C. Paul & Co.	1,606.97	
1/90 C. Howard Paul Credit to a/c	18.06	1,625.03
		x x x x

Trip #77 (cont.)

To owners 6/12/36

End policy
Exp. 2/21/36
E–22481
O–159975

Trip #78	June 8, 1936	Capt. Robt. O. Jones	
Port Reading, N.J., to Charleston, S.C. Coal			
1,044.07 tons @ 1.10 a ton		1,148.48	
Georgetown, S.C., to New York Lumber Lump sum		2,350.00	
Slops 23.86 Gas refund 4.40 Capt. a/c telegram 1.97		30.23	3,528.71
Docking Port Reading 20.00 Trim coal 93.96	Capt's. Statement 5/29/36	113.96	
Tow quarantine to anchorage, docking at Charleston		45.00	
Pilotage in and out of Charleston		108.75	
Marketing and paint Charleston		21.65	
4 keys Bolts Pliers Wrenches, etc.		2.25	
Capt's. expenses 3.00 Harbor master 2.00		5.00	
Material for all new scuppers		17.90	
Machine work and blacksmith, install scuppers		40.40	
Undocking Charleston no charge			
Towing to sea		79.32	
Tug *Hinton* and small tug *Progress* assist. and dock. G'town		40.00	
Pilotage in and out of Georgetown		143.00	
Towage out Georgetown		149.23	
Water 3.00 Gratuity stevedores 3.00		6.00	
Marketing and chandlery Ford		62.47	
Ice for sea 9.00 Door locks, radio battery 6.90 etc.		15.90	
42′ rigging wire 5.00 Phone call .75		5.75	
Caulk around hatch coamings, head of poop, and butts main deck 16 hrs. @ .40		6.40	
Laundry 2.50 Phone calls 4.60 Telegrams		7.10	
10 doz. eggs 2.00 Carpenter work 7.50 Kerosene 5.27		14.77	
Marketing in port 21.60 Boat hire 2.00		23.60	
Watchman at Cross Austin's		10.00	
Crew's wages—trip		576.52	
Captain's wages April–May		250.00	
Cook's wages in port—2 days		3.00	
Mate's wages after paid off		12.00	
Capt's. exp. in port getting sailors aboard, taxi, meals etc		16.30	

Gas 25.67 Ice 6.30 Laundry 7.90 Sulphur candles 1.02	40.89	
Dunnage for coal 27.00 Extra meat 4.86	31.86	3,528.71
Telegrams .79 .40 1.18 .51 Shipping crew 15.00	17.88	Gilmartin
Making maintopsail Martin	60.00	
Tow Red Hook to mouth of Newtown Creek	40.00	
Tow mouth of Newtown Creek to Perth Amboy and return to West Bank and water	145.00	
Commission Coal ½ Gilmartin	28.71	
Commission Lumber ⅓ Gilmartin	38.33	
Insurance advance freight Bate	13.12	
Telegrams and phone calls	8.40	
½ commission Coal C. C. Paul & Co.	28.71	
⅔ commission Lumber C. C. Paul & Co.	79.17	
Stores 155.93 Chandlery 100.28 Slops 23.86 Swan	280.07	2,588.41
		940.30

Ledger	77.40
Due by Captain	862.90
	940.30

Trip #79 September 1, 1936 Capt. Robt. O. Jones

Perth Amboy, N.J., to Jekyll Island, Ga. Coal 910.3 net tons @ 2.00	1,820.60	
Georgetown, S.C., to New York Lumber Lump sum	2,350.00	4,170.60
Gas refund 8.80 Slops to crew 24.13		32.93
		4,203.53

Docking at Perth Amboy 35.00 Trimming coal 73.15	108.15	Gilmartin 7/10/36
½ commission Coal	45.52	
½ commission Coal C. C. Paul & Co.	45.51	
Telephone and telegraph 1.26 Notary .25	1.51	
Marketing Jekyll Island	58.71	
Gas engine oil—Disch. coal 2.70 2.70	5.40	
Paid mate, running engine etc.	20.00	
Tow St. Simons to sea and sea to St. Andrews Bar 3½ miles @ 12.50	43.75	
Tow St. Andrews sea buoy to Jekyll Island to St. Andrews buoy 735 tons @ .30	220.50	
Pilotage in and out Jekyll Buoy	96.00	
Repairs Mianus engine oil cups and 2 bolts for winch, hoisting cargo	3.25	
Pilotage in Georgetown 10 feet	28.00	
Tow inward and outward Georgetown	169.82	

Trip #79 (cont.)

Item		Amount	Total
Pilotage outward Georgetown	Captain's Statement 8/27/36 at New York	115.00	
Water 3.00 Lumber .67 Georgetown		3.67	
Carpenter work and caulking		33.60	
Stores 81.85 Chandlery 75.72 Ford		157.57	
Machine and blacksmith—overhaul engine		72.90	
Gas 5.85 Kerosene 8.95 Ice for sea 10.00		24.80	
Sheet of copper—repairs to motor boat		8.00	
Doctor for mate—injured by fall		2.00	
Gratuity to stevedores		3.00	
Crew's wages on trip		703.23	
Captain's wages—June–July–August		375.00	
Phone calls 3.40 Watchman 10.00			
Sulphur candles 1.63 Ice 4.50 Laundry 8.30		14.43	
Marketing and dishes in port and at shipyard		41.87	
Help shifting twice at Cross Austin's		4.50	
Mate in port 8/20–8/25 inclus. @ 2.00		12.00	4,203.53
Capt's. expense in port and at shipyard		17.25	
Cook in port, flat rate		20.00	
Meats and vegetables—next trip		15.15	
Shipping crew and expense		15.50	
Tow sea to mouth of Newtown Creek	Gilmartin	115.00	
Tow mouth of Newtown Creek to Tebo's D. D.		40.00	
Tow Tebo's D. D. to West Bank		40.00	
Phone call		.60	
⅓ commission Lumber Gilmartin		39.17	
⅔ commission Lumber C. C. Paul & Co.		78.33	
Stores 217.34 Chandlery 296.97 Slops 24.13 Swan		538.44	3,350.53
			853.00
In hand from last trip			940.30
			1,793.30
Drydocking and painting—Robins Dry Dock			
Cleaning and washing bottom and applying one coat copper paint to 12′6″ mark, owners supplying paint		242.00	
Other repairs		121.54	
43 gals. N.J. copper paint—C. A. Woolsey		80.36	
Spanker made by Marshall and Godfrey			
Canvas #1/0 470 yds. #2 60 yds.		185.57	
Making same @ .37 yd.		196.10	
Freight shipping		6.23	831.80
			961.50

Ledger	
In hand	10.93
Due by Captain	950.57
	961.50

Trip #80 November 10, 1936 Capt. Robt. O. Jones

Georgetown, S.C., to New York Lump sum		2,350.00
Telephone and telegraph 1.89 1.26 Supplies 25.43—Ford	28.58	
Canvas last trip	48.70	
To cook last trip—in port—wages	5.85	
Asst. tow and docking in Georgetown	20.00	
1 riding pawl chock and pawl—Charleston D. D. Co.	120.00	
Water 3.00 Phone calls a/c riding pawl 3.60	6.60	
Outward towage Georgetown (Contract)	125.00	
To Captain Lucas—tug *Hinton*—Pilotage	25.00	
Lunches to Captain and car driver, bridge tolls a/c Charleston	3.35	
Lumber a/c damage to Inland Waterway Transp. Dock	10.65	
Machine, blacksmith and welding work	74.59	
Ice 9.00 Kerosene 2.68	11.68	
Stores and chandlery C. L. Ford	66.71	
Gas for car—2 trips to Charleston	3.00	
Galv. iron sheet for mast	2.00	
Carpenter work and material on mainmast	45.00	
Crew wages on trip	506.23	
Captain's wages—September and October	250.00	
Capt's. expense in port and to sch. *Edward L. Swan* for sail and hawser	15.00	
Laundry 8.80 Watchman 10.00	18.80	
Marketing 19 days, Captain, mate, and cook	32.60	
Cook's wages in port, flat rate	20.00	
Work on bobstay chainplate and head gear, repair flying jib	17.50	
Gratuity to Cross Austin machine shop, repair bobstay chainplate	3.00	
Ice and labor putting aboard—no crew	6.30	
Tow vessel to sea and return a/c hurricane report and then to sea	50.00	
Fresh meat 21.40 Gasoline 15.41	36.81	
Extract shipping master getting 3 sailors aboard a/c strike	2.25	
Ship 4 sailors and getting aboard 14.45 Telegs .41 .46 2.90 .76	19.28	
Tow sea to mouth of Newtown Creek 125.00 to W. Bank and water $70	195.00	
⅓ commission Gilmartin	39.17	
⅔ commission C. C. Paul & Co.	117.50	
Stores 205.13 Chandlery 208.66 Slops 33.91 Swan	447.70	2,334.68
		15.32
Due vessel from last trip		961.50
Due vessel		976.82

Captain's Statement

Trip #81 April 7, 1937 Capt. Robt. O. Jones

Wilmington, N.C., to New York Lumber Lump sum		2,400.00	
Slops to crew August 33.91 November 20.54	54.45		
Gas refund	3.30	57.75	
		2,457.75	
Second Special Survey No. 1—Report B-9664	110.00		
Telephone and Telegram	1.26		
Tow in and out of Wilmington	175.00		Capt's. Statement—New York
Pilotage in 10′ 15.00 Out 17′6″ 61.00	76.00		Capt's. Statement—New York
Marketing and sea stores—Wilmington	58.40		Capt's. Statement—New York
Chand. machine and blacksmith work	132.90		Capt's. Statement—New York
Cotton gauze, bandages, liniments, etc., for medicine chest	2.85		Capt's. Statement—New York
Harbor master through Bate	3.00		Capt's. Statement—New York
To mate and sailor, making new standing jib	20.00		Capt's. Statement—New York
Captain's expenses	5.30		Capt's. Statement—New York
Crew wages on trip	543.70		Capt's. Statement—New York
Capt's. wages Nov.–Dec. 1936 Jan.–Feb. 1937	500.00		Capt's. Statement—New York
Watchman Tisdale 42 hrs. @ .50 12/23 to 2/3/37	20.00		Capt's. Statement—New York
Pay-off book 1.00 Telegram .38	1.38		Capt's. Statement—New York
20. gals. kerosene 3.00 ½ ton coal 7.25	10.25		Capt's. Statement—New York
Laundry at Tisdale and shipyard	12.80		Capt's. Statement—New York
Cook's wages in port 12/24–2/14 @ .75 per day	39.75		Capt's. Statement—New York
Mate, caulking all butts outside and on deck. Waterway seam and hatch coamings, wedging, ceiling, etc.	54.00		Capt's. Statement—New York
Marketing 8 weeks, Captain, mate, and cook	104.70		Capt's. Statement—New York
Shipping 4 men, R.R. fare, exp., etc., one man to Grasselli	14.30		Capt's. Statement—New York
Captain's expense at New York, 8 weeks, Grasselli, N.J., R.R. fare to New York	34.65		Capt's. Statement—New York
Shift vessel at Tisdale, man help shift after discharge	15.00		Capt's. Statement—New York
Tow sea to Tisdale-Astoria, 2 tugs a/c high wind	150.00		
915 lbs. rope @ .05	45.75		Bate Stmt.
Insurance advance freight	26.25		Bate Stmt.
Telegraph and telephone .41 .76 3.50 1.95 Protest 1.00	7.62		Gilmartin Stmt.
Repair and adjust compass and barometer	12.00		Gilmartin Stmt.
⅓ commission Gilmartin	40.00		Gilmartin Stmt.
⅔ commission C. C. Paul & Co.	80.00		
Stores 167.05 Chandlery 173.44 Slops 30.54 Swan	361.03	2,657.89	
In debt		200.14	
In hand from last trip		976.82	
In hand		776.68	

End Policy 2/21/37
E—22990
O—166197

Trip #82 — August 13, 1937 — Capt. Robt. O. Jones

Grasselli, N.J., to Jacksonville, Fla. Phosphate residue in bulk			
807,6875 gross tons @ 2.00 per g.t.	1,615.38		
Jacksonville to Portland, Me. Lumber			
481,476 ft. @ 6.50 M	3,129.59		
Slops from crew	70.45	4,815.42	
1 flying jib #0/22—C.D. N.Y. Sailmaking Corp.	123.75		
Repairs gas engine—governor system, etc.	227.70		
Phone calls and telegrams 15.66 2.40	18.06		
Tow Tisdale Lmbr. Co. to Tebo's	50.00		
Tow Tebo's to Grasselli to sea	130.00		
Commission Phos. residue Sexton 5%	80.76		
Commission Phos. residue Paul 2½%	40.38		
Addt'l. premium Liab. insur. 2/21/36–2/21/37	19.60		
Freight insur. Jacksonville to Portland	27.50		
½ commission Lumber Sexton	78.24		
½ commission Lumber C. C. Paul & Co.	78.24		
Shipping master's fee 3.25 R.R. fare, adv. to cook to Jacksonville 22.00 Telegram 1.16	26.41		Sexton & Co.
Stores 308.54 Chandlery 371.45	679.99		Sexton & Co.
Tow sea to Jacksonville loaded			
Tow Jacksonville to sea loaded @ .36 735 tons	264.60		Capt. Statement at N.Y.
Shifting McGriffin's to Corn Point	20.00		Capt. Statement at N.Y.
Pilotage In 6′2″ 43.73 Out 17′4″ 48.83—Jacksonville	92.56		Capt. Statement at N.Y.
Fresh water 10.00 Harbor master 7.50	17.50		Capt. Statement at N.Y.
2 governor brass gears Mianus engine	10.57		Capt. Statement at N.Y.
Caulking bow ports	8.00		Capt. Statement at N.Y.
Stores 127.76 Chandlery 65.92	193.68		Capt. Statement at N.Y.
1 fore-topsail #5 Woodberry duck	130.00		Capt. Statement at N.Y.
Laundry after disch. phosphate	9.17		Capt. Statement at N.Y.
Machine and blacksmith work 44.50 9.00	53.50		Capt. Statement at N.Y.
New gaff through McGriffin Stevedore	25.00		Capt. Statement at N.Y.
Cook paid off at Jacksonville	91.04		Capt. Statement at N.Y.
Phone calls and telegrams	5.35		Capt. Statement at N.Y.
Master's exp. Jacksonville 12.00 Laundry 8.76	20.56		Capt. Statement at N.Y.
Telegram 2.57 Supplies 4.62 Marketing 103.55 Gas 10.63	121.37		Capt. Statement at N.Y.
Small marketing by cook	7.30		Capt. Statement at N.Y.
Crew wages at Portland, Me.	834.89		Capt. Statement at N.Y.
Captain's wages March–April–May	375.00		Capt. Statement at N.Y.
Paint, second hand blocks, rope, tarpaulins, main boom stick, etc.	157.83		
Docking and undocking at Portland	60.00		
Captain's expenses and stationery	11.00		

Trip #82 (cont.)

Item	Amount	Total
Cook in port and mate's part time in Portland and New York, and 2 men to tow to New York	121.36	
Fare, one man New York to Portland	6.75	
Sailor, 4 days at Portland—quit	8.00	
Repairs, sextant, rating chronometer., light list, etc.	9.70	
Marketing, New York D.D. and Perth Amboy 5/25–5/31	21.65	
Shipping 4 men, getting pictures, lunches, fares to Perth Amboy, etc.	19.30	
Boat hire at Perth Amboy taking Captain and crew ashore to sign on—6 trips	12.00	
Captain's expense dry dock, Perth Amboy and fares etc. to N.Y.	13.00	
Mate and sailor, clean bilges, etc.	10.00	4,311.01
		504.41
In hand from last trip		776.68
Due vessel		1,281.09

Trip #83 September 30, 1937 Capt. Robt. O. Jones

Item	Amount	Total
New York to Hamilton, Bermuda Coal		
$969^{16}/_{20}$ tons @ $3.25 per ton	3,151.85	
Refund on towage at Bermuda	30.00	
Jacksonville to Portland, Me. Lumber Lump sum	3,350.00	
Slops to crew 39.04 Gas refund 1.65	40.69	6,572.54

Item	Lbs.	Shillings	Pence		Amount
Liability insurance—Law. and McKim					72.80
Tow anchorage, Portland, to anchorage Red Hook, N.Y.					500.00
Tow Red Hook to Tebo's					35.00
Tow Tebo's to Perth Amboy					75.00
Tow Perth Amboy to West Bank and water					75.00
Telephone and telegraph 4.96 .35					5.31
45 gals. Brown copper paint					87.12
Services in connection with cleaning					7.50
Pilotage from Perth Amboy—17′					39.61
Insur. freight Perth Amboy to Bermuda					45.00
5% commission Coal E. Sexton & Co.					157.59
2½% commission Coal C. C. Paul & Co.					78.80
Pilotage in and out—Hamilton	14	4	0	Watlington & Conyers	70.01
Light dues 661 tons @ 3d.	8	5	3	Watlington & Conyers	40.73
Wharfage 4 days @ 6⅓d.	12	5	0	Watlington & Conyers	60.39
Telegraph arrival 4s. sailing 4s.	–	8	0	Watlington & Conyers	1.97
	35	2	3		

Margin note	Item	Amount	Location
Robbins D. D. Co	Trimming coal 87.28, Docking 27.00	114.28	
Robbins D. D. Co	2½% commission on advances 2.86, insurance 6.00	8.86	
Robbins D. D. Co	Tow Five Fathom Hole to Hamilton and to sea	300.00	
Robbins D. D. Co; Tender 5/22/37	Drydocking, clean and wash bottom, and apply one coat copper paint to 12′6″ line, exclus. of all towing & pilot.	242.00	
Tender 5/22/37	Other vessel repairs	1,442.44	
Tender 5/22/37	Ice 3.00 Fresh water 2.72	5.72	
Swan	Slops to crew (Credit to vessel's last trip)	70.45	
Swan	Slops to crew—this trip	39.04	
Swan	Stores 267.44 Chandlery 316.63	584.07	
	Phone call .76 Frt. Insur. 30.00 Jacksonville to Portland	30.76	
	½ commission Lumber Sexton	83.75	
	½ commission Lumber C. C. Paul & Co.	83.75	
Capt. Stmt.—Portland	Marketing, Fresh meat Ice etc.	86.20	Bermuda
Capt. Stmt.—Portland	Mate running engine to disch. coal, and repairs	20.00	Bermuda
Capt. Stmt.—Portland	Sailor sweep hold and bend sails after disch. to 7 P.M. Sailed next A.M.	5.00	Bermuda
Capt. Stmt.—Portland	Making half coupling, bolts, etc. for Mianus shaft	18.75	Bermuda
Capt. Stmt.—Portland	Master's exp. boat hire, entering and handling lines	16.50	Bermuda
Capt. Stmt.—Portland	Tow sea to Jacksonville to sea 735 tons @ .33	242.55	Jax.
Capt. Stmt.—Portland	Pilotage in 10′ 18.75 Out 17′4″ 48.83	67.58	Jax.
Capt. Stmt.—Portland	Water service minimum charge	10.00	Jax.
	Harbor master 7.50 Custom's ton. tax 13.22 Entry 2.50	23.22	Jacksonville
	Chandlery 124.49 Stores 175.25 Quarantine 10.00	309.74	Jacksonville
	Caulk around fo'c'sle head, waterways, and bow ports 19.50 Laundry 9.15 Master's exp. 12.00	40.65	Jacksonville
	Wages, mate deserted Jacksonville	74.50	Jacksonville
	Wages, sailors 3 days @ 60.00 paid off	6.00	Jacksonville
	Ship fee Jacksonville and exp. sailor Kolanski	8.00	Jacksonville
	Crew's wages at Portland	708.34	Portland, Me.
	R.R. fare Portland to N.Y. 4 men at 6.75 due to one green sailor and no mate	27.00	Portland, Me.
	Gratuity for paying off Saturday P.M.	5.00	Portland, Me.
	Fumigating 20.91 Fresh water 10.00	30.91	Portland, Me.
	Radio repairs and spare tubes	10.00	Portland, Me.
	Lumber for hatches 18.16 Telephone and telegraph 13.97	32.13	Portland, Me.
	Docking and undocking Portland	60.00	Portland, Me.
	Repairs pump engine 11.45 Make bolts and s. band 20.93	32.38	Portland, Me.
	1 gaff with jaw 30.00 100 fathoms mooring line 28.00	58.00	Portland, Me.
	Repair fore and mizzen sails	57.00	Portland, Me.
	Work on gaff, caulk bow ports, etc.	36.00	Portland, Me.
	Cook's wages in port 8/8–9/7/37	75.00	Portland, Me.
	Captain's wages June–July–August 1937	450.00	Portland, Me.
	Laundry Portland 7.80 Launch hire 2.00	9.80	Portland, Me.
	Marketing, stores and chandlery	451.80	Portland, Me.

Trip #83 (cont.)		
Extra stores, delayed sailing	12.15	
Tow out anchorage to sea—two river boats	40.00	
Telegrams 1.15 Capt. exp. Portland 15.00	16.15	
Shipping fee N.Y. and taxi to station	14.00	
Waiting for Portland train 2.00 R.R. fare 40.50	42.50	
Taxi to ship 1.40 Capt. exp. at N.Y.	4.65	7,458.45
In debt this trip		885.91
In hand last statement		1,281.09
Due vessel		395.18

Trip #84	January 7, 1938	Capt. Robt. O. Jones

Jacksonville, Fla., to Providence, R.I. Lumber		
441,255 ft. @ 7.50		3,309.42
Wharfage at sardine packing house instead of towing to other dock 16 days @ .75	12.00	Capt. Statement—Providence
Tow sea to Jacksonville to sea 735 tons @ .33	242.55	
Pilotage 10′6″ 20.55 in Out 17′10″ 47.25 Jacksonville	67.90	
Caulk bow ports, top of f'wd. house port side and under foc's'le head 15.80 28.80	44.60	
Fresh water 10.00 and harbor master 7.50	17.50	
Marketing and sea stores 111.67 Chandlery 90.00	202.02	
Extra sea stores—delayed sailing	17.72	
2 sailors paid off Jacksonville 47.84 46.00	93.84	
Carpenter making fore gaff and traveler for spanker, work on main boom, etc.	81.00	
Machine and blacksmith—Brennan Iron Works	38.35	
Small broken stores from Captain Chapman	6.40	
Shipping sailor, Jacksonville 7.00 Gratuity stevedores 3.50	10.50	
Laundry 6.80 Master's exp. a/c Brooks-Scanlon men 12.00	18.80	
Mate paid off at Norfolk 38.35 91.09 1.20 broken leg	130.64	
Stores 21.52 Shipping man in place of mate 3.00 Phone calls Norfolk 1.75	26.27	
Crew's wages at Providence	577.13	
Bus fare 8.50 sailor and R.R. fare mate to Norfolk 12.00	20.50	
Captain's wages—Sept.–Oct.–Nov.	450.00	
Marketing in port 11/8–12/7/37	36.75	
Cook in port 11/8–12/7/37	75.00	
Phone call .60 Laundry for sea 7.44	8.04	
Master's expense in Providence	10.00	
½ ton coal 7.65 Ice 6.00 Kerosene 4.25	17.90	
Repairs pumping engine	27.15	

110 gals. gas and drum 13.20 1 ton coal alongside vessel 13.50	26.70	
Capt's expense at N.Y. getting crew and stores and mate's fare and meal on steamer	12.25	
Docking 30.00 Tow out Providence 60.00 Water 5.00	95.00	
Ship fee, boat fare and meals on stmr. to Providence	28.50	
Wallace and Tucker night watchman	10.00	
Freight insur. Jacksonville to Providence	35.00	
Survey fee Annual Load Line insp.	32.20	
Telephone and telegraph 3.68 5.12	8.80	
Commission Sexton	82.73	
Commission C. C. Paul & Co.	82.74	2,646.48
		662.94
Due vessel from last trip		395.18
Due vessel		1,058.12

Trip #85 April 8, 1938 Capt. Robt. O. Jones

Jacksonville to Baltimore Lumber Lump sum	2,900.00	
Less a/c part of deck load lost overboard	113.18	2,786.82
Slops to crew		18.12
Cash sale of old foresail		25.00
Cash a/c telegram		1.20
		2,831.14

Pilotage In 10′6″ 20.55 Out 17′6″ 49.55 Jacksonville	70.10
Tow in and out of Jacksonville	242.55
Harbor master 7.50 Water service 10.00	17.50
Chandlery 37.50 Stores 59.50 Jacksonville	96.80
Caulking bow ports	8.00
Ship's laundry 4.80 Capt. exp. 12.00 Gratuity, etc.	16.80
Crew's wages on trip	551.96
Master's wages Dec.–Jan.–Feb.	450.00
Mate's wages in port 1/23–2/3/38	31.92
Cook's wages in port 1/23–2/3/38	30.00
Labor W. Aaron 22 days @ $1.50	33.00
Marketing in port and at railway	35.60
Capt. expenses in port—Balto.	1.75
Telephone and telegraph 11.13 6.05 1 ton coal 10.40	27.58
1 pc. 12 × 12 × 12′—heart Ga. rough pine James Lmbr. Co.	12.00
Labor Harrison and Mayhew R. B. White	15.00
Stores 237.76 Chandlery 155.16 Slops 18.12 Swan	411.04
Extra stores from Norfolk Swan	44.85

(Bracketed items from Pilotage through Capt. expenses in port: Capt. Statement—Balto.)

Trip #85 (cont.)

1 ton coal Wilcox and Ziegler	10.40	
Commission	139.34	2,496.19
		334.95
Due vessel from last trip		1,058.12
Due vessel		1,393.07

End Policy
2/21/37–2/21/38

Trip #86 June 8, 1938 Capt. Robt. O. Jones

Jacksonville, Fla., to Portland. Me. Lumber Lump sum		3,600.00
From Marshall and Godfrey a/c old clew rings	5.00	
Slops from crew Vane 3.40 Jax. S. C. Co. 14.60 Harris & Co. 8.31	36.31	41.31
		3,641.31
Telegrams and phone calls 1.26 1.86 .74	3.86	
Redman & Vane S. B. Co. 2/17/38	1,195.16	
Invoice 2/16/38: Forestaysail 71.00 Foresail 260.36 Mainsail 282.16 Mizzen 282.16 1/0 Woodberry canvas Marshall & Godfrey	895.68	
Invoice 2/16/38: 2 Tarpaulins #4 W. P. Canvas 15′6″ @ 18.75 each	37.50	
Invoice 2/16/38: 2 mast coats @ 3.00 each	6.00	
Invoice 2/16/38: 8 lbs. strip lead @ .25	2.00	
Invoice 2/16/38: 1 lb. tacks	.25	
Repair foresail and handling 27.68 3.30	30.98	
Work on water tanks, Balto. Ship Repair Co.	82.36	
Clean and repair chronometer 22.50 Chart .75	23.25	
Loane—parts for pump	3.55	
Chandlery, grub—Vane Bros.	362.02	
Freight insurance 45.00 41.25	86.25	
Liability insurance	72.80	
Tow Pier 6 to Redman & Vane Mullen	20.00	
Tow Redman & Vane to #3 anchorage Mullen	25.00	
Shipping 4 sailors and deliver aboard	13.00	
Tow sea to Jacksonville to sea 735 tons @ .33	242.55	Draft
Capt. Statement 4/13/38: Pilotage In 10′6″ 20.55 Out 17′6″ 49.55 Jacksonville	70.10	Draft
Capt. Statement 4/13/38: Lumber for trestletrees and hatches	30.69	Draft
Capt. Statement 4/13/38: Harbor master—Jacksonville	7.50	Draft
Capt. Statement 4/13/38: Caulking bow ports	8.00	Draft
Jaxville S.C. Co. 3/12/38; Capt. Statement 4/13/38: 1–3,800 lb. Patent anchor @ .04	152.00	Draft
Jaxville S.C. Co. 3/12/38; Capt. Statement 4/13/38: 180′ 1¾ stud link anchor chain 4,245 lbs. @ .04	169.80	Draft

Item	Amount	Total
Chandlery 100.59 Telephone 8.60 Grub 99.60	208.79	
Weld turnbuckle rods etc. for foretopmast support	40.80	
Fresh water 10.00 Laundry 5.80	15.80	
Gratuity stevedores 3.00 Capt's. exp. Jacksonville 10.00	13.00	
Carp. work making trestletrees for main, 1 crosstree leg, 1 outrigger, 4 hatch covers, repair binnacle box, etc.	54.00	
Sailor's wages—paid off Jacksonville 3/2/38	23.38	
Shipping sailor—Jacksonville—F. Angelhouse	5.00	
Crew's wages on trip—Paid off 3/30/38	570.48	
Bus fares to sailor signed on—Jacksonville	17.35	
Docking from stream and out	70.00	
Chandlery 140.05 Stores 181.24 Slops 8.31	329.60	
Captain's wages—March	150.00	
Captain's expense—Portland	10.00	
Extra heavy batteries for radio	14.00	
Laundry 5.35 2nd hand rope and chandlery 83.90	89.25	
New rope, paint, oil, and turpentine	16.00	
Shipping crew and expense—also fares Boothbay to Eastport	23.65	
2 power boats assist to sea	25.00	
Mate's wages in port 3/31–4/8 inclus. @ 85.00	25.50	
Cook's wages in port 3/31–4/8 @ 75.00	22.50	
Commission	180.00	5,444.40
In debt this trip		1,803.09
Due vessel from last statement		1,393.07
In debt		410.02

(Bracketed items from Extra heavy batteries through Cook's wages: Capt. Stmt. 4/13/38)

Trip #87 August 10, 1938 Capt. Robt. O. Jones

Item	Amount	Total
Jacksonville, Fla., to Portland, Me. Lumber Lump sum		3,600.00
Liab. insur. addtl. premium 2/21/37–2/21/38	26.90	
Telephone and telegrams .76 .16 .33	17.09	
1 #2 plunger for Russell pump 7.50 P/P* .98	8.48	
Port fees Jacksonville	7.50	
Tow sea to Jacksonville to sea 735 tons @ .33	242.55	
Pilotage in 10′6″ 20.55 Out 17′6″ 49.55—Jacksonville	70.10	
Making drifts and bolts, weld eye bolts and eye pads. Build up 8 eyes and 9 shackles, making 4 plates, 12 pins, spanker rigging, corners of masthead and other iron work around trestletrees, etc.	116.99	
Caulk bow ports and around new bitts aft	11.30	
Spanker topsail #5 Woodberry canvas 22″ wide, triple sewed	125.00	
Chandlery 74.54 Stores 150.55	225.09	

(Bracketed last three items: Jaxville S.C. Co.)

*Parcel Post.

Trip #87 (cont.)		
Wages, sailor paid off—Jacksonville	30.06	
Carpenter work—Jacksonville	152.00	
Lumber 15.18 Rip and dressing 2.50	17.68	
Cypress for doors and mouldings	4.20	
Fresh water 10.00 Laundry 3.75 Stevedores 3.00	16.75	
1 natural knee in the rough	5.00	
Cutting and drilling holes in knee	2.25	
Chips for main and spanker gaff	.75	
Master's exp. radio repairs and ship sailor	15.00	
Docking at Portland, Me.	35.00	
Crew's wages on trip to 6/3/38	663.07	
Mate in port 6/4—6/24/38	59.50	
Cook in port 6/5—6/25/38 paid off	52.50	
2 tons coal—salvage from burned pier	10.00	
Fresh water a/c expect to sail to Norfolk	6.30	
2 sailors putting in bow ports with mate, caulking same, etc.	4.00	
Lumber making ice box hatch	1.25	
Fog horn 20.00 Less credit for bell 12.00	8.00	
8 gals. grey paint, 1 gal. inside varnish	12.00	
Captain's wages April–May–June–July	600.00	
Phone calls 2.80 Laundry 8.30 Misc. 4.20	15.30	
Master's exp. 6/3—7/31/38 Phone calls and boat hire looking for place to beach vessel for cleaning and caulking	18.00	
Commission	180.00	
Fine a/c not renewing papers	10.00	
Mate (Davis) in port 6/24–7/25/38	50.00	2,819.61
Due vessel this trip		780.39
Due C. C. Paul & Co. from last statement		410.02
Due vessel		370.37

Trip #88 November 15, 1938 Capt. Robt. O. Jones

Sheet Harbor, Nova Scotia, to New York Lumber		
802,583 ft. @ 3.00 M		2,407.75
From Harris Co., overcharge on invoice	1.41	
From Captain Jones, a/c telegram	.78	2.19
		2,409.94
Wages in port @ 50.00 Mo. 7/24–8/28/38	64.17	
Capt's. exp. Aug. incl. phone calls to Boston and telegrams on spruce charter	8.20	

Laundry in August	Capt. Statement—Perth Amboy 10/25/38	3.15	
1 ton coal from burned pier for sea 8/30		5.00	
Captain's wages for August		150.00	
Cabin stores for sea including 3 mos. marketing		348.13	Harris Co. 500.75
Hardware in port and chandlery for sea, fresh water		108.22	
Undocking to anchorage		35.00	
Repairs to radio 8.05 Phone calls 1.35		9.40	
To tug extra for towing direct to sea and paid no pilot		15.00	
Shipping 4 sailors through mission		8.00	
Clearing at Portland, Me., for U.S.		2.50	
Harbor dues, Sheet Harbor, 9.92 Supplies for sea 26.35		36.27	Sht. Harbor Lmbr. Co.
Sick Mariners' dues 13.22 Bill of Health 1.00		14.22	90.49 Vessel
Pilotage in and Out Harbor only		25.00	115.00 Capt.
Towing to dock—fish boats		15.00	205.49
2½ commission on advances		5.04	5.04 Comm.
210 H.P. M/V* tow out through bridge and under way		20.00	210.53
Meat, fish, and vegetables		18.70	
2 phone calls to Halifax a/c sending arrival and sailing telegrams to Baltimore		.70	
Master's exp. at Halifax		7.25	
Entrance fee and tonnage tax New York		15.72	
Noting protest—Sexton's C. H. broker		1.00	
Crew's wages on trip		422.06	
Repairs to pump—Blattner Mach. Corp.		21.00	
Shipping fee and exp. cook to N. Y. and Portland		14.05	
Marketing in port and Perth Amboy—21 days		36.15	
Laundry incl. next trip		7.45	
Night watchman Cross Austin—15 nights		12.00	
Mate Davis' wages in port @ 60.00 mo. while disch. 10/5–10/19		30.00	
Cook in port disch. at Perth Amboy @ 50.00 mo. 10/5–10/23		31.73	
Sailor, clean hold 10/20–10/22 @ 1.67 a day		5.00	
Stove bolts, springs, etc. 5 & 10 store		1.20	
Captain's wages Sept. & Oct. @ 150.00 mo.		300.00	
Master's exp. at New York and Perth Amboy and boat hire at City Island on arrival—2 trips		17.50	
Pilotage in New York 17′6″ @ 1.75	Emory-Sexton	30.63	
Telegrams to Baltimore and Georgetown		1.08	
Tow City Island to mouth of Creek		90.00	
Tow mouth of creek to Perth Amboy D. D.		85.00	
Tow Perth Amboy D. D. to sea		50.00	
Shipping 3 sailors 9.00 and exp. to Perth Amboy		10.70	
Attendance fee—Sexton		25.00	

*Motor vessel.

	Trip #88 (cont.)		
	Telegrams and phone calls 4.67 2.82	7.49	
	½ commission on Lumber—B. S. Costello	60.19	
	½ commission on Lumber—C. C. Paul & Co.	60.19	
Perth Amboy Invoice 10/25/38	36 gals. Balto. brown copper paint	69.79	
Perth Amboy Invoice 10/25/38	Docking, washing off and cleaning bottom, applying 1 coat paint, keel to water line—owner's paint	170.00	
Perth Amboy Invoice 10/25/38	Vessel repairs, carpenters, caulkers, etc.	490.23	
American Bureau Invoice 10/27/38	Survey fee and expense at Perth Amboy a/c docking, load line survey, Annual survey Report C-4325	28.00	2,992.11
	In debt this trip		582.17
	In hand from last trip		370.37
	In debt		211.80

Trip #89 March 13, 1939 Capt. Robt. O. Jones

Savannah, Ga., to New York Lumber Lump sum			2,750.00
Slops a/c crew—Swan Invoice 10/26/38		19.10	
From Capt. a/c telegram—Gilmartin statement		.76	19.86
			2,769.86
Telegrams .63 .63		1.26	
Stores 144.65 Chandlery 118.95 Slops 19.10 Swan		282.70	
Teleg'ms to G'town .76 Balto. .40 Wash. .80	Gilmartin 1/23/39	1.96	
Rating chronometer 3.00 ½ ship fee—Chas. Hoyt $5	Gilmartin 1/23/39	8.00	
Tow sea to Red Hook to Tisdale Lmbr. Co. 125.00 75.00	Gilmartin 1/23/39	200.00	
Tow Tisdale, Astoria 80.00 to West Bank and filling water 10.00	Gilmartin 1/23/39	90.00	
½ commission Lumber	Gilmartin 1/23/39	68.75	
½ commission C. C. Paul & Co.		68.75	
Tow in and out Savannah		200.00	
Pilotage out Savannah 17′0″ 95.00 less 40% spec. disc. 38.00		57.00	
Making fireboard for cabin heater		12.00	
Making 2 tie bolts, furn. 4 nuts for bowsprit heel band		3.25	
Making 3 plates for bowsprit		7.00	
Repair oil housing for gas engine		2.50	
Harbor master 4.00 Fresh water 5.00 Gratuity stevedores 3.00		12.00	
Marketing at city market 11/2–11/18/38		38.65	
72 lbs. hind quarter beef for sea @ .14		10.08	
Vegetables, eggs, etc., for sea		9.15	
Ice for sea		4.50	
Paid off—sailor's wages 10/26–11/17/38 @ 50.00 mo.		38.38	

Capt's. expense and phone calls for sailor	7.35	
Crew's wages to Dec. 2, 1938 a/c trip	397.24	
3 sailors, 14 days @ 1.00 allowance a/c shorthanded from Savannah 11/19/39–12/2/38	42.00	
Marketing at New York 6 weeks	64.70	
Ship's laundry	8.76	
Lumber for wheel box of motor boat, coil box, etc.	10.88	
Lumber for stern rail Cross Austin	25.50	
Machine work, welding, and blacksmith, davits, support rod, etc.	30.75	
Truck stevedores, carrying rail patterns, iron work, etc. back and forth to Brooklyn	12.50	
Oak strips for boat ribs	2.10	
2½ tons nut coal	28.12	
Misc. items purchased by Captain	3.92	
Alien crew and departure lists	1.23	
Mate in port, repair rail and yawl 12/3/38–1/3/39 1 mo. @ 85.00	85.00	
Mate in port 1/3/–1/17/39 @ 85.00 mo.	42.50	
Cook in port 12/3/38–1/17/39 @ 50.00 mo.	75.00	
Night watchman Tisdale's 47 nights @ .50 23.50	23.50	
Captain's exp. and boat hire	15.00	
½ shipping fee—Chas. Hoyt	5.00	
Taxi bringing sailors and baggage aboard	1.95	
Clearance for Turk's Island 2.50 Custom fees 2.50	5.00	
Capt's. wages Nov.–Dec. 1938, Jan. 1939	450.00	2,450.43
		319.43
In debt from last statement		211.80
		107.63

End Policy
2/21/38–2/21/39

Trip #90 June 22, 1939 Capt. Robt. O. Jones

Sailed light from New York, Jan. 20, 1939, for Salt, East Harbor, Turk's Island, to Fernandina, Fla.		
500 tons @ 4.00	2,000	
Jacksonville to Providence, R.I. Lumber		
505,359 ft. @ 7.00 M	3,537.51	
Slops from crew—Swan Invoice 1/18/39	28.25	5,565.76
Services rendered 2/12/39 a/c fouling of vessel's anchors Turk's Island	21.18	
Frt. ins. N.Y. to Turk's Island to Fernandina	40.00	

Port	Item	Amount	Account
	Trip #90 (cont.)		
	Chandlery 131.33 Stores 187.49 Slops 28.25 Swan	347.07	
	Telephone calls and telegrams	2.20	
	½ commission Salt Whitney	50.00	
	½ commission Salt C. C. Paul & Co.	50.00	
Turk's Island	Port dues 661 tons	55.08	Kursteiner-Stubbs Salt Co.
	Bill of health 1.25 Cables 1.45 1.12	3.82	
	Inward pilotage 33.47 Stevedores 7.50	40.97	
	Commission on advances	6.00	
	27 lbs. fresh pork @ .25	6.75	Capt. Statement—Pt. Reading
	Extra pilotage 4 days anchor foul	9.00	
	Eggs 1.50 Fish 3.30 Turtle meat 2.75	7.55	
Fernandina	Fernandina entry 2.50 Tonnage tax 13.22 Port entry 2.00	17.72	
	Inspection quarantine 2/20/39	10.00	
	Crew's wages on trip Fernandina 3/3	519.46	
	4 sailors' fares Fernandina to Norfolk @ 10.90	43.60	
	12 30″ oak mast hoops @ .75	9.00	
	Phone calls for charter	5.15	
	Pilotage In 14½′ 65.00 Out 10½′ 37.00 Fernandina	102.00	
	Weld wildcat and new windlass bearings, etc. Stephen Mach. & B. Shop	72.40	
	Marketing full crew 2/20–3/6/39	51.35	
	Sailor running winch with Captain in turns, disch. salt	8.00	
	Quinn's fish boat for night work	5.00	
	Deratization exempt—inspection	10.00	
	Marketing 3/7–3/11—leaving for Jacksonville	18.01	
	Capt's. exp. Fernandina—4 mi. from town, pay off crew @ Court House	8.50	
	Tow to Jacksonville Bar Quinn's boat	50.00	
Jacksonville	Cook in port, Fernandina and Jax. 15 days and 1 mo. @ 50.00 mo.	75.00	
	Marketing A&P store Jacksonville	6.99	
	Iron and Mach. work—Brennan Iron Works	87.95	
	Tow sea to Jacksonville to sea 735 tons @ .33	242.55	
	Pilotage In 10′6″ 20.55 Out 17′6″ 49.55 Jax.	70.10	
	1 2½ H.P. pump engine complete	47.50	
	Fresh water 10.00 Harbor master 7.50	17.50	
	3 5-gal. drums Grey paint J. S. S. Co.	33.00	
	1 100 fath. 6″ 3 str. Plymouth M rope 645 lbs.	113.36	
	Chandlery 76.99 Marketing and sea stores 124.53	201.52	
	Ice in port 2.20 for sea 5.40	7.60	
	Carpenter work on vessel	140.40	
	Lumber, decking for poop	3.80	
	Lumber, decking around bitts	6.16	

Capt. Statement at Port Reading 6/20/39

Item	Amount	Total
Timber to make knee 8″ x 16″	3.00	
Lumber, moulding, nails, etc.	4.21	
Grind valves and springs for aft. engine	2.50	
Caulking bow ports	8.00	
Sailor help getting deck ready for deck load—no crew 2 days	4.00	
Laundry, cabin and for new crew	7.21	
Taxi for sailors and baggage from Balto. by bus	1.50	
Capt. exp. a/c Mr. DeMuth & McDonald of Brooks Scanlon	10.00	
Providence:		
Sailor's wages Providence by run	120.00	
Bus fare to Balto. and meals 26.20 Taxi 4.00	30.20	
Mate 181.33 Cook 50.00 Wages on trip	231.33	
Wages cook in port paid off	20.00	
Leather for pitcher pump 1.40 ½ ton nut coal 6.90	8.30	
Ice for sea to Perth Amboy and in port	6.23	
Marketing in Providence (30 days)	46.35	
Towing in and out of Providence	135.00	
Phone call to Baltimore—arrival	.50	
Taxi cook from Balto. by bus	.75	
Taxi sailors and baggage via stmr. from N.Y.	1.30	
Wallace and Tucker—Watchman	5.00	
Galley utensils, cabin and crew crockery	5.17	
Groceries and chandlery for next trip	171.27	
Capt's. exp.—phone calls to N.Y. for crew and Mr. Demuth and Wallace and party on board	13.00	
Laundry cabin and crew	6.75	
Perth Amboy marketing 1 week full crew	24.86	
Ship crew and fare 1 man to Perth Amboy	13.00	
Capt. exp. Perth Amboy and Port Reading, calling ship master and McCarren	7.50	
Master's wages—Feb. Mar. Apr. May and June	750.00	
Sea stores Port Reading 73.32 Liab. ins. Lawford & McKim 72.81	146.12	
Ship 4 sailors to Jax. 12.00 Meals 5.00 Bus fare 43.60	60.60	
Ins. difference between under and on deck rate. On deck portion of shipment	145.00	
Phone calls and telegrams	16.22	
Commission on lumber	176.88	
Shipping cook to New York	11.00	4,815.99
		749.77
In hand from last statement		107.63
Due vessel		857.40

Trip #91	November 21, 1939	Capt. Robt. O. Jones

Port Reading, N.J., to Jacksonville Coal		
574.1 tons @ 1.50		861.15
Jacksonville to Providence, R.I. Lumber		
163,798 ft. @ 7.00	1,146.58	
Sapelo Sound, Ga., to Providence Lumber		
344,233 ft. @ 7.50	2,581.75	3,728.33
		4,589.48

	Exp. R. B. White to New York and return	10.00
	Addtl. premium Liab. insur. 2/21/38–2/21/39	18.30
	Telephone and telegrams 7.25 .50 4.95 4.20	16.90
	Frt. ins. Port Reading to Jacksonville	21.25
	Boat fares 3 men New York to Providene	12.51
	35 gals. copper paint to Perth Amboy	67.57
Perth Amboy 6/15/39	Dry Dock, Perth Amboy, 6/15/39, wash off, clean bottom, apply 1 coat paint, keel to waterline, as agreed. Drill and install studs, etc., on wildcat and windlass.	55.00
	Other repairs on vessel	471.61
	Tow Perth Amboy to Reading Terminal	35.00
	McCarren—Tow Port Reading Coal Dock to Old Orchard Shoals	70.00
	Insur. diff. between under and on deck rate on deck portion of shipment of lumber	182.00
Capt. Statement at Providence 10/7/39	Gratuity to stevedores 4/19 Jacksonville	4.00
	Trimming coal Port Reading	57.50
	Harbor fees Jacksonville	7.50
	Pilotage in and out Jax. 14′6″ 36.95 13′0″ 30.40	67.35
	Tow in (partly loaded) 735 Tons @ .15	110.25
	Tow out Jacksonville 735 Tons @ .18	132.30
	Shifting McGriffin's to Corn Point	20.00
	Fresh water 10.00 Iron and machine work 15.25	25.25
	2 36″ mast hoops @ .07 Ribs for motor boat	5.04
	1 outer jib #6 Woodberry white canvas, rope with Plymouth #1 M bolt rope	98.00
	1,200 fathoms 3¼ circum. 3 strand #1 Plymouth manila rope 376 lbs. @ .18½ less 5%	66.08
	Chandlery 133.45 Stores 150.10	283.55
	Cypress for planking motor boat	3.55
	1 gal. Fre-Eze penetrating oil	3.95
	Repairs to timing gear and pump-boat engine	3.00
	Caulking bow ports	8.00
	Carpenter and helper—work on motor boat and upper hatch	66.60

Handles turned for steering wheel	4.00	
Gratuity for stevedores Jacksonville and Sapelo Sound	4.00	
Capt's. exp. Lumber parties Jacksonville and Sapelo Sound	13.25	
Laundry after discharging coal	6.85	
Marketing 10.85 .50 .75 Gas-oil 3.00 1.00 2.00 1.80 Paint 6.50	26.40	
Tow Sapelo Sound to sea	60.00	
Extra to old pilot to go over bar	5.00	
Crew's wages on trip	619.56	
Captain Davis (mate) in port at Providence, Port Reading, and on trip 5/7–8/9/39	263.50	
Repairs to engine and pouring babbit, etc.	17.45	
2 zinc strainers .50 30 gals. gas 5.70	6.20	
Tow in 8/9 Stream to Wallace and Tucker	30.00	
Tow 10/7 Wallace and Tucker to Conimicut Gas Buoy	50.00	
Shifting—dock 20.00 Water 10.00 4 bolts .78	30.78	
Wallace and Tucker night watchman 2 mos.	10.00	
Marketing 8/9–10/4 7 wks. 5 days	93.70	
Marketing 10/5–10/17/39 for full crew waiting on stores, etc. for sea	17.56	
Captain Davis in port at Providence 8/10–9/9/39	85.00	
Captain Davis in port at Providence 9/10–10/5/39 @ 85.00 mo.	73.67	
Laundry—cabin and crew	9.35	
Capt. exp. in Providence and entertainment	17.00	
Capt's. wages July–Aug. Sept.	450.00	
Shipping fee (4 sailors and cook) 15.00 Boat fare 13.75	28.75	
Meals and taxi at New York and Providence	5.15	
Capt's. exp. at New York—2 days	13.00	
Commission—Coal and lumber	229.47	4,261.70
		327.78
In hand from last statement		857.40
		1,185.18

Capt. Statement at Providence 10/7/39

Trip #92 January 22, 1940 Capt. Robt. O. Jones

Newport News, Va., to St. George, Bermuda Coal		
1,018 tons bituminous coal @ 3.00	3,054.00	
10 tons anthracite coal @ 3.00	30.00	3,084.00
From Darrell & Meyer—War Risk Ins.		43.75
Jacksonville, Fla., to Providence, R.I. Lumber		
506,801 ft. @ 7.50		3,801.01

Item		Amount	Total
Trip #92 (cont.)			
Slops from crew 21.99 Refund gas tax 7.50			29.49
			6,958.25
Frt. ins.—Hampton Roads to Bermuda to Jax. to Providence		168.00	
War risk ins. Newport News to Bermuda		43.75	
Telegrams 1.94 Slops 21.99 Grub 310.98 Chandlery 460.94		795.85	
Telegram arrival .38 sailing .38 Newport News	A. R. Hoffman & Co.	.76	
1 ton ice @ .30 per 100 lbs.	A. R. Hoffman & Co.	6.00	
Docking and undocking Pier #9	A. R. Hoffman & Co.	30.40	
Running lines 2.50 Water 449 gals. @ 1.50 M	A. R. Hoffman & Co.	3.17	
Dumping and trimming 1,018 tons @ .15	A. R. Hoffman & Co.	152.70	
Survey fee a/c ext. Load Line report #4083	A. R. Hoffman & Co.	15.25	
Beef 15.18 Eggs 1.65 Gas 33.00 Kerosene 8.50	A. R. Hoffman & Co.	59.13	
Motor oil 6.00 Agency fee enter and clearing 25.00	A. R. Hoffman & Co.	31.00	
Pilotage Newport News to sea 17′6″ @ 3.50	A. R. Hoffman & Co.	61.25	
Launch hire 2.00 Custom's clearance 2.50	A. R. Hoffman & Co.	4.50	
Cables arrival and sailing, and grub Bermuda–Darrell & Meyer		35.56	
2 unions for deck pump		2.10	
Rating chronometer 4.00 and chart .10		4.10	
Tow to anchorage 15.00 Launch hire 4.00		19.00	
Bread pans .40 Capt's. expense Norfolk 5.00		5.40	
Capt's. expense at Bermuda		10.00	
Harbor master—Jacksonville		7.50	
Medical attention to sailor—U.S.P.M. closed		2.50	
Tow sea to Jacksonville to sea 735 tons @ .33		242.55	
Pilotage In 20.55 10′6″ Out 47.55 17′6″—Jax.		70.10	
Repair turnbuckle, making shackle and pin		14.50	
Making 3⅝ studs for pump etc.		3.00	
1 pc. 10″ × 10″ × 38′ all heart LLYP* for gaff		35.00	
1 standing jib #1–22″ Woodberry W canvas		115.00	
Repair for staysail 49.00 Flying jib 68.00		117.00	
35 fathoms 5″ line 3 strand Plymouth rope—158 lbs. @ 23½		37.13	
40 lbs. 2¾″ 3 strand #1 Plymouth rope		9.40	
Chandlery 71.66–8.55=63.11 Stores 111.74		174.85	
Telegrams arrival and sailing—Jax.		1.52	
Wages—sailor paid off—Jacksonville		76.00	
Carpenters and helpers making new spanker gaff, repair 1 jaw, repair hatch, etc.		49.35	
Caulk bow ports, place iron sheet under anchor flukes		12.50	
Fresh water 10.00 Clinch washers, etc., .75		10.75	
1 turkey 4.22 Quarantine 10.00		14.22	

*Longleaf yellow pine.

Entry, tonnage tax Jacksonville	15.72	
Laundry at Jacksonville after coal cargo	8.70	
Capt's. expense getting sailor, etc.	17.20	
Crew's wages on trip	791.50	
Tow Poppasquash Pt. to Providence anchorage (12/9/39) Tow stream to Wallace & Tucker (12/9/39) and return to stream (12/26) Tow Providence to Conimicut Point Gas Buoy—12/26	135.00	
Marketing in port 13 days	22.30	
Cabin and crew laundry	9.90	
Capt's. wages Oct.-Nov.-Dec.	450.00	
Mate in port 12/10–12/21 Inclus.	36.00	
Wallace & Tucker—night watchman	5.00	
Capt's. expense at Providence	20.00	
4 phone calls to New York getting crew	2.40	
Cook paid off—not citizen 15.00—transport back to New York 2.50 1.00	18.50	
Getting supplies aboard	2.00	
Sea stores 60.04 Ice, Coal, Kerosene 33.10	93.14	
Commission coal 154.20 Lumber 190.05	344.25	4,412.40
		2,545.85
In hand from last trip		1,185.18
In hand		3,731.03

Trip #93 July 6, 1940 Capt. Robt. O. Jones

Newport News, Va., to St. George, Bermuda Coal		
997½ tons bituminous coal @ 3.00	2,992.50	
22 tons coke @ 3.00	66.00	3,058.50
Cap Haitien, Haiti, to Baltimore Logwood		
934.71 gross tons @ 6.00	5,608.27	
34.736 washed overboard Frt. paid by J. S. Young Co. @ 6.00	208.42	5,816.69
		8,875.19
From Darrell & Meyer for 22 tons coke purchased		220.00
Cash from sale of wreck pump		15.00
Slops from crew		28.20
		9,138.39
Ship cook and 4 sailors, New York to Providence, R.I.	15.00	
Transp. 2 cooks and 4 sailors, New York to Providence, R.I.	27.40	

Trip #93 (cont.)

13,000 lb. patent anchor and 3 shackles— Geo. Johnson 1/11/40	150.00	
Freight bill to Norfolk	10.50	
22 tons coke for Darrell & Meyer	220.00	
1 new spanker—Godfrey	390.00	
Frt. spanker to Norfolk 2.63. Old one sold to J. M. White 1/31/40, frt. to Balto. 5.10	7.73	
War risk insurance Newport News to Bermuda	43.75	
Ship cook to Norfolk—Saperstein	9.75	
Marine and War Risk insur. 8.62 22 T coke Tel. and Teleg. 15.51	24.13	
Frt. ins. Prov. to N. News, to Bermuda, to Haiti, to Balto.	232.50	
Liab. Ins. 2/21/40–2/21/41	72.80	
Grub 378.09 Chandlery 168.83 Slops 28.20 Swan	575.12	
Trip to quarantine 1.60 U.S.P.H. Inspect. 10.00	11.60	Allan R. Hoffman
2000′ dunnage 35.00 Dock and undock 32.00 Run lines 2.50	69.50	Allan R. Hoffman
Trimming coal 997½ tons @ .15	149.63	Allan R. Hoffman
Trimming coke 19½ tons @ .32	6.24	Allan R. Hoffman
Cash to cook, paid off at Norfolk	41.84	Allan R. Hoffman
1,870 gals. Water @ 1.50 M	2.81	Allan R. Hoffman
Premium Custom Bond load export coke	5.00	Allan R. Hoffman
20 gals. paint 46.00 Clearance fee 2.50	48.50	Allan R. Hoffman
Launch hire 10.00 Agency fee 25.00 Phone 8.15	43.15	Allan R. Hoffman
Pilotage Newport News to sea 17′ @ 3.50	59.50	Allan R. Hoffman
Provisions at Bermuda Darrell & Meyer	39.00	
Load logwood 1,000 tons @ .40=400.00 Grub 20.65	420.65	J. S. Young & Co.
Postage 1.17 Cables 2.64	3.81	J. S. Young & Co.
Discharging 934.712 tons @ .75	701.03	J. S. Young & Co.
Fresh meats, etc. 8.80 Launch help out to Old Point, Va. 15.00	23.80	N. News
Capt. exp. ashore and to Norfolk locating anchor	7.00	N. News
Medical attn.—cook 2.25 Capt. exp. getting anchor, etc., 20.00	22.25	Bermuda
20 lbs. coffee 2.00, and duty on same .62	2.62	Cap Haitien; Capt. Statement—End at Balto. 4/27/40
Fish, fruit, etc., 3.45 Fresh water 8.00	11.45	Cap Haitien; Capt. Statement—End at Balto. 4/27/40
Boatman and washing paint, etc.	14.00	Cap Haitien; Capt. Statement—End at Balto. 4/27/40
Tarring rigging, oiling booms, etc.	6.60	Cap Haitien; Capt. Statement—End at Balto. 4/27/40
1 set rudder gudgeons for motor boat	2.25	Cap Haitien; Capt. Statement—End at Balto. 4/27/40
Capt. exp. laundry and looking for cook a/c stealing stores	19.50	Cap Haitien; Capt. Statement—End at Balto. 4/27/40
Port captain, motor boat crew help get vessel under way	3.00	Cap Haitien; Capt. Statement—End at Balto. 4/27/40
Crew's wages on trip	1,140.00	Capt. Statement—End at Balto. 4/27/40
Capt's. wages Jan.-Feb.-March-April	600.00	Capt. Statement—End at Balto. 4/27/40
Cook in port 3/26–4/21/40 Paid off	67.50	Capt. Statement—End at Balto. 4/27/40

½ ton coal 6.05 Pots, pans, etc., 4.85	10.90	
Weld cable shackles, 2 pins, etc.	26.00	
Phone calls .80 Laundry, cabin and foc's'le 9.65	10.45	
Marketing 85.60 Capt's. exp. in port 5.00	90.60	
Wages—Capt. Davis in port 3/21–4/20	90.00	
Inward pilotage 3/26/40 Balto.	50.00	
Tow stream to J. S. Young & Co.	20.00	
Tonnage tax 13.22 Entry 2.50 Entrance fee 3.00	18.72	
Inspec. U.S.P.H. 10.00 Tow—Young's to Redman & Vane 20.00	30.00	
Social Security tax—1st qtr.—1940 20.44 Teleg's. 2.63	23.07	
Commission—Coal	152.93	
Commission—Logwood	290.83	6,114.41
		3,023.98
Due vessel from last trip		3,731.03
		6,755.01

End Policy Period

Trip #94 October 3, 1940 Capt. Robt. O. Jones

Newport News, Va., to St. George, Bermuda Coal		
1,009 tons @ 3.00	3,027.00	
From Wm. E. Meyer & Co.—25 tires	22.25	
From Wm. E. Meyer & Co. War Risk Ins.	43.75	3,093.00
Jacksonville, Fla., To Portland, Me. Lumber Lump sum		4,000.00
Slops from Vane Bros.		43.90
Refund gas tax		7.00
		7,143.90

Work on domestic pump, etc.	77.79
75 links #88 chain and 2 couplers	8.20
11½ lbs. nails 1.13 1 qt. Lubin Tasgon 1.13	2.26
Paint, linseed oil, dryers, etc.	125.34
Turnbuckle rods 12.00 Hinges and bolts 4.75	16.75
3 keys, 2 pawls, 2 keepers, etc.	14.00
6 shackles 5.40 Canvas duck, sail twine, etc. 50.64	56.04
R. B. White luncheons 1.90 6 tires 3.00	4.90
25 tires 20.25, and loading 2.00 Wm. E. Meyer & Co.	22.25
36 gals. Balto. brown copper paint	81.43
Vessel repairs, Redman & Vane	658.74
Telep. and teleg. 8.57 2.12 Addtl. prem. liab. ins. 55.54	66.23
Chandlery 134.19 178.07 46.40 10.51 Stores 251.05 29.40 Gas and oil 45.50	724.83

Trip #94 (cont.)

	Tow Balto. to Norfolk S. B. & D. D. Co.	150.00	
	Tow Norfolk S. B. & D. D. Co. to Newport News	60.00	
	Docking, painting to waterline and repairs—NSB&DDCo.— Day labor	1,402.00	
	Ship steward to Balto. and exp.		
	Ship 2 sailors to Norfolk and exp. and teleg. to steward and Captain	34.64	
	12 packages Magic Yeast	1.20	
	War Risk 43.75 Frt. Ins. 150.00	193.75	
	Dock and undock Pier 9 30.40 Run lines 2.50	32.90	Statement Allan Hoffman
	Dump and trimming coal 1,009 tons @ .15	151.35	
	1,571 gals. water @ 1.50 M	2.36	
	Clearance 2.50 Outward pilotage 17′6″ @ 3.50 61.25	63.75	
	Attendance fee	25.00	
	Cables 2.75	2.75	
Norfolk & N. News	Rating chronometer 3.00 Launch hire 8.00	11.00	Capt. Stmt.
	Ointment 1.38 Ice 2.10 Fresh meat 12.80	16.28	
	Capt's. exp. Norfolk and Newport News	12.00	
Bermuda	Marketing 10.06 Exchange 3.40	13.46	
	Capt's. exp. Bermuda, cigars to Meyer's stevedores	20.00	
Jacksonville	Harbor master 7.50 Caulk bow ports 8.00	15.50	Capt's. Statement—Portland 7/15/1940
	Weld 2 castings, making bolts and washers	7.50	
	Pilotage In 10′ 18.75 Out 49.55 Jacksonville	68.30	
	Tow sea to Jacksonville to sea 735 tons @ .33	242.55	
	Water 10.00 Linoleum—3 rooms 45.00	45.00	
	Entry 2.50 Tonnage tax 13.22 Jacksonville	15.72	
	Quarantine 10.00 Stores 136.82 Chandlery 51.94	198.76	
	Mizzen topsail 119.00 Life boat cover 30.50	149.50	
	Vegetable bin cover	10.50	
	Carpenter work on hatch coamings	126.00	
	Stevedores taking 5 pcs. LLYPine out of cargo for coamings	5.00	
	Laundry after coal cargo 7.30 Stevedores 5.50 Watchman	12.80	
	Utensils for galley and cabin	2.15	
	Captain's expense at Portland	15.00	
	Sailor's and cook's wages—Trip	735.50	
	Mate's wages—4/21–6/27/40	201.00	
	Cook's wages in port 6/28–7/11/40	35.00	
Bernstein & Jacobsen	Wild cat 130.00 Water tank 60.00 Russell pump 10.00		
	1 topmast 30.00 Gaff 20.00 Tires for fenders 5.00	287.28	
	269 lbs. 4″ mooring line 32.28		
	Fresh water 7.70 Cabin and foc's'le laundry 6.85	14.55	
	Rope, Mast hoops, Peak halyards, 2nd hand band and rings	25.00	
	Chandlery 379.20 Stores 301.42	680.62	
	Docking and undocking to anchorage	70.00	

Help towing out—Portland	20.00	
Rate chronometer 2.00 Ship sailor, bus fare and teleg. 6.00	8.00	
Taxi—2 sailors .75 Clearing 2.50	3.25	
Capt's. wages May-June-July 1940	450.00	
Capt's. exp. to Bath and Boothbay and Custom House a/c wildcat	20.00	
Social Security tax 2nd qtr. 1940	19.66	
Mianus Engine Co.—engine parts	40.34	
Commission Coal 154.65 Lumber 200.00	354.65	7,930.33
In debt this trip		786.43
In hand from previous statement		6,755.10
In hand and due by Captain		5,968.58

Trip #95 October 7, 1940 Capt. Robt. O. Jones

Cap Haitien, Haiti, to Baltimore Logwood		
707.81 gross tons @ 6.35	4,494.59	
200.00 gross tons @ 6.00	1,200.00	5,694.59
Shipping 3 men 9.00 Telegram .60	9.60	
Transp. taxi, baggage, and meals for same, New York to Portland	26.00	
Freight ins.—Portland—Haiti—Baltimore	180.00	
Telegrams and telephone	4.80	
Load 950 French tons @ .40	380.00	
2 cables 2.64 Medicine 1.40	4.04	
Doctor and extract sailor's tooth	3.00	
1 bbl. honey—32 gals. J. S. Young & Co.	10.00	
Marketing and sea stores	65.08	
Fresh water 14.00 Chipping windlass, etc. 16.00	30.00	
Ice daily and for sea	11.25	
Capt's. exp. Stevedores, Port Captain, Customs etc.	16.00	
Crew wages on trip to 9/16/40	946.50	
Capt's. wages—Aug. and Sept.	300.00	
Marketing 24.15 Balto. Ice 2.75	26.90	
Laundry Cabin and foc's'le	11.60	
Capt's. exp.—entertaining American Bureau Betz	10.00	
4 wrenches and 1 pair pliers	2.71	
Mate in port 9/18–9/30/40	42.00	
Entry 2.50 Tonnage tax 13.22 Ice 3.00	18.72	
Inspection service—Quarantine	10.00	
Docking—Quarantine to Young's	25.00	
Tow stage Redman & Vane to Young's to Redman & Vane	4.00	
Disch. 907.81 gross tons logwood @ .75	680.86	

Trip #95 (cont.)

Insurances on advances on Bill of Lading	44.47	
Inspection deratization—exemption	10.00	
Inward pilotage	50.00	
Labor—caulking and putting stores away	2.00	
Commission 284.73 Soc. Security tax 18.21	302.94	3,227.47
		2,467.12
In hand from last statement		5,968.58
Dividend to owners 12/19/40 5,400.00		8,435.70
1/90 C. Howard Paul	60.00	
89/90 C. C. Paul & Co.	5,340.00	5,400.00
		3,035.70

Trip #96 December 1, 1940 Capt. Robt. O. Jones

From Baltimore Light to Jacksonville to Portland, Me. Lumber 505.302 ft. Lump sum		4,000.00
Slops from crew (Capt. S. C. Co.) 9/27/40 21.55 Gas refund 2.00		23.55
		4,023.55

Ship 2 men 8.00 Fare to Old Point 19.25 Teleg. 2.39	29.64
Survey fee and exp., 2nd special survey #2, per report 9872	76.00
Telep. and teleg. 6.19 Repair and clean chronometer 25.00	31.19
Redman & Vane 24.67 Ship 4 sailors 12.40	37.07
New mizzen 1/o Mt. Vernon Godfrey Inv. 9/27/40	347.78
Gas and oil 14.15 Stores 26.75 Chandlery 104.70 Slops 21.55 Capt. Ship Chandlery Co.	167.15
Stores 183.30 Chandlery 49.30 Vane	232.60
Tow out Young's to Baltimore Light Curlett	40.00
Frt. insur. Jacksonville to Portland	67.50
Putting sail, Ice, Stores, etc. aboard Baltimore	3.50
Marketing by cook	3.40
Pilotage in 10′6″ 20.55 Out 17′6″ 49.55 Jacksonville	70.10
Fresh water 10.00 Harbor master 7.50	17.50
Work on water tanks—Brennan Iron Works	93.60
Tow sea to Jacksonville, light to sea 735 tons @ .33	242.55
Stores 131.51 Chandlery 128.84	260.35
Repair foresail 125.00 1 wire stay 44.00	169.00
1 main topsail 22″ #5 Mt. Vernon	123.00
1 coil 3¼″ 3 strand #1 Plymouth manila rope	77.16
2 sailors paid off—Jacksonville 18.00 each	36.00
Carpenter work at Jacksonville	69.00

Capt. Statement ending at Balto. 4/11/41 (bracketing the entries from "Putting sail, Ice, Stores, etc. aboard Baltimore" to "Carpenter work at Jacksonville")

Jax., S.C. Co. 629.51 (bracketing the entries from "Stores 131.51 Chandlery 128.84" to "1 coil 3¼″ 3 strand #1 Plymouth manila rope")

Repairs forward pumping engine	21.65		
Caulk bow ports and transom, etc.	16.40		
Capt. exp. gratuity to stevedores, telegs. for sailors, taxi to ship commissioner, pay off 2 men, sign on 2, etc.	20.00		
Crew wages to Portland—trip	420.00		
Fare 1 sailor to Balto. 6.90 to Jacksonville 32.48	39.38		
Advance on wages, O. Tate	12.00		
Balance wages O. Tate paid off by C. C. Paul & Co.	57.04		Capt. Statement. taken from vessel by C. G. a/c injured.
Commission	200.00		
Captain's wages Oct.–Nov 1940	300.00		
Ship 3 men at New York for Portland	12.00		
Fares to Portland 28.25 Teleg. .44 .44	29.13		
Phone calls New York to Captain at Balto. 1.90 1.20	3.10		
Stores 142.42 Gas and oil 29.60	172.02		Should be 75.00 bal. on next statement.
Machine work on hoist, engine pump, etc.	173.02		
Docking and undocking and towing past Spring Garden Point and out to sea	80.00		
Boat assistance in from West Cod ledge	20.00		
Dunnage for logwood to cover bells in wake of hatches, etc.	11.00		
Ship's laundry 9.95 Phone calls a/c crew 6.15	16.10		
Ship 1 man and getting 3 sailors from New York and sea bags 6.00 4 doz. flashlight batteries 3.30	9.30		
Help taking down Edison pump and putting in Russell pump, etc.	8.75		
8 gals. paint 12.00 Oakum 11.40 Wrench, etc., Bread and yeast .56	23.96		
Capt's. exp. stationery, Shipping commissioner, etc.	17.50	3,856.44	
		167.11	
Due vessel from last statement		3,035.70	
		3,202.81	

Trip #97 May 31, 1941 Capt. Robt. O. Jones

Item	Amount	Total
Newport News, Va., to St. George, Bermuda Coal		
1,007 gross tons @ 4.00	4,028.00	
From Wm. E. Meyer & Co. for lightening lumber	15.00	
Slops from crew Swan 12/9/40	10.32	
From Swan a/c overcharge on lightening lumber	5.00	4,058.32

Returned light to Newport News

Coal Newport News to Bermuda	
992½ gross tons bituminous coal	
10 gross tons anthracite coal	
1,002½ gross tons @ 4.00	4,010.00

Trip #97 (cont.)			
Slops from crew Swan 1/23/41	32.00		
From Haitian Agricultural Corp. for lumber	187.50	4,229.50	
Cap Haitien, Haiti, to Baltimore Logwood			
930.5786 gross tons @ 8.50		7,909.92	
		16,197.74	
Telegrams 6.08 War Risk insur. 43.75	49.83		
Frt. ins. Hampton Roads to Bermuda to Haiti	125.00		
Docking and undocking Newport News	30.40		Hoffman statement
Running lines 2.50 1,772 gals. water @ 1.50 M 2.66	5.16		Hoffman statement
Trimming coal 1,007 tons @ .15	151.05		Hoffman statement
Telegrams .56 Entering 5.00 Clearing 2.50	8.06		Hoffman statement
Premium bond a/c loading export cargo	8.00		Hoffman statement
Preparing, filing and obtain clearance permit	5.00		Hoffman statement
Phone calls 1.60 3 gals. Bakelite paint 8.25	9.85		Hoffman statement
Attendance fee 25.00 Outward pilotage 17′3″ @ 3.50 60.38	85.38		Hoffman statement
Launch service to assist vessel under way—Newport News	12.00		Capt's Statement Balto. 4/11/41
Marketing and hardware 18.60 Capt's. exp. 7.25 Gratuity trimmers	25.85		Capt's Statement Balto. 4/11/41
Marketing and blacksmith work Bermuda	26.05		Capt's Statement Balto. 4/11/41
Capt's. exp. and cigars to Mr. Meyer	18.00		Capt's Statement Balto. 4/11/41
To Mr. Barnes a/c British War Fund	5.00		Capt's Statement Balto. 4/11/41
Stores 130.05 Chandlery 264.92 Slops 10.32 Lightening lumber 20.00	425.29		
Commission 201.40	201.40		
Docking and undocking at Pier 9 Newport News	30.40		Hoffman Statement
Running lines 2.50 1,272 gals. water @ 1.50 M 1.91	4.41		Hoffman Statement
Trimming coal 991½ tons @ .15	148.88		Hoffman Statement
Marketing 18.11 Gas 24.20 Oil 9.90	52.21		Hoffman Statement
15 gals. paint 36.00 Teleg. and Telep. 1.83	37.83		Hoffman Statement
Laundry 11.95 Long distance phone calls 13.95	25.90		Hoffman Statement
Immigration service—Sunday boarding	16.66		Hoffman Statement
Custom House fees 11.66 Entry and tonnage tax 15.72 Clearing 2.50	29.88		Hoffman Statement
Entry and clearing 5.00 Fumigation 10.00	15.00		Hoffman Statement
Premium bond loading export cargo	8.00		Hoffman Statement
Preparing, filing, and obtaining clearance permit	5.00		Hoffman Statement
Launch hire—C. C. Skeeter	29.00		Hoffman Statement
Outward pilotage 17′3″	60.38		Hoffman Statement
Sending to Old Point for sailor's bag	3.00		Hoffman Statement
Attendance fee	25.00		Hoffman Statement
Lumber for Porter K. Crooks 450 pcs. 1 × 10 × 10 D4SPine @ 50.00	187.50		
2 sailors paid off at Newport News 129.17 125.00	254.17		

Launch service, assist vessel thru channel, get sails on	16.00	Capt's. Statement ending at Balto. 4/11/1941
Freshmeats a/c sailing delayed 38 lbs. @ .25	9.50	
Capt's. exp. at Newport News, hotel room, too rough to board	13.25	
Marketing 31.72 8 chickens @ .75 6.00	37.72	
Help sweeping hold, bending sails on gaffs after disch. (sailors working on sails)	7.50	
Capt's. exp. at Bermuda and assist keeping vessel in channel (anchors went out)	26.75	
Entertaining Mr. Meyer, etc., and Naval Control Cmdr.	20.00	
Cable arrival at Haiti and departure 1.32 1.32	2.64	
Loading 950 French tons logwood @ .40	380.00	
Topmast gaff 15.00 and getting same down and ashore—Sunday 10.00	25.00	
Iron bands for topmast	2.00	
Fresh provisions and sea stores	59.52	Capt's. Statement ending at Balto. 4/11/1941
21 cans tomatoes 6.30 12 tall cans evap. milk 1.20	7.50	
Fresh water 4.00 Laundry 3.00	7.00	
Men scraping 51.00 Master and crew on sails, etc.	51.00	
Gratuity stevedores and Port Captain, Haiti	15.00	
Medical attention to sailor and ointment	5.00	
Handling Mr. Crooks' lumber from on coal and stow on deck	10.00	
Crew's wages on trip	1,828.06	
Capt's. wages. Dec. 1940 Jan.-Feb.-March-April 1941	750.00	
Repairing rotator—Smola	1.50	Total bill
Balance of Deering-Winslow dunnage bill	64.00	75.00 11.00 on previous stmt
Soc. Secty. tax 4th qtr. 1940 13.30 1st qtr. 1941 31.97	45.27	
Disch. 930.5786 tons logwood @ .75	697.93	
War Risk Insur. Newport News to Bermuda	43.75	
Frt. insur. Newport News to Bermuda to Haiti to Balto.	260.00	
War Risk Insur. Haiti to Baltimore	52.50	
New flying jib #1 Mt. Vernon 107.00 Frt. to Norfolk 1.59	108.59	
Stores 115.54 Chandlery 93.15 Slops 32.00 Swan 1/23/41	240.69	
Liab. insur. 2/21/41–2/21/42	90.27	
Telep. and teleg. 11.46 Inward pilotage 50.00	61.46	
Tow north of Poplar Island Gas Buoy to Canton, Balto.	125.00	
Quarantine 10.00 Deratization exemp. certif. 10.00	20.00	
Entry 2.50 Tonnage tax 13.22 Entrance fee 5.00	20.72	
Custom's overtime a/c discharging	15.85	
Commission Coal and logwood	596.00	
Tow Young's to Booz Railway	25.00	
Tow Booz to Balto. Ship Repair Co.	25.30	
Lumber from Weyerhauser	22.81	

Trip #97 (cont.)

Repairs to ice box 40.85 Bolts and nuts 7.24	48.09	
Bolts and lag screws 4.53 Bolts .85 Washers 1.96	7.34	
Work on vessel Green 40.70 Reid 48.40 Kell 45.30	134.40	
Work on vessel Green	11.00	
Taxi .35 Cigars 1.25 Sailor's picture R. B. White .50	2.10	
Soc. Secty. tax .41 .48 .45 .11	1.45	
Railway bill Booz Bros.	1,099.28	
Railway bill Redman & Vane	900.00	
J. A. Cox Agent a/c shifting 5.00 Telep. and Teleg. 4.03	9.03	
Foretopsail, mainsail, spanker topsail—Godfrey	663.94	10,791.25
		5,406.49
Due vessel from last trip		3,202.81
Due vessel		8,609.30

End Policy period

Trip #98 August 25, 1941 Capt. Robt. O. Jones

Newport News, Va., to St. George, Bermuda Coal 1,022 gross tons @ 5.50	5,621.00	
Cap Haitien, Haiti, to Baltimore Logwood 921.80 gross tons @ 13.25	12,213.85	17,834.85
From Meyer Ltd. 50 used tires @ .45	22.50	
From Meyer Ltd. 30 gals. paint	60.00	82.50
From J. S. Young a/c Crooks' material	14.55	
From P. K. Crooks Hand lumber last trip	10.00	
From P. K. Crooks Paint Linseed oil Batteries, etc.	28.10	52.65
Refund gasoline tax		9.00
		17,979.00

American Bureau survey fee a/c completion 2nd special survey #2 Report 10360	53.00	
Weld ring, bolts, turnbuckle, etc.	6.80	
Oak lumber and labor A. Smith	8.50	
Stores 70.02 Chandlery 103.22 Capt. Ship Chandlery Co.	173.24	
Stores—daily 155.04 Sea 297.57 Chandlery .90 645.77 Vane	1,099.28	
50 used tires for Wm. H. Meyer Ltd.	22.04	
War Risk insur. 112.50 Freight insur. 350.00	462.50	
Tow Baltimore to Newport News	175.00	

Place	Item	Amount	Statement
	Running lines 2.50 Docking and undocking Pier 9 30.40	32.90	Hoffman Statement
	Dumping and trimming 1,022 T. Coal	153.30	
	1,197 gals. water @ 1.50 M	1.80	
	Marketing 20.29 10.70 3 truck 1.50, and 12 auto tires 5.40	37.89	
	20 gals. white, 20 gals. Battleship grey, 10 gals. buff pt.	100.00	
	Telegrams 2.85 Clearing 2.50	5.35	
	Entering, clearing, and Custom House papers	10.00	
	Exp. and fare—1 man Portland to Newport News	20.00	
	Shipping fee for above man	10.00	
	Auto service getting crew to launch	3.00	
	Launch hire a/c signing on crew	22.00	
	Attendance fee 25.00 Long distance phone calls 14.75	39.75	
	Preparing clearance of Haiti cargo a/c Crooks	14.55	
	Preparing, filing, and obtain Clearance permit	5.00	
	Premium Custom Bond Lading export cargo	8.00	
	Outward pilotage—Newport News to sea 17′6″ @ 4.00	70.00	
Baltimore	Marketing at Balto. 13.09 Yeast 4.05 Dishes, etc.	17.14	Capt. Stmt. Balto. 7/21/41
	Getting picture of vessel for Mr. Whip a/c suit	2.20	
	Colored cook in port—Balto. 4/15–4/23/41	27.00	
	Laundry 8.40—Balto., 1 jack plane, chisel 3.75	12.15	
	Capt's. exp. at Balto.	3.15	
Newport News	Sailor paid off at Newport News 4/14–5/19 inclus.	78.02	
	Sailor's fare—Newport News to Balto.	4.00	
	Launch service, assist vessel out of Lynnhaven Rds., Va.	20.00	
	Capt. exp. gratuity to trimmers, meals ashore for two sailors, room for one	17.50	
	Marketing and sea stores Bermuda	40.94	
Haiti	Capt. exp. gratuity stevedores, cigars, etc.	25.00	Capt's. Statement—Balto. 7/21/41
	Marketing 6.21 less 1.18 a/c postage from crew	5.03	
	1—11′ cedar skiff 20.00 Fresh water 9.00	29.00	
	Blacksmith work on motor boat	5.00	
	Boatman and labor getting vessel painted	31.20	
	Capt. exp. gratuity stevedores, Port Captain, etc.	20.00	
Balto.	Crew wages on trip	1,421.66	
	Capt's. wages—May-June-July	600.00	
	Sailor acting as boatswain—2 mos.	10.00	
	Exp. paying off aboard etc.	5.00	
	Loading 950 tons logwood @ .40	380.00	Crooks' Statement
	Marketing, coffee	82.92	
	Stamps 1.68 Cables 2.64	4.32	
	War Ris. Insur. Haiti to Balto.	50.00	
	Towing off Sandy Point, Md., to Young's—Balto.	75.00	
	Entry 2.50 Tonnage tax 13.22 Entering 5.00	20.72	

Trip #98 (cont.)		
Quarantine inspection	10.00	
Disch. 921.8 tons logwood @ .75	691.35	
1,000 gals. fresh water	1.00	
Holding mate at Boston—did not make trip	6.60	
Soc. Secty. tax—2nd qtr.—1941	27.36	
Commission Coal 281.05 Logwood 610.69	891.74	7,218.90
		10,760.10
Due vessel from last trip		8,609.30
Due vessel		19,369.40

Dividend to owners 8/25/41
1/90 = 150.00

1/90	C. Howard Paul	150.00	
89/90	C. C. Paul & Co.	13,350.00	13,500.00
			5,869.40

Trip #99 Capt. Robt. O. Jones

Cap Haitien, Haiti, to Baltimore Logwood		
953.703 gross tons @ 13.25		12,636.56
Gas refund		4.40
		12,640.96
Shipping fee 49.76 Transp. and teleg.—last trip .57	50.33	
Capt. Davis, extra a/c making last trip to Haiti	75.00	
Expense getting pilot to Baltimore Fare 12.15, Meals 1.00 Taxi 2.00	15.15	
1 pkg. yeast 1.08 26 pcs. Va. R. pine 32.10	33.18	
Addtl. premium Liab. insur. 59.35 11.51	70.86	
Repairs R.C.A. radio	9.50	
1 new Philco 124 T radio and battery	37.95	
Repairs pump and pipe from tank	19.65	
Stores 72.08 Chandlery 247.20 Capt. Ship Chandlery Co.	319.28	
Stores 291.85 Chandlery 377.67 Vane	669.52	
Shipping 2 sailors	10.00	
1 new foresail #1/0 Woodberry	332.00	
1 new tarpaulin #4 W. P. canvas	26.60	
War Risk Insur. Balto. to Haiti	52.50	
Frt. insur. Baltimore—Haiti—Baltimore	400.00	
Clearing, Consul fee, Clearance	17.50	
Telegrams 5.00 Outward pilotage 20.00	25.00	

	Item	Amount	Total	
	Tow Young's dock to Sandy Point 8/8/41	65.00		
Balto.	Ship's laundry	12.11		Capt's. Statement
	Paid cook for cleaning varnish in cabin, etc.	20.00		
	Marketing by cook 7/21–8/5/41	39.35		
	Capt's. exp. signing crew, stationery, etc.	9.15		
Haiti	Motorboat trying to pull vessel from cove and channel after being ashore, but failed	15.00		
	Tow vessel in from cove after being ashore	100.00		
	4 men working around vessel	39.00		
	Meals and 4 sailors in jail, awaiting U.S. Consul, arrested	3.05		
	Laundry 2.25 1,200 gals. fresh water 10.00	12.25		
	Marketing and fresh sea stores 9/4–9/27/41	83.45		
	Capt's. exp. a/c crew trouble and vessel ashore	23.00		
	Stevedores 10.00 Load 974.784 gross tons logwood @ .43 420.75	430.75		
	Towing out to sea	50.00		
Balto.	Crew wages on trip	1,272.94		Capt. Stmt.
	Capt. Davis' wages in port 7/20–8/4/41	66.56		
	Capt's. wages Aug.-Sept.-Oct.	600.00		
	2 sailors keeping Capt's. watch and dispute over wages	20.00		
	Quarantine	10.00		
	Pilotage in 17′—@ 5.50	93.50		
	Tow Smith's Point, Va., to Young's dock	200.00		
	Entering 5.00 Customs 2.50 Tonnage tax 13.22	20.72		
	Deratization exempt, Inspection	10.00		
	Immigration service, overtime	3.75		
	War Risk insur.—Haiti to Baltimore	52.50		
	Service of diver at Young's dock	30.00		
	Assisting diver	3.00		
	Social Security tax	23.32		
	Commission	631.83		
	Discharging 953.703 tons logwood	715.28	6,819.53	
			5,821.43	
	Due vessel from last trip		5,869.40	
			11,690.83	
	Due vessel from trip #99		11,690.83	
	For old rope sold to ram *Edwin and Maud*	17.05		
	For old rope sold to C. C. Paul & Co.	24.20		
	From Parry Shipping Co. a/c vessel bills	500.00	541.25	
			12,232.08	
	Stove pipe, Floor boards, etc.	24.25		
	Stores 29.54 Copper paint 90.31 Vane 10/11/41	119.85		
	Tow Balto. to Norfolk from Young's 10/28/41	225.00		

Trip #99 (cont.)

Drydocking and repairs to vessel Norfolk S. B. Co. Contract 11/5/41		2,050.53	
Pipe and fittings 3.57 Muffler and nipple 10.48		14.05	
Tow Norfolk to Redman & Vane, Balto. 11/4/41		225.00	
Telephone and telegraph		10.26	
1 boom—Patapsco Dry Dock Co.		50.00	
Work on boom and install fittings		160.00	
Elec. weld sheet traveler		8.00	
Repairs to vessel—Redman & Vane 12/1/41		306.41	
Chandlery 38.15 4.85 = 43.00—8.00 credit		35.00	
Cash to Captain Jones 10/28	20.00		
Cash to Mrs. Jones 11/1	100.00		
Cash to Captain Jones 11/7	80.00		
Cash to Mrs. Jones 12/1	100.00		
Cash to Captain Jones 12/16	100.00		
Captain's wages Nov.–Dec. 1941		400.00	
Ship's laundry		5.00	
Cash to J. E. Hanger a/c Captain Jones		84.00	
Exp. R. B. White to Norfolk		37.17	
Paid cook—daily stores Oct. 41.42 Nov. 36.39		77.81	
Tow 3 masts—Wathen's to Smith's		3.00	
Repairs to clock 3.60 Hardware .45 .25 Phone .85		5.15	
Wages E. Green 11/17–11/22/41		19.80	
Wages—cook A. Brown—10/11–10/31/41		77.00	
Wages—cook A. Brown—11/1–11/30/41		110.00	
Wages C. Loveitt 10/11–10/31/41		77.00	
Wages C. Loveitt 11/1–11/5/41		18.32	
Wages C. Loveitt 11/24–11/30/41		25.67	
Transp. Loveitt—Maine to Balto.		8.00	
Wages G. Lindquist 10/26–10/31/41		16.00	
Wages G. Lindquist 11/1–11/30/41		80.00	
Notary fee		.50	
Social Security tax 1.15 3.99		5.14	
Social Security tax Jones		8.00	
A. Stronski—Repairs, welding, etc.		10.90	
Capt's. Ship Chandlery Co.—use of boat a/c diver 12.00 and tow boom, Curtis Bay to vessel 7.00		19.00	
1 box candy 2.00 1 rule .70		2.79	
Liab. insur. addtl. premium		51.95	4,370.46
			7,861.62
Less amount due by Captain R. O. Jones when he left vessel			2,999.01
Amount in hand and due vessel when sold to Albert Shipping Co., Inc., New York, N.Y.			4,862.61

1/90 = 54.029

89/90	C. C. Paul & Co.	4,808.50	
1/90	C. Howard Paul	54.03	4,862.61
			x x x x

Vessel sold for	40,000.00	
Commission a/c sale	2,000.00	38,000.00

1/90 = 422.222

89/90	C. C. Paul & Co.	37,577.78	
1/90	C. Howard Paul	422.22	38,000.00
			x x x x

Checks to owners 12/31/41

Appendix C

Figures and Facts

Statement of Cost of Schooner *Albert F. Paul*

Baltimore, Maryland
October 23, 1917

Contract with W. G. Abbott for hull	$40,000.00
Allowance to Mr. Abbott	750.00
Bonus money	2,000.00
George Taulane Sons, sails	1,900.00
William F. Wilson, rigger	1,142,70
C. M. Struven & Co., a/c outfit	13,304.01
J. S. Beacham & Bro., spars, painting and extra carpentry work	3,778.42
Redman-Vane Shipbuilding Co., painting etc.	56.26
Wm. E. Woodall & Co., hauling	121.59
Geo. W. Ilgenfritz, blacksmith	113.62
Captain Southard, wages, railroad fare, hotel bills, incidentals	1,094.71
W. S. Biggs, ironwork	3,157.60
W. S. Bier, tank and freight	276.93
W. D. Hollhes, loading bowsprit	5.00
Fare to Washington, Shipping Board, a/c masts	1.50
J. L. Gilbert & Bro., screens, table and wood work	120.57
J. F. Corcoran & Co., galvanizing iron work	294.34
Mullen, towing in harbor	26.00
Mianus Motor Works, engine for yawl	204.90
W. G. Abbott, for cartage and freight on outfit and extras	969.47
Carving trailboards	26.00
H. D. McCollough & Son, plumber	700.00
Watchman at Baltimore	64.00
Hughes & Sons Transp. & Towing Co., towing to Baltimore	1,400.00
J. W. Neilly, galvanizing link and chain	21.73
Rohde & Sons Co., building boats and cutting numbers	277.28
Otto Schmidt, medicines	54.60
E. J. Codd Co., rudder supporter	165.00

Maury, Donnelly, Williams Co., trip and harbor ins.	481.25
Duffer, Baggott & Co., copper wire and rods	15.69
John J. Nigl, plumbing and supplies	58.12
R. H. Dougherty, making davits	226.85
Geo. D. Summers, furniture for the cabin	179.70
I. Franklin & Son, blacksmith work	264.37
The Gibson & Kirk Co., furnishing and putting up hand rails, etc.	94.21
Duer, brass screws, knobs, and buttons	4.06
Chronometer	200.00
Mianus Motor Works, engine for forward house	1,502.87
J. F. Fisher, surveyor	195.37
Ten certificates of ownership	2.00
John E. Hand & Sons Co., nautical supplies	10.30
	$75,261.02

Paid in full for hull	$40,000.00
Paid bonus to carpenters	2,000.00
Paid account outfit	15,300.00
Paid account outfit	9,000.00

C. C. Paul, Managing owners

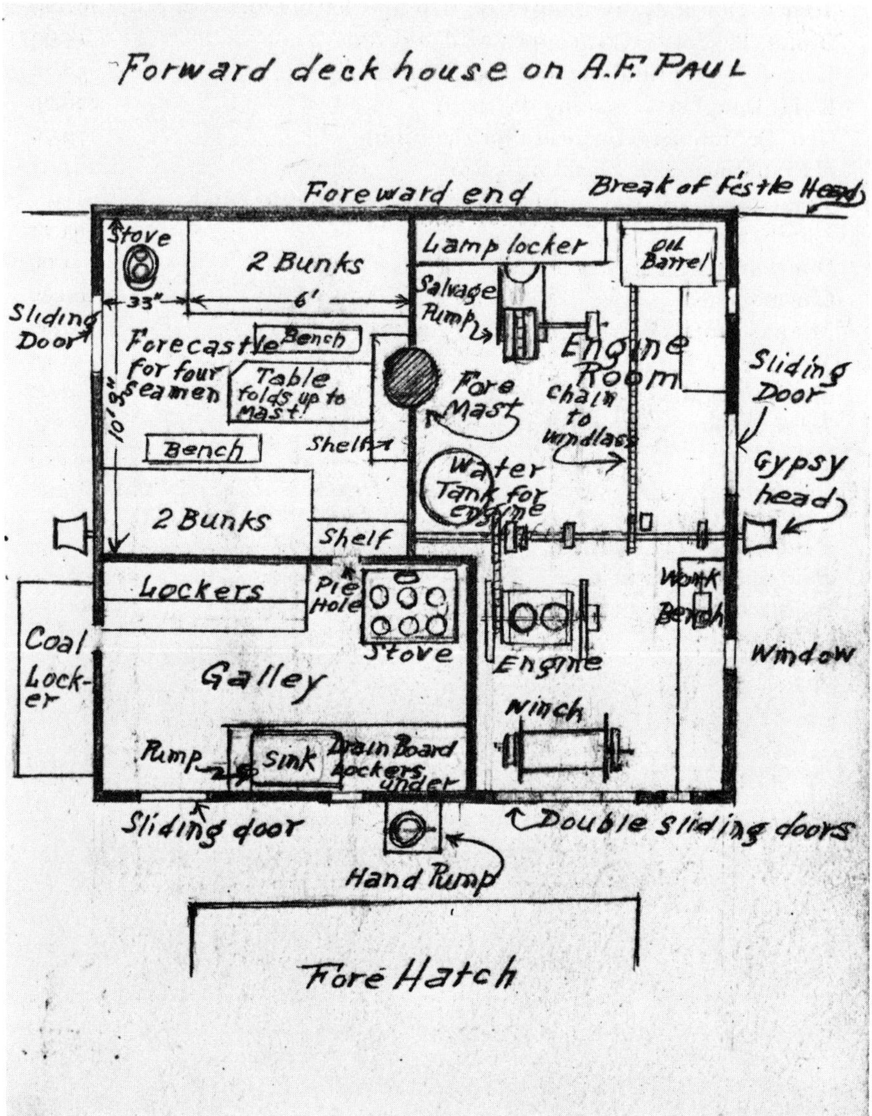
Forward deck house on A.F. PAUL
Foreward end
Break of fo'c'stle Head
Stove
2 Bunks
33"
6'
Sliding Door
Forecastle for four seamen
Bench
Table folds up to mast!
10'9"
Bench
Shelf
2 Bunks
Shelf
Lamp locker
Oil Barrel
Salvage Pump
Engine Room
Fore Mast
chain to windlass
Water Tank for engine
Sliding Door
Gypsy head
Lockers
Pie Hole
Stove
Coal Locker
Galley
Engine
Work Bench
Window
Winch
Pump
Sink
Drain Board lockers under
Sliding door
Double sliding doors
Hand Pump
Fore Hatch

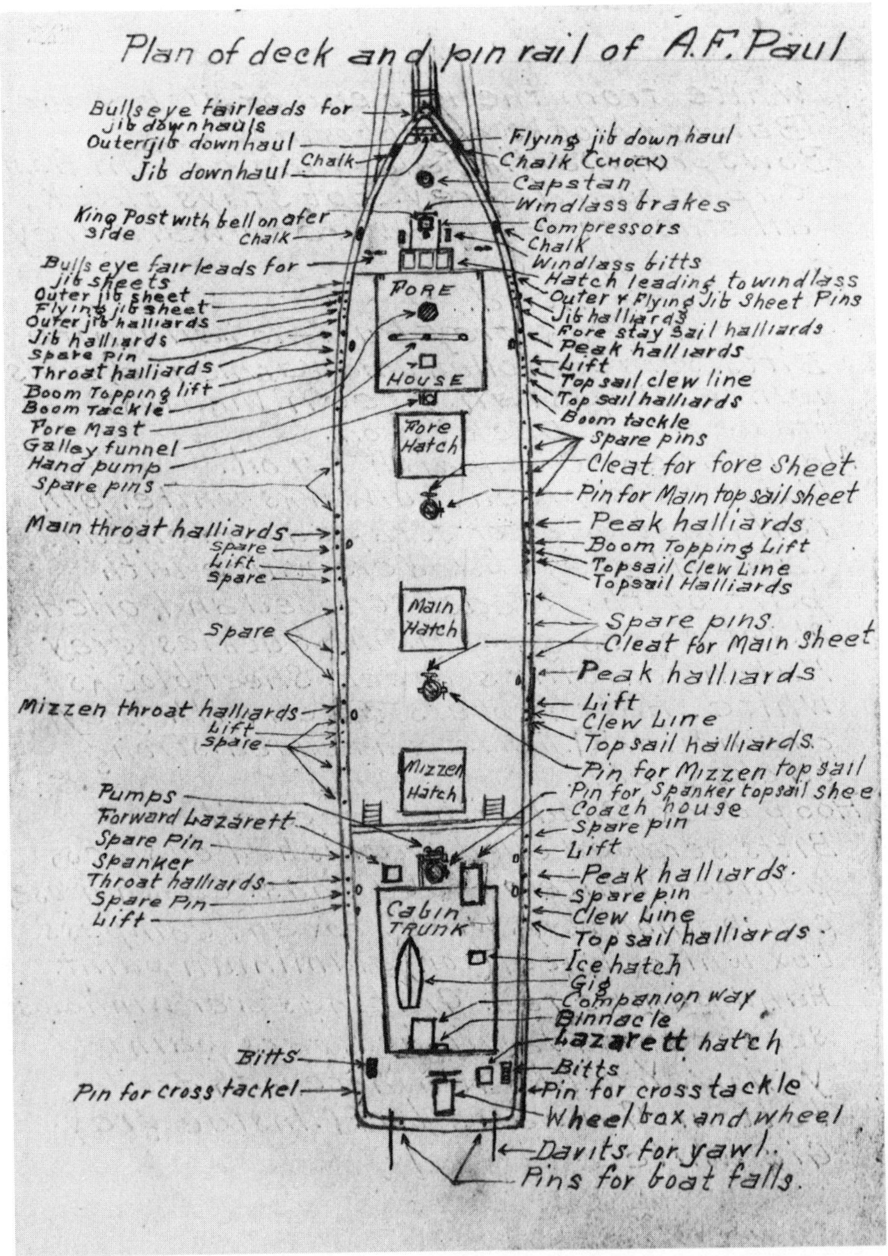
Plan of deck and pin rail of A.F. Paul
Bullseye fairleads for jib downhauls
Outer jib downhaul
Chalk
Jib downhaul
Flying jib down haul
Chalk (CHOCK)
Capstan
Windlass brakes
King Post with bell on after side
Chalk
Compressors
Chalk
Windlass bitts
Bulls eye fair leads for jib sheets
Hatch leading to windlass
Outer jib sheet
Flying jib sheet
Outer jib halliards
Jib halliards
Spare Pin
Throat halliards
Boom Topping lift
Boom Tackle
Fore Mast
Galley funnel
Hand pump
Spare pins
Outer & Flying Jib Sheet Pins
Jib halliards
Fore stay sail halliards
Peak halliards
Lift
Top sail clew line
Top sail halliards
Boom tackle
Spare pins
Cleat for fore Sheet
Pin for Main top sail sheet
FORE
HOUSE
Fore Hatch
Main throat halliards
Spare
Lift
Spare
Peak halliards
Boom Topping Lift
Topsail Clew Line
Topsail Halliards
Main Hatch
Spare
Spare pins
Cleat for Main sheet
Peak halliards
Mizzen throat halliards
Lift
Spare
Lift
Clew Line
Top sail halliards
Mizzen Hatch
Pin for Mizzen top sail
Pumps
Forward Lazarett
Spare Pin
Spanker
Throat halliards
Spare Pin
Lift
Pin for Spanker topsail shee
Coach house
Spare pin
Lift
Peak halliards
Spare pin
Clew Line
Top sail halliards
Cabin TRUNK
Ice hatch
Gig
Companion way
Binnacle
Lazarett hatch
Bitts
Pin for cross tackel
Bitts
Pin for cross tackle
Wheel box and wheel
Davits for yawl
Pins for boat falls

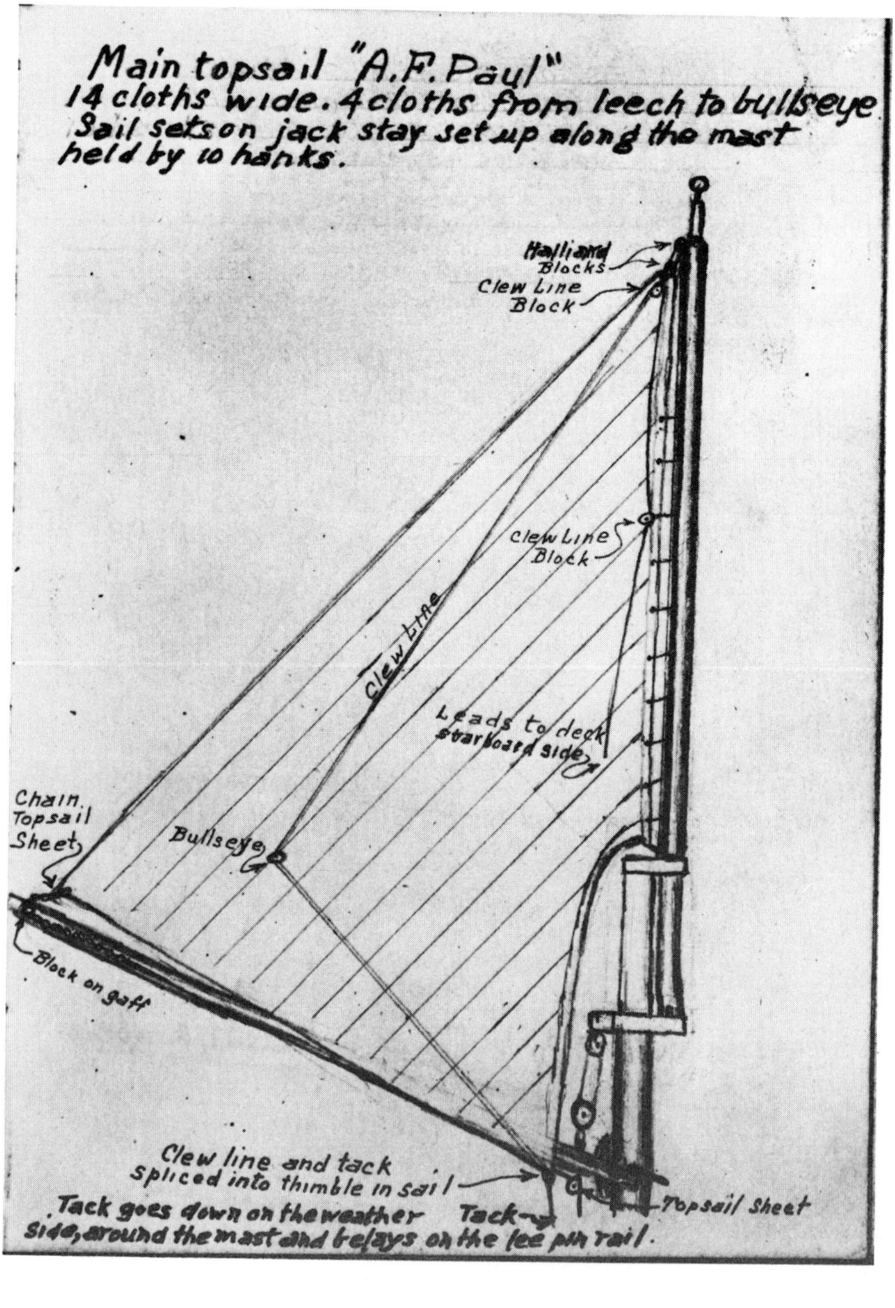
Main topsail "A.F. Paul"
14 cloths wide. 4 cloths from leech to bullseye
Sail sets on jack stay set up along the mast
held by 10 hanks.
Halliard Blocks
Clew Line Block
Clew Line Block
Clew Line
Leads to deck starboard side
Chain Topsail Sheet
Bullseye
Block on gaff
Clew line and tack spliced into thimble in sail
Tack goes down on the weather side, around the mast and belays on the lee pin rail.
Tack
Topsail Sheet

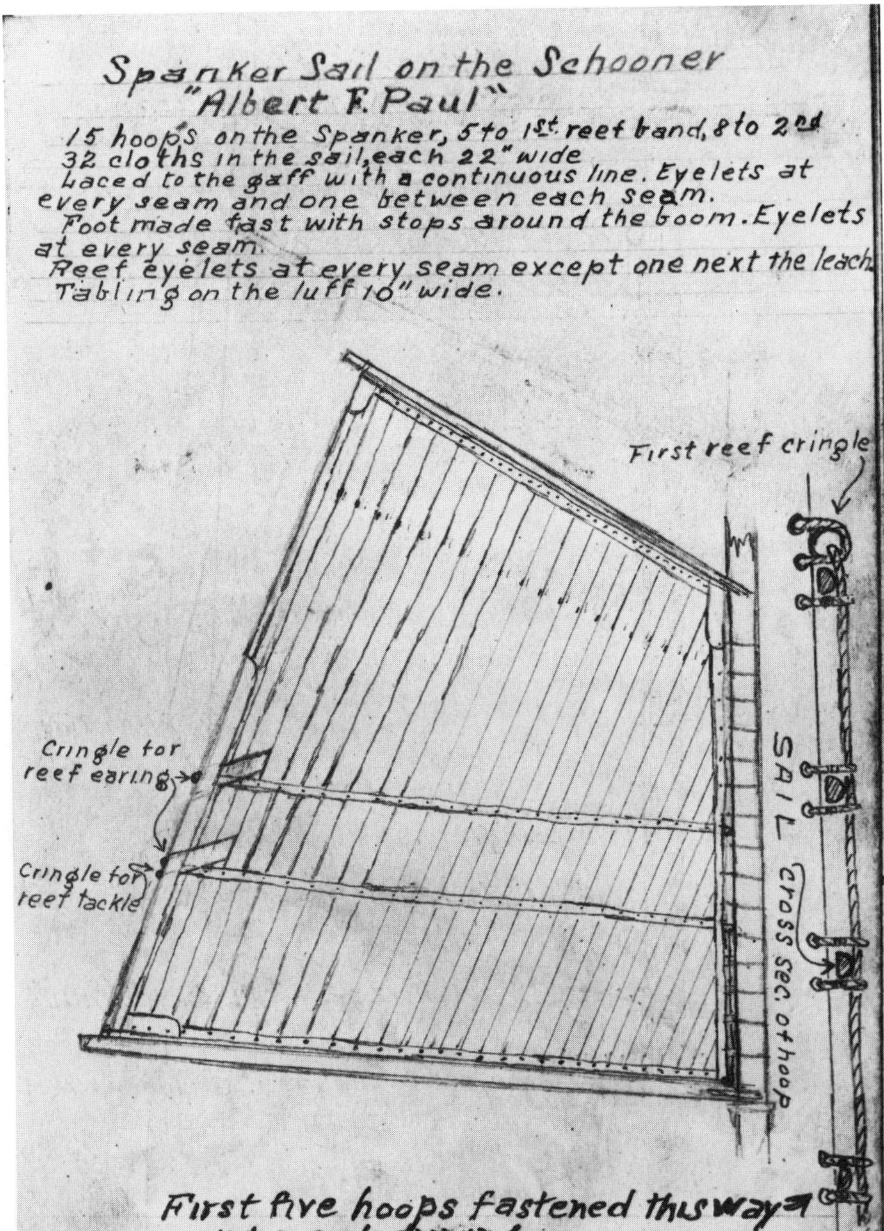
Spanker Sail on the Schooner
"Albert F. Paul"
15 hoops on the Spanker, 5 to 1st reef band, 8 to 2nd
32 cloths in the sail, each 22" wide
Laced to the gaff with a continuous line. Eyelets at every seam and one between each seam.
Foot made fast with stops around the boom. Eyelets at every seam.
Reef eyelets at every seam except one next the leach.
Tabling on the luff 10" wide.
First reef cringle
Cringle for reef earing
Cringle for reef tackle
SAIL
cross sec. of hoop
First five hoops fastened this way
Not a scale drawing.

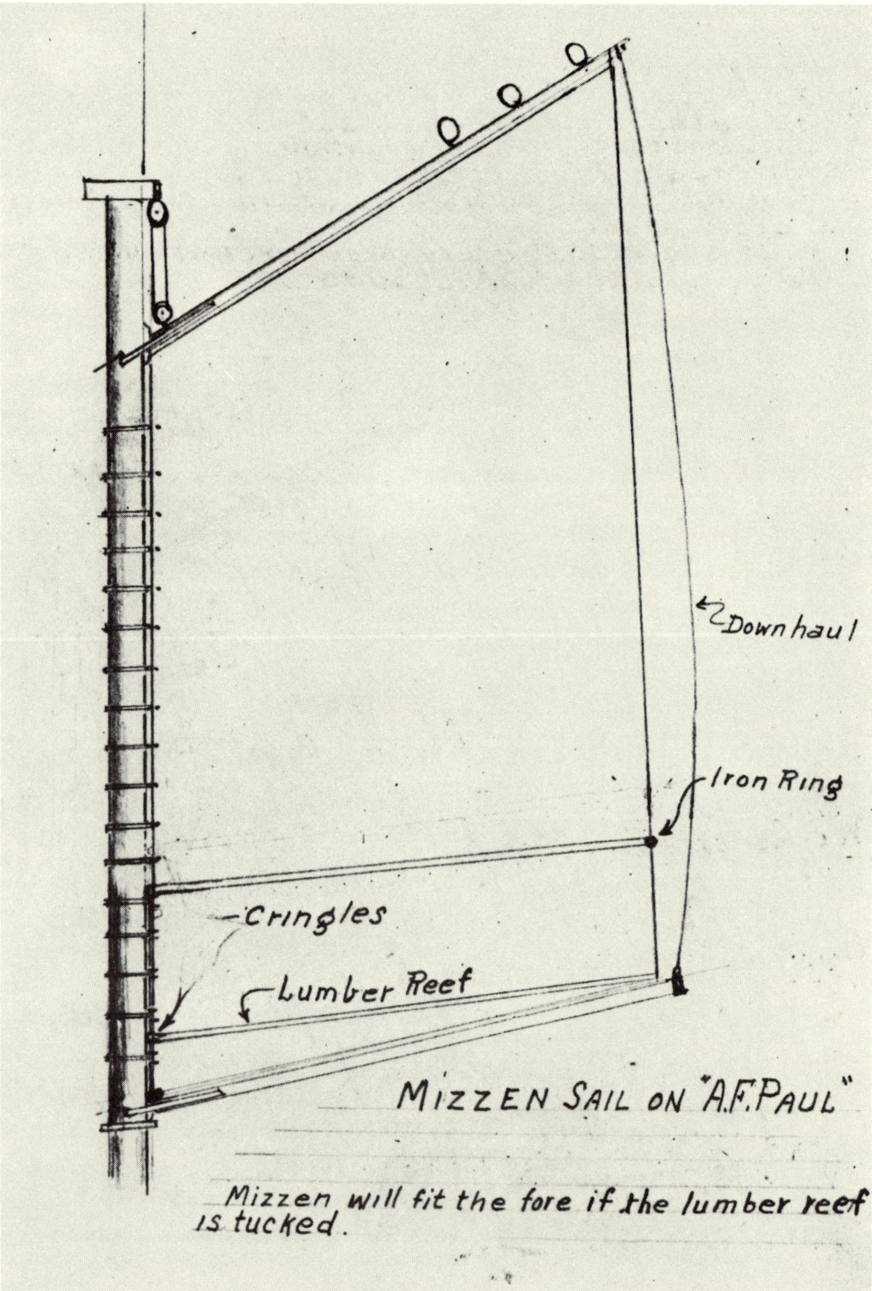
Downhaul
Iron Ring
Cringles
Lumber Reef
MIZZEN SAIL ON "A.F. PAUL"
Mizzen will fit the fore if the lumber reef is tucked.

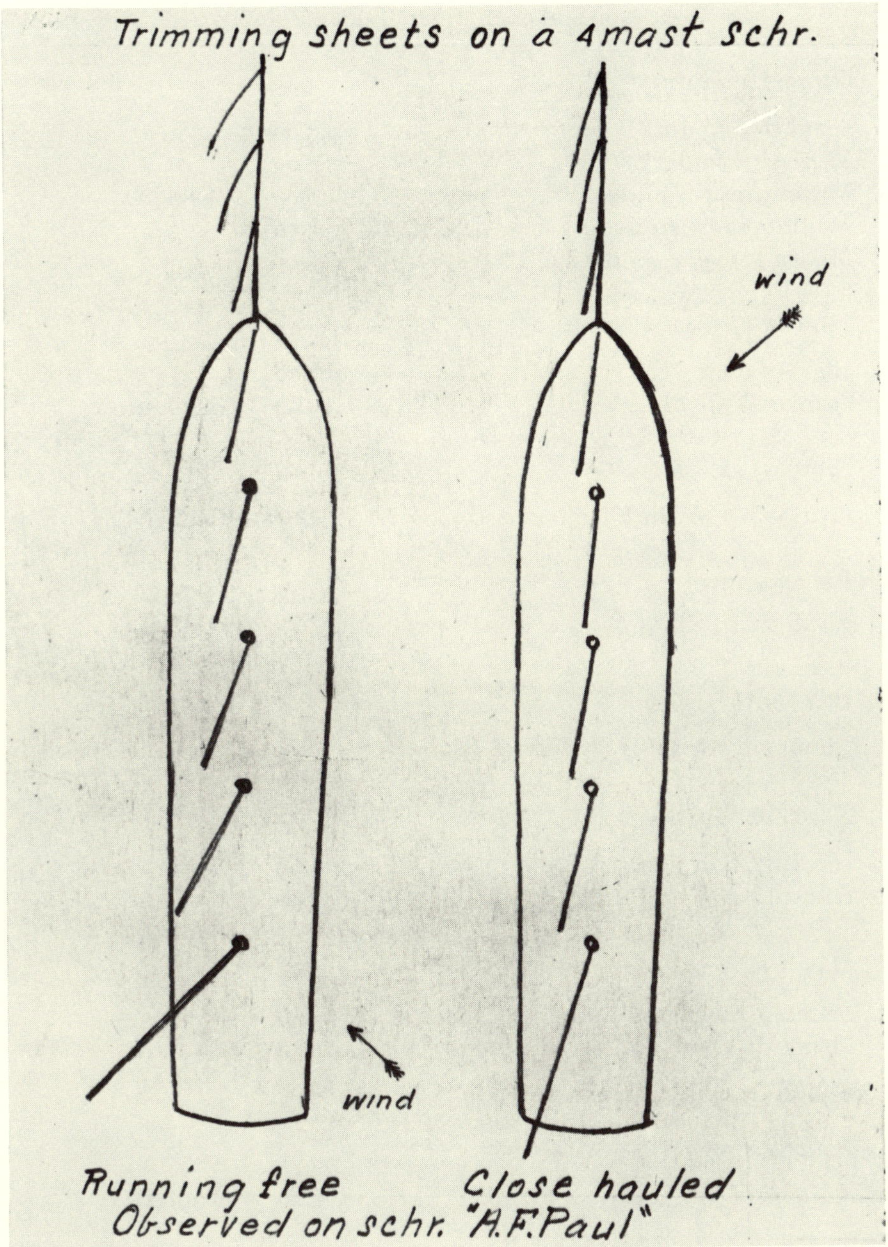
Trimming sheets on a 4mast schr.
wind
wind
Running free
Close hauled
Observed on schr. "A.F. Paul"

MEMORANDUM OF SAILS—Material and Cost

Schooner *Albert F. Paul*

Item	Cost	Maker
October 25, 1922		
Spanker #0 duck	$345.00	
Mizzen #0 duck	280.00	
Mizzen cover #6 duck	40.00	Taulane
Main topsail #4 duck	105.00	
Mizzen topsail #4 duck	105.00	
January 2, 1924		
Jib #0 duck	105.00	
Spanker Topsail #4 duck.	105.00	Taulane
February 28, 1924		
Flying jib #2 duck	105.00	Taulane
June 20, 1923		
Forestaysail #0 duck	105.00	Taulane
July 23, 1924		
Jib topsail 186 yards #5 duck @ 68¢	126.48	Taulane
November 19, 1924		
Foresail #1/0 duck	315.00	
Foresail cover #6 duck	48.00	Taulane
March 16, 1925		
Mainsail cover #6 duck	52.50	
Flying jib cover #6 duck	19.50	Taulane
Jib cover #6 duck	23.00	
January 8, 1926		
Mainsail #0 duck	325.00	Taulane
January 11, 1927		
Spanker topsail #4 duck	115.00	Taulane

September 23, 1927		
Mizzen sail #0 duck	325.00	Taulane
March 26, 1928		
Mizzen topsail #4 duck	110.00	Taulane
October 18, 1928		
Foresail #0 duck	300.00	Taulane
December 24, 1928		
Forestaysail #0 duck	105.00	Taulane
January 29, 1929		
Spanker #1/0 duck	400.00	
Cover for new spanker	65.00	Taulane
March 29, 1930		
Mainsail #0 Woodberry duck	310.00	L. Martin & Son
March 22, 1930		
Flying jib #2 duck	115.00	
Fore topsail #4 duck	115.00	Taulane
September 12, 1930		
Main topsail #4 duck	110.00	Taulane
January 26, 1931		
Jib topsail #5 duck	120.00	Taulane

Observations by James S. McCullough

Bending a Fore and Aft Sail

Lower the boom and gaff down as far as possible. Hoist the throat a little, and trice up all the hoops except the lower ones that are made fast with the jack rope. Stretch the sail out along the deck under the boom, and bolt the tack in the boom and the throat in the gaff. Haul out the foot of the sail, and bolt it in the band on the end of the boom. Use the donkey engine and messenger if a large sail. Tie the foot stops (square knot).

Haul out the head of the sail and bolt into the band on the end of the gaff. Use donkey engine if a large sail. Pass the lace line around the gaff and through eyelets in the head of the sail. Begin in the middle of the sail, and work both ways. Bend the hoops, using white spun yarn. Start with the lower hoop of the ones triced up. Each hoop must be made fast. After all the hoops that were triced up have been bent, hoist the sail and reeve off the jack rope securing the balance of the hoops.

Manipulation of Fore and Aft Sails

Setting a topsail in light wind
Sheet home, haul up the sail, down tack.

Setting a topsail in strong wind
Sheet home, tack down, and masthead the sail.

Taking in a foresail, blowing
Run the vessel off enough to blanket the foresail with the main and mizzen, and lower it.

Tieing up a sail
Start with the stop nearest the mast.

Shaking out a reef
Slack down the peak a little, loosen the reef points beginning in the middle and working toward both ends. Let go the tack lashing and reef earing last. Set the sail.

Reefing a fore and aft sail
Slack off the lee lift and lower the sail down, the peak all the way down, and secure the gaff to the lee rail with the downhaul. Steady the boom with the boom tackle and sheet. All hands lay along the boom, and pull the sail from the foot to the reef band, up on the boom. Put a piece of parcelling around the sail in the wake of the reef earing. Hook the reef earing in the band on the end of the boom, reeve one end through the reef cringle. Heave the reef band taut along the boom with the donkey engine and messenger leading

through a snatch block secured in line and abaft the boom. The messenger is hooked to a bowline tied in the end of the reef earing that is rove through the reef cringle. After the reef band is hove out taut, take the free end of the reef earing, pass it through the reef cringle the opposite way to the other end, then around the sail through the cringle and heave it taut with a heaver. Hold the other end of the earing, come up the messenger, and cast it off. Pass it around the boom and through the reef cringle until only enough to knot remains. Heave each turn tight with the heaver. Pass the other end of the earing around the boom and through the cringle but in an opposite direction, heaving each turn tight. Knot the ends of the earing with a square knot, and stop off the ends with rope yarns. In the meantime other hands have tied the reef points, three overhand knots, square knots.

Hoist the sail until the luff is almost stretched and the hoops are clear for passing the tack lashing. After the tack lashing is passed, knot it with a square knot or three overhand knots and stop the ends with rope yarns and set the sail.

Nicknames Used Aboard Coasting Schooners along the Atlantic Coast in the 1930s

Gaff-Topsail Christ
Miserable Christ
Sou'western
Bergen Pete
Black Pete
Parkhouse John
Barehead Johnson
Dopey Andrew
Sore-eyed Martin
Even So
Western-Ocean Nelson
Step and a Half
Soap-Box Wilson
Chew-Tobacco Olsen
Alphabetical Olsen
(A. B. C. Olsen)
Russian Sam
Russian Otto
Keegan
Mad Mike Jensen
Black Charlie
Scotty the Boar
Bullshit Burns
Broken-Nose Scotty
Moonface Mullins
Patty the Pig
Hold-Fast McCarthy
Stomping John
Nick the Greek

Stores List for the *Albert F. Paul* from Wm. H. Swan & Sons Inc.,

Norfolk, Virginia, on trip #92, departing from Newport News to Bermuda on January 15, 1940

January 12, 1940

3½	barrels family beef
85	pounds fresh HQ beef
10	pounds pork sausage
½	barrel extra prime pork, lean
1	35 lb. keg pig's feet
3	covered smoked hams
3	sides smoked bacon, covered
3	smoked shoulders, covered
6	8 lb. tins lard
40	pounds cabin butter in tins
1	5 lb. box YA [Yellow American] cheese
1	crate US graded fresh eggs
4	98 lb. bags Gold Medal flour
10	pounds white corn meal
1	case regular size pkgs. rolled oats
12	pkg. corn flakes
12	pkgs. Cream of Wheat
12	pkgs. Aunt Jemima Pancake flour
50	pounds rice
20	pounds green peas
15	pounds split peas
15	pounds white beans
15	pounds Y S [Yellow Split] beans
10	pounds red kidney beans
20	pounds lima beans
2	pounds barley
5	pounds minute tapioca
6	pkgs. macaroni
3	4 lb. pkgs. vermicelli
2	pkgs. corn starch
50	pounds N F [Newfoundland] codfish
5	kits mackerel
2	kits tongues and sounds
1	kit herring
2	boxes smoked herring
6	1½ lb. pkgs. table salt

50 pounds coarse salt
600 pounds potatoes
1 bushel white onions
½ bushel beets
1 bushel yellow turnips
1 bushel carrots
1 dozen cabbages
½ basket cooking apples
½ basket table apples
2 dozen oranges
6 #2 tins pineapple juice
9 #1 tins tomato juice
5 pounds cabin tea
45 pounds Swan's Special cabin coffee
200 pounds granulated sugar
1 gallon molasses
1 gallon Karo syrup
6 pounds raisins
6 pkgs. currants
15 1 lb. pkgs. prunes
15 pounds evaporated [dried] apples
10 pounds evaporated peaches
10 1 lb. pkgs. evaporated apricots
¼ pound nutmeg
½ pound ginger
½ pound black pepper
12 pkgs. Magic yeast
12 pkgs. Fleischman's yeast
5 pounds baking powder
1 8 oz. jar prepared mustard
3 pounds curry powder (tins)
1 pail—2 gals. plain pickles
1 pail—2 gals. mixed pickles
6 quarts sweet pickles
1 quart dill pickles
3 bottles stuffed olives
3 14 oz. bottles tomato catsup
1 gallon salad oil
1 gallon vinegar
12 cans dog food
2 doz. tins #1 Maine clams
2 doz. tins #1 pink salmon

4 doz. tins Norwegian sardines
4 doz. tins kippered herring
2 doz. tins condensed milk
1 case tall evaporated milk
1 case baby evaporated milk
1 doz. 4 lb. tins roast beef
2 doz. tins corned beef
2 doz. tins sausage meat
1 doz. tins tripe
1 doz. tins 2s sweet corn
2 doz. tins 2s green peas
2 doz. tins 2s string beans
2 doz. tins 2½s tomatoes
2 doz. tins 2½s spinach
1 doz. tins 2s beets
4 doz. tins assorted soups
2 doz. tins pumpkin
1 doz. tins blueberries
½ doz. tins cranberry sauce
1 doz. tins 2½s peaches
½ doz. tins 2½s pineapple
½ doz. tins 2½s apricots
2 #2 tins apples
6 tins 2½s cherries
6 tins mincemeat
6 tins baked beans
2 7 lb. tins crew jam
12 jars assorted cabin jam
2 8 oz. bottles vanilla extract
2 8 oz. bottles lemon extract
6 pkgs. Jello
2 gross safety matches
8 doz. tins (small) Prince Albert tobacco
8 cartons Lucky Strike cigarettes
200 White Owl cigars
25 pounds cabin pilot bread
1 doz. tins lima beans
1 ton ice

Chandlery List for the *Albert F. Paul* from Wm. H. Swan & Sons Inc.

Norfolk, Virginia, on Trip #92, departing from Newport News to Bermuda on January 15, 1940

January 12, 1940

20 fathoms 1″ circum. Manila
5 pounds marlin
10 pounds 2-Y [two-ply] manila spunyarn
15 fathoms 15-thd. [thread] ratline
½ bale spun oakum
25 yards 10 oz. duck
6 balls cotton twine
5 pounds cotton waste
5 pounds Cities Service Gas Engine grease
12 flashlight unit cell batteries
1 6-cell Hot Shot battery
5 gallons gas engine oil
50 gallons gasoline
15 gallons raw linseed oil and 3 cans
6 B-lip chimneys
5 pounds putty
1 quart Dixon's aluminum
6 sheets emery cloth
2 4″ flat paint brushes
1 1½″ wood chisel
2 6″ saw files for small hand saws
1 hand cross cut saw 7-T
10 pounds 3″ wire nails
36 deck spikes 6″ × ½″ galv.
2 pounds ¾″ galv. tacks
1 14″ marlinspike
5 pounds tallow
42 pounds mast grease
1 bag cement
1 #7 cabin corn broom
2 deck corn brooms #8 RC
4 30″ mast hoops and fittings
Pins for 8″, 12″, and 14″ blocks
2 galv. buckets
1 14″ double block with becket and shackle
1 5″ × 8″ American ensign

2 pounds chrome yellow
4 gals. OS [outside] white paint DH [deck house]
1 gal. BCP [Baltimore Copper Paint] Pea Green paint
1 doz. large pkgs. Gold Dust
6 tins Dutch Cleanser
1 scrub brush
2 tins lye
3 rolls toilet paper
2 pts. liquid metal polish
1 wall galley lamp
1 dish basket
1 iron griddle for pancakes
1 pc. white oak 6″ × 6″ × 60″ D4S [dressed sides]
6 1¼″ washers
6 1½″ washers
1 feather duster
250′ signal halyard, 9-thd. manila 8½#
1 Nautical Almanac
1 Hydrographic chart
3 barrels to hold drinking water supply
1 spanker from Baltimore and one to go back
1 anchor from Baltimore with shackles

Paint Scheme of
the Four-Masted Schooner *Albert F. Paul*—1933

Outside hull

Bottom, red copper paint

Waterline to rail, grey with yellow band along sheer strake

Scroll work on bow yellow

Transom black with name and hailing port, "Baltimore, Md.," white

Nameboards on bows and quarters, black with white letters

Buffalo rail and taff rail, white

Deck house and cabin trunk, white—corners scraped and varnished

Covering board around the bottom, green; around the top, mast color (buff)

Deck on forward house, canvas painted green

Deck on cabin trunk, wood painted green

Masts, booms, and gaffs

Deck to saddle, white

Saddle to lower band, scraped and greased

Mast lower band to trestle trees, mast color

Crosstrees, trestletrees, spreaders, bands, and blocks, white

Doublings, mast color

Topmasts, scraped and greased

Trucks, white; balls, yellow

Gaffs, mast color; ends from after peak halliard block, white

Jaws, scraped and oiled

Booms, scraped and oiled; ends from sheet blocks aft, white

Jaws, white except sides which are scraped and oiled

Jibboom, scraped and varnished from cap to outer foretopmast stay and white from there to end of jibboom

Bands and blocks on jibboom, white

Bowsprit, martingale, and jibboom from cap inboard, grey

Bobstays, black; all other chain and wire forward, grey

Anchors, black

Fo'c'sle head

Margin plank, grey

Buffalo rail, white

Bitts, scraped, oiled, and varnished, ends, white

Capstan, green

Windlass brake, green

Deck, tar oil

Main deck, oiled with tar oil

Waterways, green, bulwarks, white, pin rail, mast color or scraped and oiled

Cap rail, grey

Ladders, white with part of the tread scraped and oiled

Mast coats, green

Turnbuckles, grey

Hatch coamings, green

Sheet blocks, white

Hatch covers, green with grey diamond thereon

Inside of hatch, red

Strongbacks, green

Poop deck, oiled with linseed oil

Bitts, scraped, oiled, and varnished on sides, painted white on top and ends

Coach house, companionway, wheel box, and compass box (binnacle), white

Wheel, (iron) aluminum paint

Hand pumps, red

Gratings over windows, scraped and varnished; bars painted yellow

Yawl boat, white with green bottom, gunwales, buff, inside, grey

Gig, white

Purnell T. White. Following McCullough's two trips in the *Albert F. Paul* in the spring and summer of 1933 he signed on the four-masted schooner *Purnell T. White* in October of that year on a trip from New York to Georgetown, South Carolina, and return. Bound south, the schooner encountered a gale off Cape Hatteras, North Carolina. To record that event, McCullough later sketched the *White* hove to on the starboard tack under forestaysail, and reefed main, and mizzen sails riding out the storm.

Appendix D

Schooner *Purnell T. White*

Paint Scheme of the Four-Masted Schooner *Purnell T. White*—1933

Outside hull

- Bottom, red copper paint
- Hull, waterline to rail, grey with red stripe along sheer strake
- Transom, black with name and home port in white letters
- Cap rail, green
- Scroll work (eagle's head) at bow, red
- Bulwarks inside, white
- Pin rail, buff or mast color
- Waterways, green
- Buffalo rail, white
- Anchors, grey

Forward deck house

- House white; covering board at bottom, green; covering board at top, buff; top, grey

Cabin trunk

- House white with corners scraped and varnished; frames of bars in the windows, varnished; covering board around bottom, green; covering board around top, buff, cabin top, grey; reef plank and ice hatch, grey; tops of skylight, coach house, and companionway, buff

Poop deck

- Steering wheel box, white with buff top
- Bitts scraped and varnished, tops and ends painted white
- Taff rail, white

Masts, booms, and gaffs

- Mast coats, green
- Mast from deck to saddle, including the saddle, white
- Mast from saddle to futtock band, scraped and greased

Futtock band to cap, buff except crosstrees
Bands around mast head, and blocks, white
Doublings of topmast, buff
Cap to truck, scraped and greased
Short truck, white
Booms, jaws white, boom buff to bail band, white from bail band to end of boom
Spanker boom, white from lift band to end
Gaffs, jaws white, gaff buff to after peak halliard block and then white to end of gaff
All blocks aloft, white; mast hoops, buff
Bowsprit, jibboom, and martingale—bowsprit, grey
Jibboom, grey from inboard and to cap; buff from cap to band on the end, and white from the band to the end
Martingale, buff

Hatches, deck fittings—Hatch coamings, grey; hatch covers, grey with green square
King plank, green
Mast coats, green
Blocks on deck, green
Capstan, red
Lazarette hatches, grey
Yawl boat, white and buff

Sail Particulars of the Four-Masted Schooner *Purnell T. White*

Spanker

Sixteen mast hoops; 5 hoops to reef band; 29 cloths to reef band; jack line runs up to 7th hoop. Reef point in every seam; foot stop in every seam. Five eyelets to every 3 cloths in the head.

Mizzensail

Seventeen mast hoops; 2 reef bands. First reef band, a lumber reef with no points rove in it, located between the first and second hoops, nearer the first hoop. Second reef band between the 6th and 7th hoop in the middle. Jack line runs to 5th hoop. When sail is set, the boom is about 4 feet above the break of the poop and clears the coach house by about 18 inches.

Mainsail

Seventeen mast hoops; two reef bands. First reef band a lumber reef with no points rove, located between the first and second hoops, nearer the first hoop. The second reef band is at the 6th hoop on the main. The jack line runs to the reef cringle at the 6th hoop. Seventeen cloths at the head and 18½ at the foot. When mainsail is set, the end of the boom is about 4 feet above the mizzen saddle. Sail when set, 9 inches from mast.

Foresail

Altogether 16 hoops; two reef bands, the first reef band runs from the tack to about 3 feet above the foot at the leech. The second reef band is at the 6th hoop. The jack line runs to the 6th hoop. Seventeen full cloths, 1½ more cloths at the foot. The leech of the sail runs about 2 feet 6 inches below a line through the tack and parallel to the waterline.

Forestaysail

Fifteen cloths, 17 hanks, foot stops at every seam. When sail is set, the boom is parallel to the waterline and in line with first hoop on the foresail. Jack line runs to 9th hank.

Jib

Fourteen cloths, 24 hanks; foot stops at every seam. Boom parallel to waterline when sail is set and about 3 feet above the forestaysail boom. Jack line runs up to 10th hank.

Flying jib

Seven and one half cloths on the foot; 29 hanks.

Mizzen topsail

Ten cloths to the tack at the masthead; 15 cloths to the lower tack; 9 hoops.

Measurements on the Four-Masted Schooner *Purnell T. White*

Bow to capstan on foredeck	12 feet
Capstan to forward house	11 feet
Fore end of fore house to foremast	10 feet 6 inches
Fore house	24 feet long
Fore house	7 feet high
Fore hatch to mainmast	6 feet 3 inches
Fore traveler to mainmast	3 feet 6 inches
Deck to top of mainmast saddle	4 feet 3 inches
Cabin trunk	30 feet long
Companionway	5 feet × 3 feet 3 inches
Top of after cabin to top of companionway	2 feet 4 inches
Taffrail	34 inches high
Break of poop to coach house	5 feet 6 inches
Cabin trunk side to taffrail	4 feet
Forward lazarette hatch	4 feet × 4 feet × 16 inches
Steering wheel diameter	4 feet 8 inches
Cabin trunk to wheelbox	4 feet 8 inches
Wheelbox to taffrail	1 foot 9 inches
Spanker sheet traveler to taffrail	1 foot 9 inches
Mainmast centerline to mizzenmast centerline	37 feet
Bulwarks at break of fo'c'sle	4 feet 9 inches
Bulwarks	4 feet high
Cap rail	15 inches wide
Mainmast	2 feet diameter
Main gaff diameter	9 inches
Main boom	34 feet 6 inches long
Main gaff	34 feet long
Forestaysail boom	28 feet long
Forestaysail boom to foremast	5 inches
Spanker sheet	45 fathoms long

Index

Other Books by Robert H. Burgess

This Was Chesapeake Bay
Chesapeake Circle
Coasting Captain (edited)
Steamboats Out of Baltimore (collaborated)
Sea, Sails and Shipwreck
The *Sea Serpent* Journal: Hugh McCulloch Gregory's
Voyage Around the World in a Clipper Ship, 1854–55 (edited)
Chesapeake Sailing Craft, Part I
Louis J. Feuchter, Chesapeake Bay Artist